HCSB

HOLMAN CHRISTIAN STANDARD BIBLE: SOLO

AN UNCOMMON DEVOTIONAL

SOLO

NAVPRESS

Discipleship Inside Out®

HCSB

NAVPRESS
Discipleship Inside Out®

NavPress is the publishing ministry of The Navigators, an international Christian organization and leader in personal spiritual development. NavPress is committed to helping people grow spiritually and enjoy lives of meaning and hope through personal and group resources that are biblically rooted, culturally relevant, and highly practical.

For a free catalog go to www.NavPress.com
or call 1.800.366.7788 in the United States or 1.800.839.4769 in Canada.

INTRODUCTION TO *SOLO*

The devotional you hold is unique. It isn't designed to teach you to study the Bible but rather to develop a conversation between you and God. The devotions found in *Solo* are based on the classical method of *lectio divina*: reading, thinking, praying, and living Scripture with the intention of inviting an infinite, omniscient God into your life — as it is, no gloss, no veneer. Lectio divina is more Bible basking than Bible study, as it teaches you to absorb and meditate on Scripture, converse with God openly, and live out what has become a part of you: His Word.

But it's not easy. Lectio divina takes practice, and lots of it. You will have to learn to be quiet, to silence the voices of responsibility, self, family, and even religion in order to hear what God has to say to you. Try not to view the elements of lectio divina as steps to be checked off your to-do list. Instead, allow them to meld together in the intentional process of listening to God, of focusing on Him and learning what He would have from you and for you, His beloved. Don't worry if no lightning strikes or brilliant revelations come. Sometimes devotion means just sitting in the presence of God.

We know the four elements of lectio divina as Read, Think, Pray, and Live. Each element has a purpose, but don't be surprised if they overlap and weave into each other. Remember as you dive into this devotional that lectio divina is about wholeness: whole practice, whole Bible, whole God.

Read. Thoughtfully, leisurely, faithfully — read the epic love story that is the Bible. Yes, love story. The Bible is the chronicle of God's love for His people from the darkness before Eden to eternity with Him in heaven. You are in it, I am in it, and, most important, God is in it. Here you will meet Him face-to-face.

Eugene Peterson called the Bible "a book that reads us even as we read it." That's an uncommon sort of book, and it requires an uncommon sort of read. Knowing facts about God doesn't change your relationship with Him, so take the time to splash around in the Word, to absorb it, to discover what God has to say to you each day.

In each *Solo* devotion, you will find a Scripture passage but also a reference to an expanded passage. I encourage you to read them both, slowly, attentively, and repeatedly. As Peterson said, "The Bible is given to us in the first place simply to invite us to make ourselves at home in the world of God . . . and become familiar with the way God speaks and the ways in which we answer him with our lives." No Scripture passage exists in a vacuum. Whenever you can, take the time to stretch beyond the passage put before you to understand the larger context in which it is found. The more you read, the more you will understand about yourself and this God who created you.

Think. Each subtle, significant, powerful word of Scripture is meant for you. One word may speak today and another tomorrow, but God sent each of them straight into your life. So listen. Go into your reading with a clean slate. Don't bring what you think you need to hear, what others have said, or what you've been taught about a particular passage. Don't bring fear that you'll misinterpret the text. This is about what God has to say to you.

Our lives are full of static. Whether it's our to-do lists, our emotions, or just plain noise, it can be hard to sift out God's voice from all the racket. By meditating on each word, by turning it over and over in your mind, you will discover that as God Himself is infinitely complex, so His thoughts have subtle meaning beyond the rote. The more you think about what you read, the more familiar you will become with His voice.

Pray. God yearns to converse with you. And He wants far more than just "thanks for this, can I please have that" prayer. Respond to Him in dialogue. That means it's as much about listening as it is about speaking. Open your ears and your heart to hear His voice. Sing praises or laments; write your thoughts in a journal; dance or prostrate yourself before Him. Pray.

Maybe God has challenged you. Tell Him how you feel, but always remember that what He asks, He asks for your good. He is loving and merciful, not manipulative and harsh. If you come across something in your reading that you don't understand, tell Him about it. Ask Him about it. Fill your prayers with Scripture. Using the words you have read helps you ensure that your prayers line up with God's Word and intention for your life.

It's easy for us in our culture of doing to want to skim over this part. Don't. Even if you are quiet and God is quiet, you are learning to communicate with Him.

Live. You can read, think, and pray all day, but unless you live in God's Word as well, you miss the point. The Bible says, "In the same way faith, if it doesn't have works, is dead by itself" (James 2:17). If you have taken God's Word to heart and truly made it part of you, it will by its very nature change you. And when it does, you will find yourself called to act. There will come a time when God takes you to the end of yourself then asks you to go further. He wants you to put yourself at His disposal, to go and do what He asks, even the impossible. When that time comes, you will need the Word He has seared on your heart to give you comfort and strength. This is the "life . . . in abundance" of which Jesus spoke (John 10:10).

///

Solo. One on one. Just you and God.

The *Solo* devotions are tailored to help you learn to listen to what God wants to say to you through His Word. You will find that every seventh day is marked as a day of reflection, a time to sit back and let God guide your thoughts and prayers back to themes and Scripture from the previous week. Don't be afraid to reflect, and don't be afraid to go back. Each time you read these devotions, you may find that God has something new to say, for though He is the same always, you change a little each day as He shapes you into the person He designed you to be.

Also, there may be times when you need to hear God's voice on a specific issue. For those times, we have provided an index of topics that will guide you to a devotion that may be just what you need.

And so begins the journey.

DESIRE FOR RECONCILIATION

GENESIS 3:1-10

¹ Now the serpent was the most cunning of all the wild animals that the LORD God had made. He said to the woman, "Did God really say, 'You can't eat from any tree in the garden'?"

² The woman said to the serpent, "We may eat the fruit from the trees in the garden. ³ But about the fruit of the tree in the middle of the garden, God said, 'You must not eat it or touch it, or you will die.'"

⁴ "No! You will not die," the serpent said to the woman. ⁵ "In fact, God knows that when you eat it your eyes will be opened and you will be like God, knowing good and evil." ⁶ Then the woman saw that the tree was good for food and delightful to look at, and that it was desirable for obtaining wisdom. So she took some of its fruit and ate it; she also gave some to her husband, who was with her, and he ate it. ⁷ Then the eyes of both of them were opened, and they knew they were naked; so they sewed fig leaves together and made loincloths for themselves.

⁸ Then the man and his wife heard the sound of the LORD God walking in the garden at the time of the evening breeze, and they hid themselves from the LORD God among the trees of the garden. ⁹ So the LORD God called out to the man and said to him, "Where are you?"

¹⁰ And he said, "I heard You in the garden and I was afraid because I was naked, so I hid."

READ

Read the passage, Genesis 3:1-10, carefully.

THINK

For many of us, these are familiar verses. The first two chapters of Genesis speak of God's amazing Creation. Chapter 3 speaks of the rebellion of humankind. And the remainder of the message details God's intricate and loving plan to redeem, restore, and reconcile creation back to Himself after what happened in Genesis 3. God's plan hinges on what happened in the garden. How does this passage speak to your situation today?

PRAY

There is no better way to begin to understand God's plan than to grasp our separation from Him because of sin and our desperate need for Him to reconcile our relationship. Take some time to confess those areas where you have deliberately rebelled against God.

LIVE

Knowing that you and everyone else on earth have rebelled against God, what do you feel? In what ways does this knowledge affect the way you live your life?

Reread verse 9. If God knows everything, why did He call out to Adam asking, "Where are you?"

In verse 10, Adam responds to God's question by saying, "I heard You in the garden and I was afraid because I was naked, so I hid." When are you most tempted to hide?

1

WRESTLING IN THE NIGHT

GENESIS 32:22-32

²² During the night Jacob got up and took his two wives, his two female slaves, and his 11 sons, and crossed the ford of Jabbok. ²³ He took them and sent them across the stream, along with all his possessions.

²⁴ Jacob was left alone, and a man wrestled with him until daybreak. ²⁵ When the man saw that He could not defeat him, He struck Jacob's hip socket as they wrestled and dislocated his hip. ²⁶ Then He said to Jacob, "Let Me go, for it is daybreak."

But Jacob said, "I will not let You go unless You bless me."

²⁷ "What is your name?" the man asked.

"Jacob," he replied.

²⁸ "Your name will no longer be Jacob," He said. "It will be Israel because you have struggled with God and with men and have prevailed."

²⁹ Then Jacob asked Him, "Please tell me Your name."

But He answered, "Why do you ask My name?" And He blessed him there.

³⁰ Jacob then named the place Peniel, "For I have seen God face to face," he said, "and I have been delivered." ³¹ The sun shone on him as he passed by Penuel — limping because of his hip. ³² That is why, to this day, the Israelites don't eat the thigh muscle that is at the hip socket: because He struck Jacob's hip socket at the thigh muscle.

READ

Read the passage slowly. (To find out about Jacob's fear of meeting his brother, Esau, whom he had tricked many years before, read the expanded passage.)

THINK

Read the passage aloud this time and pause after each of the three questions in the text (verses 27,29). Jacob, whose name means "manipulator," had made elaborate plans to reconcile with Esau in a generous, peaceful way. Then he stayed behind, which was uncharacteristic of such a quintessential deal maker. There with the night sounds and the smell of the brook, Jacob encountered "a man." Was this man an angel, a God-man, Jesus? (It's okay that we don't know for sure.)

1. Picture yourself in this passage. Are you Jacob? Are you an invisible bystander watching it all?
2. What moment in this passage resonates with you most?

   ☐ wanting desperately to be blessed
   ☐ wanting desperately to know more of God
   ☐ other:

PRAY

Depending on what resonated with you, pray about what you desperately want from God. To avoid letting your mind wander, try writing down your prayer, listening for words from God in response.

LIVE

Sit quietly before God, imagining the night sounds and the smell of running water. Try to be comfortable with God in this wild atmosphere. What does it feel like to trust and to reveal the desires of your heart? Be honest if you feel uncomfortable. What would you like it to feel like? Rest in that.

A PICTURE OF FORGIVENESS

GENESIS 50:15-21

¹⁵ When Joseph's brothers saw that their father was dead, they said to one another, "If Joseph is holding a grudge against us, he will certainly repay us for all the suffering we caused him."

¹⁶ So they sent this message to Joseph, "Before he died your father gave a command: ¹⁷ 'Say this to Joseph: Please forgive your brothers' transgression and their sin — the suffering they caused you.' Therefore, please forgive the transgression of the servants of the God of your father." Joseph wept when their message came to him. ¹⁸ Then his brothers also came to him, bowed down before him, and said, "We are your slaves!"

¹⁹ But Joseph said to them, "Don't be afraid. Am I in the place of God? ²⁰ You planned evil against me; God planned it for good to bring about the present result — the survival of many people. ²¹ Therefore don't be afraid. I will take care of you and your little ones." And he comforted them and spoke kindly to them.

READ

Take some time before you begin to rest in silence. Let your mind settle. Silently read the passage.

THINK

Read the passage again, this time aloud, listening specifically for a word or phrase that touches your heart. When you finish, close your eyes. Recall the word or phrase, taking it in and mulling it over. After a few moments, write it down. Don't write anything else.

PRAY

Read the passage aloud again, searching for how forgiveness is illustrated in the text. Think about what it feels like to be the forgiver, as well as what it feels like to be the forgiven. How is this expression of love meaningful to you? Briefly note your thoughts.

Read the text one last time, then stop and listen for what God is inviting you to do or become this week. Perhaps His invitation will have to do with a new perspective on who you are in His eyes, or maybe you sense an action He is calling you to take. After your prayer, write down what you feel invited to do.

LIVE

Take time to meditate on the following quote from *The Book of Common Prayer*, and let it become your own: "Let not the needy, O Lord, be forgotten; nor the hope of the poor be taken away."[1]

LEARNING TO PAY ATTENTION

EXODUS 3:1-6

¹ Meanwhile, Moses was shepherding the flock of his father-in-law Jethro, the priest of Midian. He led the flock to the far side of the wilderness and came to Horeb, the mountain of God. ² Then the Angel of the LORD appeared to him in a flame of fire within a bush. As Moses looked, he saw that the bush was on fire but was not consumed. ³ So Moses thought: I must go over and look at this remarkable sight. Why isn't the bush burning up?

⁴ When the LORD saw that he had gone over to look, God called out to him from the bush, "Moses, Moses!"

"Here I am," he answered.

⁵ "Do not come closer," He said. "Remove the sandals from your feet, for the place where you are standing is holy ground." ⁶ Then He continued, "I am the God of your father, the God of Abraham, the God of Isaac, and the God of Jacob." Moses hid his face because he was afraid to look at God.

READ

Read the passage aloud.

THINK

Moses is shepherding his father-in-law's sheep. In the distance he sees a bush in flames, but the bush mysteriously doesn't burn up. He walks closer, perhaps expecting a miracle, only to have a more unique encounter than he ever imagined. He interacts with the living God.

When have you experienced a unique encounter with the living God? What was your burning bush like?

What do you think God meant when He said, "Remove the sandals from your feet, for the place where you are standing is holy ground."?

God is holy. What difference does that make in your life?

PRAY

Ask God to reveal Himself to you today in a fresh way, a way that He has never revealed Himself before.

LIVE

Moses heard from God when he paid attention. Like Moses, we often encounter God when we pay attention to what's going on around us. Find a quiet place and spend a few moments in utter silence, paying attention to those aspects of your life that you often neglect: people, situations, quiet moments, creation, and so on. As you do this, look for God waiting there to interact with you.

THE BREAD GOD HAS GIVEN

EXODUS 16:9-16

⁹ Then Moses told Aaron, "Say to the entire Israelite community, 'Come before the LORD, for He has heard your complaints.'" ¹⁰ As Aaron was speaking to the entire Israelite community, they turned toward the wilderness, and there in a cloud the LORD's glory appeared.

¹¹ The LORD spoke to Moses, ¹² "I have heard the complaints of the Israelites. Tell them: At twilight you will eat meat, and in the morning you will eat bread until you are full. Then you will know that I am Yahweh your God."

¹³ So at evening quail came and covered the camp. In the morning there was a layer of dew all around the camp. ¹⁴ When the layer of dew evaporated, there were fine flakes on the desert surface, as fine as frost on the ground. ¹⁵ When the Israelites saw it, they asked one another, "What is it?" because they didn't know what it was.

Moses told them, "It is the bread the LORD has given you to eat. ¹⁶ This is what the LORD has commanded: 'Gather as much of it as each person needs to eat. You may take two quarts per individual, according to the number of people each of you has in his tent.'"

READ

Read the passage aloud. If you'd like, read the expanded passage to get a picture of the complaining that came before this and the obsessive hoarding that came after. Both give us a picture of the neediness of the Israelites at this time.

THINK

Read the passage again slowly, pausing to feel each emotion of the Israelites:

- the deep neediness of complaining
- the excitement of seeing the glory of God visible in the cloud
- the perplexity of seeing this strange bread from heaven
- the satisfaction of having enough

Then consider: If you were to complain to God right now, what would your complaint be? (Don't choose this yourself; wait and let it come to you.) In what ways, if any, have you been perplexed by God's response to your complaining? How might God have truly provided enough but you didn't recognize it as God's bread from heaven—exactly what you needed?

PRAY

If you haven't formally complained to God about this matter, do so. Ask God to show you how He has provided you with enough, even though you still might wonder.

LIVE

Sit in the quiet and feel God's "enoughness" in your body. Where do you feel it? In arms that are full? In a quiet mind? In a stomach that feels full? In muscles that work well? If you can really mean it, try delighting in this enoughness.

5

GOD REVEALS HIMSELF

EXODUS 33:21–34:7

²¹ The LORD said, "Here is a place near Me. You are to stand on the rock, ²² and when My glory passes by, I will put you in the crevice of the rock and cover you with My hand until I have passed by. ²³ Then I will take My hand away, and you will see My back, but My face will not be seen."

¹ The LORD said to Moses, "Cut two stone tablets like the first ones, and I will write on them the words that were on the first tablets, which you broke. ² Be prepared by morning. Come up Mount Sinai in the morning and stand before Me on the mountaintop. ³ No one may go up with you; in fact, no one must be seen anywhere on the mountain. Even the flocks and herds are not to graze in front of that mountain."

⁴ Moses cut two stone tablets like the first ones. He got up early in the morning, and taking the two stone tablets in his hand, he climbed Mount Sinai, just as the LORD had commanded him.

⁵ The LORD came down in a cloud, stood with him there, and proclaimed His name Yahweh. ⁶ Then the LORD passed in front of him and proclaimed:

Yahweh — Yahweh is a compassionate and gracious God, slow to anger and rich in faithful love and truth, ⁷ maintaining faithful love to a thousand generations, forgiving wrongdoing, rebellion, and sin. But He will not leave the guilty unpunished, bringing the consequences of the fathers' wrongdoing on the children and grandchildren to the third and fourth generation.

READ

Read the passage slowly. To get a broader feel for what's happening, quickly read the expanded passage.

THINK

During a second read, explore the nooks and crannies of God's communication with Moses, noticing words that embellish your mental picture of who God is or of the situation at hand. The third time, listen for one or two of God's words that especially impress you. Choose one word or phrase, then take time to repeat it to yourself, letting it interact with your thoughts, feelings, and desires.

PRAY

Deeply ponder the quality of God that the word or phrase portrays. Share with Him what's striking to you about this aspect of His character. Explore what makes you desirous of someone with this trait. If more thoughts, feelings, or desires come to the surface, open up to them and ask God to clarify how they expand or even alter your understanding of this part of His personality. End your prayer by letting the word or words drift through your mind and heart again.

LIVE

Envision the ways God is present to you right now. What posture does He have (for example, standing tall, sitting near)? What expression is on His face? If He speaks to you, what tones does His voice hold? Ask Him to enhance — and correct, if necessary — in the coming months this picture of how you see Him, through the Bible passages you read and through your experiences.

DAY 7

GOD ENCOUNTERS

On this seventh day, review and reflect on all you have read this week. Take the time to revel in the ways you've encountered God in the past six days.

THE NECESSITY OF SACRIFICE

LEVITICUS 4:32-35

³² "Or if the offering that he brings as a sin offering is a lamb, he is to bring an unblemished female. ³³ He is to lay his hand on the head of the sin offering and slaughter it as a sin offering at the place where the burnt offering is slaughtered. ³⁴ Then the priest must take some of the blood of the sin offering with his finger and apply it to the horns of the altar of burnt offering. He must pour out the rest of its blood at the base of the altar. ³⁵ He is to remove all its fat just as the fat of the lamb is removed from the fellowship sacrifice. The priest will burn it on the altar along with the fire offerings to the LORD. In this way the priest will make atonement on his behalf for the sin he has committed, and he will be forgiven."

READ

Read the passage in a very soft voice, maybe even a whisper. Focus intently on each word as you read.

THINK

We might be tempted to believe that Leviticus is a confusing and irrelevant book, but it has some direct implications for our lives. In Leviticus we find specific rules and regulations from Yahweh, given to distinguish His people, the nation of Israel, from every other culture. God commanded the offering of many different types of sacrifices: burnt, grain, fellowship, sin, and guilt. Each of these served a specific purpose for interaction with God. For example, a sin offering was given for confession, forgiveness, and cleansing.

Why do you think God prescribed offerings to be done in such a unique way? Is He cruel to require that animals be killed to make offerings to Him? Why or why not? Why don't we do these types of sacrifices today?

Why does God take sin so seriously? When we sin, what sort of sacrifices are we required to bring to God?

PRAY

Ask God to help you understand the severity of your own sin. Thank God that He sent Jesus, the Lamb of God, to come and be the sacrifice for your sins.

LIVE

Knowing that God has provided the ultimate sacrifice through His Son, Jesus, consider sharing this great truth with someone today. As you drive, walk, work, and relax, whisper under your breath, "Thank You, Jesus," each time you remember the sacrifice He made for your sins.

LETTING GO OF SIN

LEVITICUS 16:20-22

²⁰ "When he has finished purifying the most holy place, the tent of meeting, and the altar, he is to present the live male goat. ²¹ Aaron will lay both his hands on the head of the live goat and confess over it all the Israelites' wrongdoings and rebellious acts — all their sins. He is to put them on the goat's head and send it away into the wilderness by the man appointed for the task. ²² The goat will carry on it all their wrongdoings into a desolate land, and he will release it there."

READ

Read the passage slowly. (Read the expanded passage to see how the scapegoat is sent off.)

THINK

The practice in this passage may seem odd today. It was also odd in those days because instead of killing a near-perfect animal, this animal would be allowed to live.

Read the passage again.

1. Picture yourself laying your hands on this precious animal's head. Even better, hold a stuffed animal, figurine, or even your pet, and put your hands on its head.
2. Confess to God your acts of rebellion, your bad attitudes, and your harsh thoughts about others.
3. Experience the feeling of transferring your sin to this animal. (Don't feel sorry for the animal. God didn't give it the capacity to take on hurt or guilt from your sin.)
4. See yourself sending it off as it takes your sin far away from you.

PRAY

What do you wish to say to God about having sent your sins off without you?

LIVE

Quiet your mind and wait on God to show you situations in which you need to remember what you just did. Practice resting assured of God's love in those situations as you are resting assured now.

9

MY HOLY NAME

LEVITICUS 22:1-8

[1] The LORD spoke to Moses: [2] "Tell Aaron and his sons to deal respectfully with the holy offerings of the Israelites that they have consecrated to Me, so they do not profane My holy name; I am Yahweh. [3] Say to them: If any man from any of your descendants throughout your generations is in a state of uncleanness yet approaches the holy offerings that the Israelites consecrate to the LORD, that person will be cut off from My presence; I am Yahweh. [4] No man of Aaron's descendants who has a skin disease or a discharge is to eat from the holy offerings until he is clean. Whoever touches anything made unclean by a dead person or by a man who has an emission of semen, [5] or whoever touches any swarming creature that makes him unclean or any person who makes him unclean — whatever his uncleanness — [6] the man who touches any of these will remain unclean until evening and is not to eat from the holy offerings unless he has bathed his body with water. [7] When the sun has set, he will become clean, and then he may eat from the holy offerings, for that is his food. [8] He must not eat an animal that died naturally or was mauled by wild beasts, making himself unclean by it; I am Yahweh."

READ

Get comfortable. Take time to clear your mind, then focus only on this activity. Read the passage silently. Now read it once more, aloud.

THINK

As you read God's statements about Himself and about the priests, what is your reaction? Notice whether you are drawn toward God as you read or repelled from God. Talk to Him about this. Explore what might be causing your response. Ask Him to show you more of yourself—the memories, opinions, and feelings you bring to Him on this day.

PRAY

Silently pray the passage. Praying in your own words by responding to what you're reading is okay at first. But as you continue, use the words of the passage as your prayer. Perhaps you will repeat to your soul "He is Yahweh" or ask Him to increase your belief that He is holy. Ask God to show you how this truth interacts with your first reaction.

LIVE

Use this silent time simply to rest in the presence of the holy God who has just made Himself known to you. Let go of your own words and let yourself enjoy the experience.

DON'T FORGET

NUMBERS 9:4-5,9-12

[4] So Moses told the Israelites to observe the Passover, [5] and they observed it in the first month on the fourteenth day at twilight in the Wilderness of Sinai. The Israelites did everything as the LORD had commanded Moses. . . .

[9] Then the LORD spoke to Moses: [10] "Tell the Israelites: When any one of you or your descendants is unclean because of a corpse or is on a distant journey, he may still observe the Passover to the LORD. [11] Such people are to observe it in the second month, on the fourteenth day at twilight. They are to eat the animal with unleavened bread and bitter herbs; [12] they may not leave any of it until morning or break any of its bones. They must observe the Passover according to all its statutes."

READ

Read the passage five times, each time focusing on a different aspect of it.

THINK

As humans, we are forgetful people, and as forgetful people we need tangible reminders — symbols — of who God is and what He's done. Therefore, as God commanded, many Jewish homes celebrate Passover around the time of Easter to remember all that God orchestrated to bring them out of bondage in Egypt and into the Promised Land. Under what circumstances are you most prone to forget who God is and what He's done for you?

PRAY

Take a stroll down memory lane. Think about the times when God was evident and at work. Allow your memories to guide your prayers of gratitude for all He has done.

LIVE

Create a symbol that will remind you of God's faithfulness in your life. Maybe it's a photograph of your close friends or a rock you picked up during a hike. Put this symbol in a place where you will see it often. When you look at it, be reminded and thank God for His blessings.

A DIFFERENT STORY

NUMBERS 14:17-24

¹⁷ "So now, may my Lord's power be magnified just as You have spoken: ¹⁸ The LORD is slow to anger and rich in faithful love, forgiving wrongdoing and rebellion. But He will not leave the guilty unpunished, bringing the consequences of the fathers' wrongdoing on the children to the third and fourth generation. ¹⁹ Please pardon the wrongdoing of this people, in keeping with the greatness of Your faithful love, just as You have forgiven them from Egypt until now."

²⁰ The LORD responded, "I have pardoned them as you requested. ²¹ Yet as surely as I live and as the whole earth is filled with the LORD's glory, ²² none of the men who have seen My glory and the signs I performed in Egypt and in the wilderness, and have tested Me these 10 times and did not obey Me, ²³ will ever see the land I swore to give their fathers. None of those who have despised Me will see it. ²⁴ But since My servant Caleb has a different spirit and has followed Me completely, I will bring him into the land where he has gone, and his descendants will inherit it."

READ

Read the passage aloud slowly. Keep in mind that this is the prayer of Moses after ten of the twelve members of the Israelite scouting party to the Promised Land expressed doubt that they could make their home in that land, even with God's help. (Read the expanded passage to learn more about the depths of the Israelites' doubt.)

THINK

Read the passage again slowly, noting (a) qualities of God that stand out, (b) qualities of Caleb's response to God, and (c) whatever else comes to you.

What impresses you most about God? Why?

What impresses you most about Caleb? Why?

How do you respond to God's willingness to forgive so many Israelites even though He seems to think they do not have the capacity to be used by Him?

PRAY

Ask God to show you where you fit in this passage. How might you be tempted to not obey God? How might God be calling you to live a different story — to be one who has "a different spirit" from others, who follows God passionately even though it might involve risks (for example, loving the unlovely, pursuing a career that makes less money, admitting to others the mistakes you've made)?

LIVE

Imagine what it would feel like to have such trust in God that you would be willing to take whatever next steps God presents to you. Imagine what it would be like to be so different from others that you might be excluded because of it.

GOD OF THE CITIES OF REFUGE

NUMBERS 35:9-15

[9] The LORD said to Moses, [10] "Speak to the Israelites and tell them: When you cross the Jordan into the land of Canaan, [11] designate cities to serve as cities of refuge for you, so that a person who kills someone unintentionally may flee there. [12] You will have the cities as a refuge from the avenger, so that the one who kills someone will not die until he stands trial before the assembly. [13] The cities you select will be your six cities of refuge. [14] Select three cities across the Jordan and three cities in the land of Canaan to be cities of refuge. [15] These six cities will serve as a refuge for the Israelites and for the foreigner or temporary resident among them, so that anyone who kills a person unintentionally may flee there."

READ

Read the passage without worrying about specifics; just try to understand its overall idea.

THINK

God wanted communities to try suspected murderers justly in court, but He also planned "cities of refuge" as a refuge from would-be avengers until the trial could be held. Spend time thinking about the God who is making Himself known here. Jot down a few words to describe Him.

PRAY

For a moment, set aside this passage. Check in with yourself—explore recent thoughts, feelings, and events in your life and how you've responded to them. What's primarily on your heart today? Is anything troubling you?

Bring your thoughts to the God who created cities of refuge. Read the verses again. As you do, picture God entering the room. How do you relate to His presence? Share with Him what you've been thinking, if you can. Does doing so make you uncomfortable? Why or why not?

LIVE

Think about what it's been like for you to be with the God who is both a God of justice and a God of refuge. Has it left you with questions or with new thoughts on how you want to deal with your sin in the future? Make note of anything that seems significant.

DAY 14

GOD ENCOUNTERS

On this seventh day, review and reflect on all you have read this week. Take the time to revel in the ways you've encountered God in the past six days.

LISTEN!

DEUTERONOMY 6:1-9

¹ "This is the command — the statutes and ordinances — the LORD your God has instructed me to teach you, so that you may follow them in the land you are about to enter and possess. ² Do this so that you may fear the LORD your God all the days of your life by keeping all His statutes and commands I am giving you, your son, and your grandson, and so that you may have a long life. ³ Listen, Israel, and be careful to follow them, so that you may prosper and multiply greatly, because Yahweh, the God of your fathers, has promised you a land flowing with milk and honey.

⁴ "Listen, Israel: The LORD our God, the LORD is One. ⁵ Love the LORD your God with all your heart, with all your soul, and with all your strength. ⁶ These words that I am giving you today are to be in your heart. ⁷ Repeat them to your children. Talk about them when you sit in your house and when you walk along the road, when you lie down and when you get up. ⁸ Bind them as a sign on your hand and let them be a symbol on your forehead. ⁹ Write them on the doorposts of your house and on your gates."

READ

Stand in a posture signifying respect for and full attention to God's Word. Read the passage aloud.

THINK

This passage is extremely important among Jewish people. In Jesus' time, every good Jew would recite it as soon as he woke up in the morning and right before he went to bed at night. The passage is referred to as the *Shema,* which comes from the Hebrew "to listen" or "to hear." If you visit the Western Wall in Jerusalem today, you will see Jews fervently praying in front of it. They will have leather straps wrapped around their arms and tiny boxes (called phylacteries) containing Scriptures tied to their arms and foreheads.

How seriously do you take the words of God?

PRAY

Slowly and reverently, pray the words found in verses 4 and 5: "The LORD our God, the LORD is One. Love the LORD your God with all your heart, with all your soul, and with all your strength." Repeat these words over and over again, letting what the words ask of you to sink into your heart.

LIVE

Memorize the words you just prayed, and pray them as often as you remember them.

LIVE IN HIS PRESENCE

DEUTERONOMY 10:12-21

¹² "And now, Israel, what does the LORD your God ask of you except to fear the LORD your God by walking in all His ways, to love Him, and to worship the LORD your God with all your heart and all your soul? ¹³ Keep the LORD's commands and statutes I am giving you today, for your own good. ¹⁴ The heavens, indeed the highest heavens, belong to the LORD your God, as does the earth and everything in it. ¹⁵ Yet the LORD was devoted to your fathers and loved them. He chose their descendants after them — He chose you out of all the peoples, as it is today. ¹⁶ Therefore, circumcise your hearts and don't be stiff-necked any longer. ¹⁷ For the LORD your God is the God of gods and Lord of lords, the great, mighty, and awesome God, showing no partiality and taking no bribe. ¹⁸ He executes justice for the fatherless and the widow, and loves the foreigner, giving him food and clothing. ¹⁹ You also must love the foreigner, since you were foreigners in the land of Egypt. ²⁰ You are to fear Yahweh your God and worship Him. Remain faithful to Him and take oaths in His name. ²¹ He is your praise and He is your God, who has done for you these great and awesome works your eyes have seen."

READ

Read the passage aloud slowly.

THINK

Read it aloud slowly again.

1. What phrase is most memorable?
2. What quality of God stands out to you? Why?
3. What command stands out to you? Why?

PRAY

Here are some ways to pray back the passage. Use as many of these suggestions as you wish.

- Express to God your thoughts about living in His presence. Has living in His presence been important to you or not?
- Express to God those areas in which you would guess He considers you "stiff-necked." (Pause and let this come to you. Don't necessarily go with the first thing that comes to mind.)
- Express to God your feelings about the have-nots you know (widows, orphans, foreigners). Talk to God honestly about how willing or unwilling you've been to include such people in your life.

LIVE

Experiment with living in God's presence while caring for the rest of the world. Relax. Quiet yourself. Just be.

YOU WERE ONCE SLAVES

DEUTERONOMY 24:10-15,17-22

¹⁰ "When you make a loan of any kind to your neighbor, do not enter his house to collect what he offers as security. ¹¹ You must stand outside while the man you are making the loan to brings the security out to you. ¹² If he is a poor man, you must not sleep in the garment he has given as security. ¹³ Be sure to return it to him at sunset. Then he will sleep in it and bless you, and this will be counted as righteousness to you before the LORD your God.

¹⁴ "Do not oppress a hired hand who is poor and needy, whether one of your brothers or one of the foreigners residing within a town in your land. ¹⁵ You are to pay him his wages each day before the sun sets, because he is poor and depends on them. Otherwise he will cry out to the LORD against you, and you will be held guilty. . . .

¹⁷ "Do not deny justice to a foreigner or fatherless child, and do not take a widow's garment as security. ¹⁸ Remember that you were a slave in Egypt, and the LORD your God redeemed you from there. Therefore I am commanding you to do this.

¹⁹ "When you reap the harvest in your field, and you forget a sheaf in the field, do not go back to get it. It is to be left for the foreigner, the fatherless, and the widow, so that the LORD your God may bless you in all the work of your hands. ²⁰ When you knock down the fruit from your olive tree, you must not go over the branches again. What remains will be for the foreigner, the fatherless, and the widow. ²¹ When you gather the grapes of your vineyard, you must not glean what is left. What remains will be for the foreigner, the fatherless, and the widow. ²² Remember that you were a slave in the land of Egypt. Therefore I am commanding you to do this."

READ

Read the passage, noting especially the three scenarios and God's instructions for how to respond to them.

THINK

What common theme links the three scenarios? Write it down in one sentence. Get a picture in your mind of what this God is like — One who would give such instructions to His people. What stands out to you about Him? Jot that down too.

PRAY

Sit with your eyes closed. Think about a recent encounter with someone who might relate to you like the neighbor, hired hand, foreigner, or fatherless child described in the passage. Perhaps you spoke a few words to a homeless beggar, or you listened to someone at school or work who was upset. When faced with the person's need, what did you feel? What thoughts popped into your head? What did you do? Take a few moments to explore with God what was going on in your heart during the encounter.

LIVE

Now look back at the theme you wrote down from the passage and at the traits you noticed about God. How do you picture this God responding to you as you think about the situation you faced? Do you sense Him speaking a personal message to you? What is it? (If you have a tendency to assume what God's response would be, say, something similar to what an authority figure in your life might say, resist that.) If you feel clueless about what God might be saying to you, offer this up to Him and ask Him to show you in the coming weeks.

17

LEAVING A LEGACY

DEUTERONOMY 34:1-4

[1] Then Moses went up from the plains of Moab to Mount Nebo, to the top of Pisgah, which faces Jericho, and the LORD showed him all the land: Gilead as far as Dan, [2] all of Naphtali, the land of Ephraim and Manasseh, all the land of Judah as far as the Mediterranean Sea, [3] the Negev, and the region from the Valley of Jericho, the City of Palms, as far as Zoar. [4] The LORD then said to him, "This is the land I promised Abraham, Isaac, and Jacob, 'I will give it to your descendants.' I have let you see it with your own eyes, but you will not cross into it."

READ

Read the passage the way you might to a room full of children. Articulate your words. Use inflections. Sound excited as you read.

THINK

Moses was the leader of the nation of Israel for the latter part of his life. He was mostly obedient and faithful, but there were times of disobedience. Because of that, God told Moses that the Israelites would enter the Promised Land but that he would not. In chapter 34 Moses dies atop Mount Nebo, located in the modern-day country of Jordan, just to the east of the Dead Sea in Israel.

Why do you think God takes disobedience so seriously? What have been some consequences of your own disobedience?

Are you able to trust the promises of God, even if you never end up seeing them? Why or why not?

PRAY

Ask God to help you live a life of faith and obedience, the kind of life that honors Him at all times.

LIVE

Think of Moses-like people you know — older, godly individuals living faithfully for God. Consider connecting with them and getting to know them and their stories.

COURAGEOUS WHEN IT COUNTS

JOSHUA 1:1-9

¹ After the death of Moses the LORD's servant, the LORD spoke to Joshua son of Nun, who had served Moses: ² "Moses My servant is dead. Now you and all the people prepare to cross over the Jordan to the land I am giving the Israelites. ³ I have given you every place where the sole of your foot treads, just as I promised Moses. ⁴ Your territory will be from the wilderness and Lebanon to the great Euphrates River—all the land of the Hittites—and west to the Mediterranean Sea. ⁵ No one will be able to stand against you as long as you live. I will be with you, just as I was with Moses. I will not leave you or forsake you.

⁶ "Be strong and courageous, for you will distribute the land I swore to their fathers to give them as an inheritance. ⁷ Above all, be strong and very courageous to carefully observe the whole instruction My servant Moses commanded you. Do not turn from it to the right or the left, so that you will have success wherever you go. ⁸ This book of instruction must not depart from your mouth; you are to recite it day and night so that you may carefully observe everything written in it. For then you will prosper and succeed in whatever you do. ⁹ Haven't I commanded you: be strong and courageous? Do not be afraid or discouraged, for the LORD your God is with you wherever you go."

READ

As you read the passage, imagine that you wrote these words yourself and are now reflecting on what you wrote.

THINK

Israel is grieving the loss of its trusted leader, Moses. But with every ending comes a new beginning. In the midst of the mourning, God approaches Joshua and assures him that he is the man to lead the people into the Promised Land. God promises Joshua that He will be with him and that the land will be given to the nation of Israel. God commands Joshua to be courageous and tells him to remain committed to the study of His Word.

Read verse 9 again. Is embracing these words in your life hard or easy? At what times are you scared? Why? When you are fearful, what can you do about it?

PRAY

Be blatantly honest with God about your fears, worries, concerns, and anxieties. Tell Him exactly why you are scared, and be assured that He hears you. Thank Him for listening. Then reread the passage, personalizing the words by making God's words to Joshua your very own.

LIVE

When you find yourself in situations that expose your fears, remember the promises of God—His presence and His guidance for you into the future.

SLOW DOWN AND INQUIRE

JOSHUA 9:3-9,11,14-16

³ When the inhabitants of Gibeon heard what Joshua had done to Jericho and Ai, ⁴ they acted deceptively. They gathered provisions and took worn-out sacks on their donkeys and old wineskins, cracked and mended. ⁵ They wore old, patched sandals on their feet and threadbare clothing on their bodies. Their entire provision of bread was dry and crumbly. ⁶ They went to Joshua in the camp at Gilgal and said to him and the men of Israel, "We have come from a distant land. Please make a treaty with us."

⁷ The men of Israel replied to the Hivites, "Perhaps you live among us. How can we make a treaty with you?"

⁸ They said to Joshua, "We are your servants."

Then Joshua asked them, "Who are you and where do you come from?"

⁹ They replied to him, "Your servants have come from a far away land because of the reputation of the LORD your God. For we have heard of His fame, and all that He did in Egypt. . . . ¹¹ So our elders and all the inhabitants of our land told us, 'Take provisions with you for the journey; go and meet them and say, "We are your servants. Please make a treaty with us."' . . . ¹⁴ Then the men of Israel took some of their provisions, but did not seek the LORD's counsel. ¹⁵ So Joshua established peace with them and made a treaty to let them live, and the leaders of the community swore an oath to them. ¹⁶ Three days after making the treaty with them, they heard that the Gibeonites were their neighbors, living among them.

READ

Read the passage slowly. Keep in mind that the people of Gibeon were afraid because Joshua had conquered Jericho and Ai.

THINK

Read the passage slowly again. The people of Gibeon repeatedly flattered Joshua in order to get their way. He accepted their evidence without inquiring after God. Is there a place in your life where you are susceptible to offers and flattery, so you form attachments without asking God for input? (*Attachments* refers to relationships and commitments to people, tasks, and organizations.)

PRAY

Ask God to help you go over your attachments by moving through the following questions as if God were sitting next to you with His arm around you.

What attachments, if any, have you formed because you think the people involved do something for you?

What attachments, if any, have you rushed into without investigating further, especially by asking God what you need to know about the situation?

Ask God to show you where, if at all, you need to back off from an attachment.

LIVE

Wait with an open heart for anything God might say to you. If nothing comes to you, ask God to make it apparent in the next few weeks if there's anything you need to know about your attachments.

DAY 21

GOD ENCOUNTERS

On this seventh day, review and reflect on all you have read this week. Take the time to revel in the ways you've encountered God in the past six days.

WE WILL WORSHIP

JOSHUA 24:16-24

¹⁶ The people replied, "We will certainly not abandon the LORD to worship other gods! ¹⁷ For the LORD our God brought us and our fathers out of the land of Egypt, out of the place of slavery, and performed these great signs before our eyes. He also protected us all along the way we went and among all the peoples whose lands we traveled through. ¹⁸ The LORD drove out before us all the peoples, including the Amorites who lived in the land. We too will worship the LORD, because He is our God."

¹⁹ But Joshua told the people, "You will not be able to worship Yahweh, because He is a holy God. He is a jealous God; He will not remove your transgressions and sins. ²⁰ If you abandon the LORD and worship foreign gods, He will turn against you, harm you, and completely destroy you, after He has been good to you."

²¹ "No!" the people answered Joshua. "We will worship the LORD."

²² Joshua then told the people, "You are witnesses against yourselves that you yourselves have chosen to worship Yahweh."

"We are witnesses," they said.

²³ "Then get rid of the foreign gods that are among you and offer your hearts to the LORD, the God of Israel."

²⁴ So the people said to Joshua, "We will worship the LORD our God and obey Him."

READ

Read the passage, paying special attention to what it shows you about the nature of the human heart.

PRAY

As you read of the Israelites' passionate desire to follow God ("We will certainly not abandon the LORD!"), what is your reaction to them? When you take a bird's-eye view of the history of Israel, noticing their many rebellions against God and inability to stay committed, what does it make you think and feel? Do you relate to Israel at all—in their desire, in their failure, or both? Talk to God about your thoughts and feelings, eventually sitting quietly to listen for His response.

THINK/LIVE

Write about your prayer experience. What was it like for you? What stood out to you about the Israelites? About yourself? About God? If you contemplated your own fickleness or zeal, do you sense that God is leading or challenging you in some way regarding this? Make a note of anything that seems significant.

WHEN YOU CAN'T TAKE THE CREDIT

JUDGES 7:1-7

¹ Jerubbaal (that is, Gideon) and everyone who was with him, got up early and camped beside the spring of Harod. The camp of Midian was north of them, below the hill of Moreh, in the valley. ² The LORD said to Gideon, "You have too many people for Me to hand the Midianites over to you, or else Israel might brag: 'I did it myself.' ³ Now announce in the presence of the people: 'Whoever is fearful and trembling may turn back and leave Mount Gilead.'" So 22,000 of the people turned back, but 10,000 remained.

⁴ Then the LORD said to Gideon, "There are still too many people. Take them down to the water, and I will test them for you there. If I say to you, 'This one can go with you,' he can go. But if I say about anyone, 'This one cannot go with you,' he cannot go." ⁵ So he brought the people down to the water, and the LORD said to Gideon, "Separate everyone who laps water with his tongue like a dog. Do the same with everyone who kneels to drink." ⁶ The number of those who lapped with their hands to their mouths was 300 men, and all the rest of the people knelt to drink water. ⁷ The LORD said to Gideon, "I will deliver you with the 300 men who lapped and hand the Midianites over to you. But everyone else is to go home."

READ

As you read the passage, underline the words that stick out to you or surprise you.

THINK

The book of Judges is filled with violence. Christians struggle to understand how God's redemptive plan can involve these events. Yet God's power is at work when the Israelites battle foreign, pagan armies. God uses Gideon to lead the nation into battle for His purposes. But as He guides Gideon, He asks much of him. God cuts Gideon's army down from thirty-two thousand men to ten thousand, and eventually to three hundred. God wants to show *His* power through Gideon. He wants Israel to credit Him.

When have you accomplished things in your own strength and taken all the credit while forgetting about God? When have you accomplished things that seemed big and impossible, knowing you did so only because God intervened?

PRAY

Write a list of huge requests you have for God — things so large that if they came to fruition, you would know they did so only because God intervened. Spend time praying through this list.

LIVE

Review your list on a regular basis, watching for God's incredible — and at times subtle — intervention. As you see God's faithfulness, thank Him often that He is a caring friend.

TALKING WITH GOD

JUDGES 13:2-3,6-9,17-20

² There was a certain man from Zorah, from the family of Dan, whose name was Manoah; his wife was unable to conceive and had no children. ³ The Angel of the LORD appeared to the woman and said to her, "It is true that you are unable to conceive and have no children, but you will conceive and give birth to a son." . . .

⁶ Then the woman went and told her husband, "A man of God came to me. He looked like the awe-inspiring Angel of God. I didn't ask Him where He came from, and He didn't tell me His name. ⁷ He said to me, 'You will conceive and give birth to a son. Therefore, do not drink wine or beer, and do not eat anything unclean, because the boy will be a Nazirite to God from birth until the day of his death.'"

⁸ Manoah prayed to the LORD and said, "Please Lord, let the man of God you sent come again to us and teach us what we should do for the boy who will be born."

⁹ God listened to Manoah, and the Angel of God came again to the woman. She was sitting in the field, and her husband Manoah was not with her. . . .

¹⁷ Then Manoah said to Him, "What is Your name, so that we may honor You when Your words come true?"

¹⁸ "Why do you ask My name," the Angel of the LORD asked him, "since it is wonderful."

¹⁹ Manoah took a young goat and a grain offering and offered them on a rock to the LORD, and He did a wonderful thing while Manoah and his wife were watching. ²⁰ When the flame went up from the altar to the sky, the Angel of the LORD went up in its flame. When Manoah and his wife saw this, they fell facedown on the ground.

READ

Read the passage aloud slowly. Manoah and his wife will become Samson's parents, and so God prepares them for this task. (Read the expanded passage to hear even more of the story.)

THINK

Read the passage aloud slowly again, taking note of the back-and-forth conversation between God and this couple. It forms a picture of what an interactive life with God might be like.

Notice the conversational interaction: who listened; who asked questions.

Would you have asked the question Manoah asked ("What is Your name?") or a different question?

How would it be to talk to God when lying facedown (see verse 20)?

PRAY

Try this: Lie facedown on the floor or the ground as Manoah and his wife did. Ask God for further instruction about something in your life. Notice what it's like to talk to God in this position. Don't get up too soon.

LIVE

Rest your forehead on the ground with your arms above you. Just "be" before God this way.

LET ME BE AVENGED

JUDGES 16:25-30

²⁵ When they were drunk, they said, "Bring Samson here to entertain us." So they brought Samson from prison, and he entertained them. They had him stand between the pillars.

²⁶ Samson said to the young man who was leading him by the hand, "Lead me where I can feel the pillars supporting the temple, so I can lean against them." ²⁷ The temple was full of men and women; all the leaders of the Philistines were there, and about 3,000 men and women were on the roof watching Samson entertain them. ²⁸ He called out to the LORD: "Lord GOD, please remember me. Strengthen me, God, just once more. With one act of vengeance, let me pay back the Philistines for my two eyes." ²⁹ Samson took hold of the two middle pillars supporting the temple and leaned against them, one on his right hand and the other on his left. ³⁰ Samson said, "Let me die with the Philistines." He pushed with all his might, and the temple fell on the leaders and all the people in it. And the dead he killed at his death were more than those he had killed in his life.

READ

Sit quietly and let your thoughts settle. Now read the passage silently. Let the events of the story filter into your heart and interact with your present state of mind.

THINK

What stands out to you about Samson's dramatic action and the ending of his life? Do you resonate with his deep desire for justice to be served? What do you observe about how he acted on that desire for revenge?

PRAY

Read the passage a second time, looking specifically for a word or phrase about Samson's desire for revenge or justice that is meaningful to you. Maybe his act angers you, or you feel a similar desire. When you finish reading, close your eyes. Recall the word or phrase and sit quietly, mulling it over. Let it stimulate you into a dialogue with God.

LIVE

Read the passage a third time, watching how God interacts with Samson and with the Philistines: Although God does not directly act or speak in the passage, He grants Samson's request to avenge himself, and He allows the Philistines to lose their lives. What stands out to you about God's involvement (or lack of involvement)? Talk with Him about your perception of Him in this passage. Be open to what He may be showing you through what you read.

WELCOMING THE STRANGER

RUTH 3:1-2,4,8-13,16-18

¹ Ruth's mother-in-law Naomi said to her, "My daughter, shouldn't I find security for you, so that you will be taken care of? ² Now isn't Boaz our relative? Haven't you been working with his female servants? This evening he will be winnowing barley on the threshing floor. . . . ⁴ When he lies down, notice the place where he's lying, go in and uncover his feet, and lie down. Then he will explain to you what you should do." . . .

⁸ At midnight, Boaz was startled, turned over, and there lying at his feet was a woman! ⁹ So he asked, "Who are you?"

"I am Ruth, your slave," she replied. "Spread your cloak over me, for you are a family redeemer."

¹⁰ Then he said, "May the Lord bless you, my daughter. You have shown more kindness now than before, because you have not pursued younger men, whether rich or poor. ¹¹ Now don't be afraid, my daughter. I will do for you whatever you say, since all the people in my town know that you are a woman of noble character. ¹² Yes, it is true that I am a family redeemer, but there is a redeemer closer than I am. ¹³ Stay here tonight, and in the morning, if he wants to redeem you, that's good. Let him redeem you. But if he doesn't want to redeem you, as the Lord lives, I will. Now lie down until morning." . . .

¹⁶ She went to her mother-in-law, Naomi, who asked her, "How did it go, my daughter?"

Then Ruth told her everything the man had done for her. ¹⁷ She said, "He gave me these six measures of barley, because he said, 'Don't go back to your mother-in-law empty-handed.'"

¹⁸ Naomi said, "My daughter, wait until you find out how things go, for he won't rest unless he resolves this today."

READ

Read the passage slowly. Naomi is Ruth's mother-in-law, the mother of Ruth's deceased husband.

THINK

Read the passage again slowly, this time keeping in mind that Ruth is a foreign Moabite woman while Naomi and Boaz are Israelites. Ruth is different from them in nationality, background, and age.

Who do you identify with most: Naomi or Boaz, the older, wiser Israelites, or Ruth, the younger, foreign woman?

Imagining you are the person you identified with, how does it feel to hear or say the term *daughter*? (Again, this was unusual because of their differences in nationality.)

What might God be saying to you about the "strangers" in your life?

What might God be telling you about the places in your life where you feel like a stranger?

PRAY

Thank God for how He provides for those who are strangers and aliens, that He isn't partial to just one group. Ask God how you might partner with Him in this.

LIVE

In the quiet, consider God's attentiveness to all people. Is there someone specific He brings to mind? Today and in the next few days, look for opportunities to pay attention to the stranger in the same way God does.

DECIPHERING GOD'S VOICE

1 SAMUEL 3:8-10

8 Once again, for the third time, the LORD called Samuel. He got up, went to Eli, and said, "Here I am; you called me."

Then Eli understood that the LORD was calling the boy. 9 He told Samuel, "Go and lie down. If He calls you, say, 'Speak, LORD, for Your servant is listening.'" So Samuel went and lay down in his place.

10 The LORD came, stood there, and called as before, "Samuel, Samuel!"

Samuel responded, "Speak, for Your servant is listening."

READ

As you read the passage, imagine yourself in the story, watching the situation from the back of the room.

THINK

At the beginning of 1 Samuel, Hannah wanted to give birth to a son, but she was barren. She prayed earnestly, crying out to the Lord. God heard her prayer, and she gave birth to Samuel. She dedicated him to the temple, where he ministered under Eli the priest. Scholars believe Samuel was a teenager when the events of this passage occurred.

Does hearing God so clearly seem possible? How do you decipher between His voice and the other voices in your life? Samuel needed Eli's guidance for this. What people around you could help you discern when God is trying to communicate with you and what He's saying?

PRAY

Often the most effective way to hear God's voice is to still our minds and quiet our hearts for a considerable amount of time. Set aside twenty minutes in a quiet place and make yourself comfortable. Invite God to communicate with you. Don't read or pray. Just listen and be, bringing your mind back if it wanders.

LIVE

Sometime in the next week, schedule another twenty minutes of silence and once again listen and wait for God to speak to you. Don't give up. Your patience will pay off.

DAY 28

GOD ENCOUNTERS

On this seventh day, review and reflect on all you have read this week. Take the time to revel in the ways you've encountered God in the past six days.

IS GOD ENOUGH?

1 SAMUEL 8:1,3-7,9-10,19-22

¹ When Samuel grew old, he appointed his sons as judges over Israel. . . .
³ However, his sons did not walk in his ways — they turned toward dishonest gain, took bribes, and perverted justice.

⁴ So all the elders of Israel gathered together and went to Samuel at Ramah. ⁵ They said to him, "Look, you are old, and your sons do not follow your example. Therefore, appoint a king to judge us the same as all the other nations have."

⁶ When they said, "Give us a king to judge us," Samuel considered their demand sinful, so he prayed to the LORD. ⁷ But the LORD told him, "Listen to the people and everything they say to you. They have not rejected you; they have rejected Me as their king. . . . ⁹ Listen to them, but you must solemnly warn them and tell them about the rights of the king who will rule over them."

¹⁰ Samuel told all the LORD's words to the people who were asking him for a king. . . .

¹⁹ The people refused to listen to Samuel. "No!" they said. "We must have a king over us. ²⁰ Then we'll be like all the other nations: our king will judge us, go out before us, and fight our battles."

²¹ Samuel listened to all the people's words and then repeated them to the LORD. ²² "Listen to them," the LORD told Samuel. "Appoint a king for them."

Then Samuel told the men of Israel, "Each of you, go back to your city."

READ

Read the passage aloud slowly.

THINK

The Israelites wanted God, but they were afraid they'd miss out if they didn't have a king like the other nations. They wanted to fit in with the other nations by having a king lead them and fight their battles for them. Read the passage again, this time deeply feeling the determination of the Israelites and the disappointment of Samuel.

1. Who do you resemble most? (a) Samuel — being confronted by people asking him to make changes he believes are wrong, or (b) the Israelites — wanting to be like others?
2. If you chose *a*, converse with God about this as Samuel did: What would you like to say to God regarding these demands? If *b*, how would you finish this sentence: I want to be like _____. If you continue wanting to be like a certain person, how might it cheat you out of what God wants for *you*?
3. What would your life look like if you trusted God to give you what you need, regardless of how odd that may seem when compared to other people's lives?

PRAY

Be honest with God about any frustration of wanting to be like others or frustration with those who do. Ask God to show you the advantages of trusting Him more with these things.

LIVE

While you sit in a quiet place, practice feeling okay being different from other people. If you can, view that difference as special or chosen. Relax with a sense of God's hand on you.

29

MAY THE LORD BE WITH YOU

1 SAMUEL 17:31-40

³¹ What David said was overheard and reported to Saul, so he had David brought to him. ³² David said to Saul, "Don't let anyone be discouraged by him; your servant will go and fight this Philistine!"

³³ But Saul replied, "You can't go fight this Philistine. You're just a youth, and he's been a warrior since he was young."

³⁴ David answered Saul: "Your servant has been tending his father's sheep. Whenever a lion or a bear came and carried off a lamb from the flock, ³⁵ I went after it, struck it down, and rescued the lamb from its mouth. If it reared up against me, I would grab it by its fur, strike it down, and kill it. ³⁶ Your servant has killed lions and bears; this uncircumcised Philistine will be like one of them, for he has defied the armies of the living God." ³⁷ Then David said, "The LORD who rescued me from the paw of the lion and the paw of the bear will rescue me from the hand of this Philistine."

Saul said to David, "Go, and may the LORD be with you."

³⁸ Then Saul had his own military clothes put on David. He put a bronze helmet on David's head and had him put on armor. ³⁹ David strapped his sword on over the military clothes and tried to walk, but he was not used to them. "I can't walk in these," David said to Saul, "I'm not used to them." So David took them off. ⁴⁰ Instead, he took his staff in his hand and chose five smooth stones from the wadi and put them in the pouch, in his shepherd's bag. Then, with his sling in his hand, he approached the Philistine.

READ

While you read, let the scenario unfold in your mind. When David describes grabbing a bear by its fur, hear the roaring and grunting. Feel the ponderous weight of the bronze helmet, and then the light, smooth weight of the stones in your hand.

THINK

What one particular event, character, or feature of the story stands out to you? Take time to concentrate on that. Are you drawn to David's courage? Maybe you're surprised when David rejects Saul's armor. Consider what your own reaction would be, and then consider how the characters in the story reacted. As you meditate, allow God to show you more about yourself, Him, and the way life is.

PRAY/LIVE

Priest and author Henri Nouwen wrote, "Make the conscious choice to move the attention of your anxious heart away from [the] waves and direct it to the One who walks on them and says, 'It's me. Don't be afraid.' . . . Look at him and say, 'Lord, have mercy.' Say it again and again, not anxiously but with confidence that he is very close to you and will put your soul to rest."[2] (To read the rest of the story, see John 6:16-21.)

What do you feel anxious about, if anything? What might happen if you shifted your attention "away from [the] waves" and "to the One who walks on them"? What concrete thing could you do to help redirect your attention?

HONORING AND VALUING OTHERS

1 SAMUEL 26:7-11

⁷ That night, David and Abishai came to the troops, and Saul was lying there asleep in the inner circle of the camp with his spear stuck in the ground by his head. Abner and the troops were lying around him. ⁸ Then Abishai said to David, "Today God has handed your enemy over to you. Let me thrust the spear through him into the ground just once. I won't have to strike him twice!"

⁹ But David said to Abishai, "Don't destroy him, for who can lift a hand against the Lord's anointed and be blameless?" ¹⁰ David added, "As the Lord lives, the Lord will certainly strike him down: either his day will come and he will die, or he will go into battle and perish. ¹¹ However, because of the Lord, I will never lift my hand against the Lord's anointed. Instead, take the spear and the water jug by his head, and let's go."

READ

Hold this book in your hands. As you read the passage, pace the room or walk outside. As you do, consider the speed at which you are reading. Take your time and find a rhythm of reading that matches your pace. (For example, if you are reading fast, walk fast.)

THINK

Earlier in 1 Samuel, God anointed David to be the future king of Israel, even though Saul was still on the throne. This man, overcome with cruelty, jealousy, evil, and insecurity, then repeatedly attempted to take David's life. For many years, David hid from Saul's army.

One night, David and Abishai sneak into Saul's camp, and there Abishai notices the perfect opportunity to kill Saul. But David refuses. David is so certain of God's sovereignty that he refuses to kill Saul.

We all have enemies, big or small, and desire for them to come to ruin. As you read the expanded passage, ponder the interchange between Saul and David in verses 21-24.

PRAY

Think of the people you consider your enemies. Pray for them and ask God to help you honor them, even though doing so may seem impossible.

LIVE

Seek out intentional opportunities to honor those who dishonor you and to value the lives of those who do not value you.

PAIN, DISAPPOINTMENT, AND HEARTBREAK

2 SAMUEL 1:24-27

²⁴ Daughters of Israel, weep for Saul,
who clothed you in scarlet, with luxurious things,
who decked your garments with gold ornaments.
²⁵ How the mighty have fallen in the thick of battle!
Jonathan lies slain on your heights.
²⁶ I grieve for you, Jonathan, my brother.
You were such a friend to me.
Your love for me was more wonderful
than the love of women.
²⁷ How the mighty have fallen
and the weapons of war have perished!

READ

King Saul (who tried to kill David many times) and his son, Jonathan (David's best friend), are dead. If possible, read the expanded passage, the song of lament David wrote in response to the news of their deaths.

THINK

Sometimes pain and suffering are the central emotions of our hearts. We cannot avoid pain and suffering, but we can control how we respond to them. David's reaction is to be honest and open about the pain rather than avoid it or pretend it isn't there.

What is your response to heartbreak? Do you think David's response is healthy? Why or why not? What thoughts and feelings go through you as David honors the evil king in death?

PRAY

Think of the pain and heartbreak you have experienced in your lifetime. Maybe that pain is a current reality. Though doing so may be difficult, spend time expressing your pain in a lament to God. See Him attentively listening to you and reaching out to comfort you. What does it feel like to be comforted?

LIVE

Live knowing that God is loving enough to listen to you and big enough to care for you in your pain.

GOD'S TRACK RECORD WITH ME

2 SAMUEL 7:18,20-23,28-29

¹⁸ Then King David went in, sat in the LORD's presence, and said, "Who am I, Lord GOD, and what is my house that You have brought me this far? . . . ²⁰ What more can David say to You? You know Your servant, Lord GOD. ²¹ Because of Your word and according to Your will, You have revealed all these great things to Your servant.

²² "This is why You are great, Lord GOD. There is no one like You, and there is no God besides You, as all we have heard confirms. ²³ And who is like Your people Israel? God came to one nation on earth in order to redeem a people for Himself, to make a name for Himself, and to perform for them great and awesome acts, driving out nations and their gods before Your people You redeemed for Yourself from Egypt. . . .

²⁸ "Lord GOD, You are God; Your words are true, and You have promised this grace to Your servant. ²⁹ Now, please bless Your servant's house so that it will continue before You forever. For You, Lord GOD, have spoken, and with Your blessing Your servant's house will be blessed forever."

READ

Read the passage aloud slowly.

THINK

Read the passage even more slowly and deliberately, considering every word. Listen for the line that resonates with you and read it again after you finish the passage. Pause. Consider any of the following issues, letting God nudge you.

- In what ways has God changed you that you can be grateful for?
- What has God brought you out of?
- How has God been heroic regarding you (performing "great and awesome acts, driving out nations and their gods before Your people")?
- What would you like to ask God for regarding the future?

PRAY

Pray through the passage, innovating and personalizing your prayer according to the questions in the Think section.

LIVE

Give this a try: Consider the line from the passage that caught your attention and put it to a tune from a song you already know (or make a tune up, if you wish). Sing that line and then sit in the quiet. Sing it again and sit in the quiet. Sing it one more time and sit in the quiet.

HONORING OTHERS

2 SAMUEL 9:8-13

[8] Mephibosheth bowed down and said, "What is your servant that you take an interest in a dead dog like me?"

[9] Then the king summoned Saul's attendant Ziba and said to him, "I have given to your master's grandson all that belonged to Saul and his family. [10] You, your sons, and your servants are to work the ground for him, and you are to bring in the crops so your master's grandson will have food to eat. But Mephibosheth, your master's grandson, is always to eat at my table." Now Ziba had 15 sons and 20 servants.

[11] Ziba said to the king, "Your servant will do all my lord the king commands."

So Mephibosheth ate at David's table just like one of the king's sons. [12] Mephibosheth had a young son whose name was Mica. All those living in Ziba's house were Mephibosheth's servants. [13] However, Mephibosheth lived in Jerusalem because he always ate at the king's table. His feet had been injured.

READ

Read the passage slowly, setting yourself inside the throne room. Look at David up close — the imposing crown, the rugged face that's seen countless wars, the lavish surroundings. Now see Mephibosheth, "a dead dog" hunched in fear, embarrassed and uncomfortable. How might he have come into the room with his feet injured? What feelings rise up in you as you see the story play out? What questions come to mind?

THINK

Pause to become aware of how you relate to what is unfolding here. Which character do you identify with, if any? Why?

PRAY

Read the story a second time, being aware of memories, thoughts, or ideas it triggers. Read it one last time, listening for how the story's message about honoring others relates to what is in you today. Spend time meditating on what you discover.

LIVE

Ask God if there is something He is specifically inviting you to do based on your reading today. Is there anything standing in your way of responding? Explore it with God. Talk to Him about what holds you back from following Him completely.

DAY 35

GOD ENCOUNTERS

On this seventh day, review and reflect on all you have read this week. Take the time to revel in the ways you've encountered God in the past six days.

AN ABSALOM MOMENT

2 SAMUEL 15:3-6

³ Absalom said to him, "Look, your claims are good and right, but the king does not have anyone to listen to you." ⁴ He added, "If only someone would appoint me judge in the land. Then anyone who had a grievance or dispute could come to me, and I would make sure he received justice." ⁵ When a person approached to bow down to him, Absalom reached out his hand, took hold of him, and kissed him. ⁶ Absalom did this to all the Israelites who came to the king for a settlement. So Absalom stole the hearts of the men of Israel.

READ

Read the passage five times.

THINK

There are points in our lives (more often than we would like to admit) when we attempt consciously and subconsciously to promote ourselves in unhealthy and selfish ways. We puff ourselves up, brag about our accomplishments, and embellish the truth.

Absalom, the son of King David, promotes himself for selfish gain in front of those who came to the city gate. The text says he "stole the hearts of the men of Israel."

When are you most tempted to steal the hearts of everyone in _____? Think about your most recent Absalom moment. Consider the roots of your temptation and how you might avoid it in the future.

PRAY

Spend time inviting God to remind you that He loves you just the way you are, that you cannot earn His approval. Welcome God to show you your true identity as His child, an identity that is defined not by what you do, but by who you are and to whom you belong.

LIVE

Ask a good friend to gently keep you accountable when you begin to promote yourself in front of others. Be ready to accept your friend's input.

LOVING THOSE IN THE HERE AND NOW

2 SAMUEL 19:1-8

¹ It was reported to Joab, "The king is weeping. He's mourning over Absalom." ² That day's victory was turned into mourning for all the troops because on that day the troops heard, "The king is grieving over his son." ³ So they returned to the city quietly that day like people come in when they are humiliated after fleeing in battle. ⁴ But the king hid his face and cried out at the top of his voice, "My son Absalom! Absalom, my son, my son!"

⁵ Then Joab went into the house to the king and said, "Today you have shamed all your soldiers — those who rescued your life and the lives of your sons and daughters, your wives, and your concubines. ⁶ You love your enemies and hate those who love you! Today you have made it clear that the commanders and soldiers mean nothing to you. In fact, today I know that if Absalom were alive and all of us were dead, it would be fine with you!

⁷ "Now get up! Go out and encourage your soldiers, for I swear by the LORD that if you don't go out, not a man will remain with you tonight. This will be worse for you than all the trouble that has come to you from your youth until now!"

⁸ So the king got up and sat in the gate, and all the people were told: "Look, the king is sitting in the gate." Then they all came into the king's presence.

Meanwhile, each Israelite had fled to his tent.

READ

Read the passage aloud slowly. Absalom had rebelled against his father, David, and taken over Israel. As David mourns Absalom, the people who defended David and brought him back with honor are listening.

THINK

Read the passage aloud slowly again. David did what we often do. He lived in regret. He wanted what he used to have and what he couldn't now have. As a result, he undervalued and discouraged the people who had stood by him and helped him.

1. Who do you identify with more: David or the army?
2. Consider their feelings: David living in regret; the army feeling ignored and discarded.
3. Consider their next steps: David turning his heart to the people around him who loved him; the army speaking up and stating their needs to a hurting person.

PRAY

Pray for yourself and others, especially that they'll see and implement any possible next steps (for example, moving out of regret and valuing the people in front of them, or speaking up to someone who is devaluing others).

LIVE

Let your mind rest in glad appreciation for those who stand by you. Ask God for opportunities to bless them. Then in the dailiness of life, look for those opportunities.

GOD FEELS THE PAIN

2 SAMUEL 24:13-17,25

¹³ So Gad went to David, told him the choices, and asked him, "Do you want three years of famine to come on your land, to flee from your foes three months while they pursue you, or to have a plague in your land three days? Now, think it over and decide what answer I should take back to the One who sent me."

¹⁴ David answered Gad, "I have great anxiety. Please, let us fall into the LORD's hands because His mercies are great, but don't let me fall into human hands."

¹⁵ So the LORD sent a plague on Israel from that morning until the appointed time, and from Dan to Beer-sheba 70,000 men died. ¹⁶ Then the angel extended his hand toward Jerusalem to destroy it, but the LORD relented concerning the destruction and said to the angel who was destroying the people, "Enough, withdraw your hand now!" The angel of the LORD was then at the threshing floor of Araunah the Jebusite.

¹⁷ When David saw the angel striking the people, he said to the LORD, "Look, I am the one who has sinned; I am the one who has done wrong. But these sheep, what have they done? Please, let Your hand be against me and my father's family." . . .

²⁵ He built an altar to the LORD there and offered burnt offerings and fellowship offerings. Then the LORD answered prayer on behalf of the land, and the plague on Israel ended.

READ

Skim the expanded passage. Now read the excerpt three times carefully.

THINK/PRAY

Set the text aside and imaginatively replay the story, inserting yourself as a character in it. Perhaps you will be one of David's elders, or David himself.

What do you think and feel as you hear God's words of discipline? What do you experience as you walk through this tension-filled and tragic day? What do you see? Hear? Smell? What questions do you have for God? Are you angry? Afraid? Talk to Him.

As the end of the day approaches and you see God's interaction with the angel, what is that like for you? When God's heart is changed by David's prayers, what thoughts and feelings bubble up in you? Express them to God.

LIVE

C. S. Lewis wrote, "[Each sinful act leaves a mark] on that tiny central self which no one sees in this life but which each of us will have to endure — or enjoy — for ever. One man may be so placed that his anger sheds the blood of thousands, and another so placed that, however angry he gets, he will only be laughed at. But the little mark on the soul may be much the same in both."[3] Are there any "little marks" on your soul that you haven't talked about with God? Explore recent experiences, reactions, thoughts, and feelings you've had. What do they tell you about what's inside your heart? Talk to God about this, and make note of any action you feel He is leading you to.

A DREAM FULFILLED

1 KINGS 5:1-5

¹ Hiram king of Tyre sent his servants to Solomon when he heard that he had been anointed king in his father's place, for Hiram had always been friends with David.

² Solomon sent this message to Hiram: ³ "You know my father David was not able to build a temple for the name of Yahweh his God. This was because of the warfare all around him until the LORD put his enemies under his feet. ⁴ The LORD my God has now given me rest all around; there is no enemy or crisis. ⁵ So I plan to build a temple for the name of Yahweh my God, according to what the LORD promised my father David: 'I will put your son on your throne in your place, and he will build the temple for My name.'"

READ

Read the passage aloud slowly.

THINK

Read the passage aloud slowly again, especially verses 3-5.

1. Listen for the words or phrases that stand out to you, perhaps one of these:

   - "build a temple for the name of Yahweh his God"
   - "warfare all around him until the LORD put his enemies under his feet"
   - "The LORD my God has now given me rest all around; there is no enemy or crisis."
   - "I plan to build a temple for the name of Yahweh my God, according to what the LORD promised my father David."

   These phrases indicate that David lived an interactive life with God and that Solomon is attempting to do the same. They also refer to David and Solomon's dream coming true. David had wisely let go of his dream of building the temple, while Solomon was now taking the next step by implementing the dream.

2. What dreams have you had?
3. What dreams have you let go of or picked up?

PRAY

Talk to God about the phrases in the passage that hint at dreams you have. Ask God to give you wisdom about whether you need to let go of these dreams or pick them up. Ask God for vision and power to take your next step.

LIVE

Relish the peace that God gives, knowing that dreams don't have to be realized today. Maybe ponder and pursue your next step. Put on the idea of readiness and see if it fits.

HEAR MY PRAYERS

1 KINGS 8:22-30

²² Then Solomon stood before the altar of the LORD in front of the entire congregation of Israel and spread out his hands toward heaven. ²³ He said:

> LORD God of Israel, there is no God like You
> in heaven above or on earth below,
> keeping the gracious covenant with Your servants
> who walk before You with their whole heart.
> ²⁴ You have kept what You promised to Your servant,
> my father David. You spoke directly to him
> and You fulfilled Your promise by Your power as it is today.
> ²⁵ Therefore, LORD God of Israel, keep what You promised
> to Your servant, my father David: You will never fail to have a man
> to sit before Me on the throne of Israel, if only your sons guard
> their walk before Me as you have walked before Me.
> ²⁶ Now LORD God of Israel, please confirm what You promised
> to Your servant, my father David.
>
> ²⁷ But will God indeed live on earth?
> Even heaven, the highest heaven, cannot contain You,
> much less this temple I have built.
> ²⁸ Listen to Your servant's prayer and his petition,
> LORD my God, so that You may hear the cry and the prayer
> that Your servant prays before You today,
> ²⁹ so that Your eyes may watch over this temple night and day,
> toward the place where You said: My name will be there,
> and so that You may hear the prayer
> that Your servant prays toward this place.
> ³⁰ Hear the petition of Your servant and Your people Israel,
> which they pray toward this place. May You hear in Your
> dwelling place in heaven. May You hear and forgive.

READ

Read the passage.

THINK

What's your immediate reaction to Solomon's candid prayer to God? Think about the statements Solomon makes and the things he asks God to do. Are they things you could let yourself ask of God? Or do they indicate a belief in qualities of God that you have not encountered or experienced? Which qualities?

PRAY

Read Solomon's prayer again, this time listening for what stands out to you as representing the lack of belief you noticed in yourself when you read the passage the first time. Explore your reaction more deeply, paying attention to what it tells you about yourself. Maybe you feel that you can bring to God only desires that are completely selfless, or perhaps you don't trust that He loves you. Share with God what you uncover.

LIVE

Ignatius of Loyola once said, "Everything that one turns in the direction of God is prayer." No matter what has arisen in you during this time — irritation, fear, desire, disinterest, lack of trust in God — it can all be prayer when shared with Him; it's all part of your conversation with God. Notice how Solomon lets his anxiety and insecurity spill into his prayer to God, and allow yourself to do the same.

IDOL FACTORIES

1 KINGS 12:27-33

²⁷ "If these people regularly go to offer sacrifices in the LORD's temple in Jerusalem, the heart of these people will return to their lord, Rehoboam king of Judah. They will murder me and go back to the king of Judah." ²⁸ So the king sought advice.

Then he made two golden calves, and he said to the people, "Going to Jerusalem is too difficult for you. Israel, here is your God who brought you out of the land of Egypt." ²⁹ He set up one in Bethel, and put the other in Dan. ³⁰ This led to sin; the people walked in procession before one of the calves all the way to Dan.

³¹ Jeroboam also built shrines on the high places and set up priests from every class of people who were not Levites. ³² Jeroboam made a festival in the eighth month on the fifteenth day of the month, like the festival in Judah. He offered sacrifices on the altar; he made this offering in Bethel to sacrifice to the calves he had set up. He also stationed the priests in Bethel for the high places he had set up. ³³ He offered sacrifices on the altar he had set up in Bethel on the fifteenth day of the eighth month. He chose this month on his own. He made a festival for the Israelites, offered sacrifices on the altar, and burned incense.

READ

Each time you read this passage, focus on the sentence "This led to sin."

THINK

Israel at this time was split into two sections: the northern and the southern kingdoms. Jeroboam was ruling in the northern kingdom. He erected two golden calves (as Aaron had at Sinai in Exodus). In addition to calves, he erected forbidden shrines and created a sacred holiday.

Instead of placing his entire trust in Yahweh, Jeroboam chose to erect idols to be the center of worship for the people in his kingdom. Under his leadership, the significance of worshiping the Lord God was lessened and eventually lost.

Sneering at such blatant disrespect of the living God is easy for us. But even though we don't erect golden calves, our focus on certain things eclipses our worship of God. John Calvin said that our hearts are idol factories.

Meditate on some of the golden calves in your life that eclipse your worship of God. These could be reputation, power, wealth, identity, fame, church, relationships — anything that takes your eyes off God.

PRAY

Spend time confessing your golden calves. Ask the Holy Spirit to pinch you each time you turn to them.

LIVE

Be aware that your heart is an idol factory. Recognize that idols come in all shapes and sizes. When you find yourself bowing a knee to them, return to the Lord in humility.

41
42

DAY 42

GOD ENCOUNTERS

On this seventh day, review and reflect on all you have read this week. Take the time to revel in the ways you've encountered God in the past six days.

WHEN TRUSTING GOD IS A HANDFUL

1 KINGS 17:7-16

[7] After a while, the wadi dried up because there had been no rain in the land.

[8] Then the word of the LORD came to him: [9] "Get up, go to Zarephath that belongs to Sidon and stay there. Look, I have commanded a woman who is a widow to provide for you there." [10] So Elijah got up and went to Zarephath. When he arrived at the city gate, there was a widow woman gathering wood. Elijah called to her and said, "Please bring me a little water in a cup and let me drink." [11] As she went to get it, he called to her and said, "Please bring me a piece of bread in your hand."

[12] But she said, "As the LORD your God lives, I don't have anything baked — only a handful of flour in the jar and a bit of oil in the jug. Just now, I am gathering a couple of sticks in order to go prepare it for myself and my son so we can eat it and die."

[13] Then Elijah said to her, "Don't be afraid; go and do as you have said. But first make me a small loaf from it and bring it out to me. Afterward, you may make some for yourself and your son, [14] for this is what the LORD God of Israel says, 'The flour jar will not become empty and the oil jug will not run dry until the day the LORD sends rain on the surface of the land.'"

[15] So she proceeded to do according to the word of Elijah. Then the woman, Elijah, and her household ate for many days. [16] The flour jar did not become empty, and the oil jug did not run dry, according to the word of the LORD He had spoken through Elijah.

READ

Read the passage aloud slowly.

THINK

Read the passage slowly again. This time notice the repetitive phrases and words that seem to shimmer. Are there any in this passage that you sense God saying directly to you?

1. How do you resemble Elijah, the loner who was perhaps content by the solitary wadi but now has to venture into Palestinian territory and ask a widow for her last dime?
2. How do you identify with the widow and feel that Elijah is asking too much? How difficult is it for you to give up the last handful of flour? Hold out your hand in front of you. Open and close it. Imagine that the amount of flour your hand could hold is all that stands between you and death.
3. How do you think the widow felt every time she put her hand in the jar and there was another handful of flour?

PRAY

Ask God what might be your jar of flour today — something that needs filling up. It's okay to tell God He's asking too much. At first, the widow did just that. Trusting God is a process.

LIVE

Consider how it would feel to trust God this much. How would your life be different if you trusted God with just a little more every single morning, as the widow did?

BECAUSE HE HUMBLED HIMSELF

1 KINGS 21:20-29

²⁰ Ahab said to Elijah, "So, you have caught me, my enemy."

He replied, "I have caught you because you devoted yourself to do what is evil in the LORD's sight. ²¹ This is what the LORD says: 'I am about to bring disaster on you and will sweep away your descendants:

> I will eliminate all of Ahab's males,
> both slave and free, in Israel;

²² I will make your house like the house of Jeroboam son of Nebat and like the house of Baasha son of Ahijah, because you have provoked My anger and caused Israel to sin. ²³ The LORD also speaks of Jezebel: The dogs will eat Jezebel in the plot of land at Jezreel:

> ²⁴ He who belongs to Ahab and dies in the city, the dogs will eat,
> and he who dies in the field, the birds of the sky will eat.' "

²⁵ Still, there was no one like Ahab, who devoted himself to do what was evil in the LORD's sight, because his wife Jezebel incited him. ²⁶ He committed the most detestable acts by going after idols as the Amorites had, whom the LORD had dispossessed before the Israelites.

²⁷ When Ahab heard these words, he tore his clothes, put sackcloth over his body, and fasted. He lay down in sackcloth and walked around subdued. ²⁸ Then the word of the LORD came to Elijah the Tishbite: ²⁹ "Have you seen how Ahab has humbled himself before Me? I will not bring the disaster during his lifetime, because he has humbled himself before Me. I will bring the disaster on his house during his son's lifetime."

READ

Read the passage, putting yourself into the scene as much as you can.

THINK

Imagine yourself as Elijah, noticing what you think and feel throughout this tale. (See the expanded passage for more details.) Read the passage again until you reach God's words to Ahab and Jezebel, and the description of what they have done to defy Him. Pause there.

PRAY

As you picture yourself speaking God's words of judgment to Ahab, listen to what you are saying. What does God's anger toward this enemy make you feel? Do you feel the same anger God does over the injustice? If not, what does Ahab's sin make you feel? When you picture the three of you there — Ahab, God, you — what position is your body inclined to take toward each of them? Talk to God about your response.

Now return to the passage, and continue reading where you left off. When you reach the part about Ahab's repentance in humbling himself, hear God tell you about His change of mind. What does this make you feel? Where do your thoughts go? Talk to God about your response.

LIVE

Meditate on the following prayer from *The Book of Common Prayer*: "The Lord is full of compassion and mercy: O come, let us adore him."[4] Notice what your response is. If there is something you need to repent of today, go to God and receive His mercy. If you want to adore Him for His compassion, spend time doing so. If you don't want to adore God, take time to open yourself to the reality that He is praiseworthy. Don't force yourself to feel things you don't feel or to say things you don't mean, but do consider the reality acknowledged in the prayer.

FALSE HOPES?

2 KINGS 4:20,24-29

²⁰ So he picked him up and took him to his mother. The child sat on her lap until noon and then died. . . .

²⁴ Then she saddled the donkey and said to her servant, "Hurry, don't slow the pace for me unless I tell you." ²⁵ So she set out and went to the man of God at Mount Carmel.

When the man of God saw her at a distance, he said to his attendant Gehazi, "Look, there's the Shunammite woman. ²⁶ Run out to meet her and ask, 'Are you all right? Is your husband all right? Is your son all right?'"

And she answered, "Everything's all right."

²⁷ When she came up to the man of God at the mountain, she clung to his feet. Gehazi came to push her away, but the man of God said, "Leave her alone — she is in severe anguish, and the LORD has hidden it from me. He hasn't told me."

²⁸ Then she said, "Did I ask my lord for a son? Didn't I say, 'Do not deceive me'?"

²⁹ So Elisha said to Gehazi, "Tuck your mantle under your belt, take my staff with you, and go. If you meet anyone, don't stop to greet him, and if a man greets you, don't answer him. Then place my staff on the boy's face."

READ

Read the passage, preferably including the expanded passage.

THINK

Have you ever felt the bitter sting of shattered hopes and desires? The barren woman from Shunem knows the sting intimately — her grief here seems to confirm the doubt she experienced earlier when the holy man, Elisha, prophesied that she would have a son. At the time of the prophecy, not wanting to get her hopes up, she wouldn't even let on that she desired a son. Now she seems to wish she'd never hoped at all.

Notice Elisha's response to the woman in her fear, grief, and regret. Take several minutes to think about this. How might Elisha's response reflect God's response to her? What might God have been feeling as He watched her struggle with her son's death?

PRAY

Explore your own heart to see if there are any deep desires there that you are afraid to trust God with. Can you tell Him why you hold back? Ask Him to show you His response to your desires and to help you trust Him more, just as the Shunammite woman trusted Elisha enough to expose her anguish to him.

LIVE

Henri Nouwen wrote, "At every moment you have to decide to trust the voice that says, 'I love you. I knit you together in your mother's womb' (Ps. 139:13)."[5] Ponder this quote. What might your life look like if you were to take God at His word, believing that He knows all about you and cares for you as tenderly as Elisha cared for the Shunammite? How might you pray differently? Live differently?

45

INVESTING IN PEOPLE

2 KINGS 11:17–12:2

[17] Then Jehoiada made a covenant between the LORD, the king, and the people that they would be the LORD's people and another covenant between the king and the people. [18] So all the people of the land went to the temple of Baal and tore it down. They broke its altars and images into pieces, and they killed Mattan, the priest of Baal, at the altars.

Then Jehoiada the priest appointed guards for the LORD's temple. [19] He took the commanders of hundreds, the Carites, the guards, and all the people of the land, and they brought the king from the LORD's temple. They entered the king's palace by way of the guards' gate. Then Joash sat on the throne of the kings. [20] All the people of the land rejoiced, and the city was quiet, for they had put Athaliah to death by the sword in the king's palace.

[21] Joash was seven years old when he became king.

[1] In the seventh year of Jehu, Joash became king and reigned 40 years in Jerusalem. His mother's name was Zibiah, who was from Beer-sheba. [2] Throughout the time Jehoiada the priest instructed him, Joash did what was right in the LORD's sight.

READ

Read the passage aloud slowly, keeping in mind that Jehoiada is a priest of Judah at a time when Judah has been worshiping Baal instead of God.

THINK

Read the passage again slowly, trying to picture the priest Jehoiada and his young pupil, Joash, who becomes one of the few good kings of Judah.

1. What about Jehoiada do you most admire or dislike?
2. How would you like, or not like, to resemble Jehoiada as a teacher and leader? (Think of a teacher as anyone from whom others learn, and think of a leader as anyone who finds others following him or her. Even in friendships, sometimes one friend is the teacher and the other is the student, although they may not realize it.)

PRAY

Pray for people who look up to you — either for good or bad. In that case, you are their teacher and leader. Ask God who He is asking you to reach out to as an informal teacher or leader. Or you may want to simply pray about what you pass on to others.

LIVE

Sit in the quiet with God, holding before Him those who follow you or look up to you. You might wish to ask God, "What do I need to know about myself as a teacher or leader?" Ideas might not come to you right away. Note those that do, and keep watch for them in the coming days and weeks.

GOD'S KINDLED WRATH

2 KINGS 22:11-17

[11] When the king heard the words of the book of the law, he tore his clothes. [12] Then he commanded Hilkiah the priest, Ahikam son of Shaphan, Achbor son of Micaiah, Shaphan the court secretary, and the king's servant Asaiah: [13] "Go and inquire of the LORD for me, the people, and all Judah about the instruction in this book that has been found. For great is the LORD's wrath that is kindled against us because our ancestors have not obeyed the words of this book in order to do everything written about us."

[14] So Hilkiah the priest, Ahikam, Achbor, Shaphan, and Asaiah went to the prophetess Huldah, wife of Shallum son of Tikvah, son of Harhas, keeper of the wardrobe. She lived in Jerusalem in the Second District. They spoke with her.

[15] She said to them, "This is what the LORD God of Israel says, 'Say to the man who sent you to Me: [16] This is what the LORD says: I am about to bring disaster on this place and on its inhabitants, fulfilling all the words of the book that the king of Judah has read, [17] because they have abandoned Me and burned incense to other gods in order to provoke Me with all the work of their hands. My wrath will be kindled against this place, and it will not be quenched.'"

READ

Read the passage once aloud to get a feel for what's happening.

THINK

Read the passage again. As you do, listen for words or images that especially impact you, such as wrath that "will not be quenched" or the king tearing his clothes.

PRAY

Take time to silently repeat this word or phrase from the passage or to let the image play itself out in your mind. See how it meshes with your thoughts, feelings, and memories. Eventually let your contemplation lead you to consider whether there are any questionable or sinful areas of your life that you have been ignoring lately. Can you tell why you've been ignoring them? Bring them before God. What is your posture?

LIVE

Picture this God whose wrath, or anger, is kindled. What's it like to be before Him? Now see Jesus, the mediator between the holy God pictured in this passage and the sinful people God loves. Turn to Jesus and together examine your heart. Watch His response to the sinful areas you noticed. What is He inviting you to do in response to what you see? Respond to His invitation. Watch God the Father accept Jesus' redemption of your sin — see God's wrath cool — and experience being welcomed back into full fellowship with Him once more.

UNITED WARRIORS

1 CHRONICLES 11:10-11

[10] The following were the chiefs of David's warriors who, together with all Israel, strongly supported him in his reign to make him king according to the LORD's word about Israel. [11] This is the list of David's warriors:

Jashobeam son of Hachmoni was chief of the Thirty; he wielded his spear against 300 and killed them at one time.

READ

Read the passage and underline every verb or action word.

THINK

David's warriors were willing to risk their lives by crossing the Philistine military camp in order to bring David water from the Bethlehem well. What incredible friendships!

Discuss this passage with a friend or spiritual mentor. What do you think about the idea of becoming united warriors with others? Is it awkward? Is it worth the effort?

PRAY

Tell God about any worries or insecurities you have about uniting with others. Pray for the discernment to choose a few mature, like-minded people to join with you and the boldness to ask them for help.

LIVE

Approach these individuals and ask them to become God's warriors with you.

DAY 49

GOD ENCOUNTERS

On this seventh day, review and reflect on all you have read this week. Take the time to revel in the ways you've encountered God in the past six days.

EXPANDED PASSAGE:
1 CHRONICLES 16:7-36, "DAVID'S PSALM OF THANKSGIVING"

SHOUT FROM THE MOUNTAINTOPS

1 CHRONICLES 16:23-29

23   Sing to the LORD, all the earth.
     Proclaim His salvation from day to day.
24   Declare His glory among the nations,
     His wonderful works among all peoples.

25   For the LORD is great and highly praised;
     He is feared above all gods.
26   For all the gods of the peoples are idols,
     but the LORD made the heavens.
27   Splendor and majesty are before Him;
     strength and joy are in His place.
28   Ascribe to the LORD, families of the peoples,
     ascribe to the LORD glory and strength.
29   Ascribe to Yahweh the glory of His name;
     bring an offering and come before Him.
     Worship the LORD in the splendor of His holiness.

READ

Read the passage aloud slowly, keeping in mind that "ascribe to" here means something like "give credit to."

Read the passage aloud again, but do it this time as if you are speaking convincingly, first to "all the earth" (verse 23 addresses the entire planet, including the vegetation and animals of the earth), then to all the "families of the peoples" (verse 28, all nations, all tribes, all classes of people).

THINK

Read the passage again silently and ponder the following:

1. Consider the words you most relish. What phrase did you particularly enjoy saying as you read the passage dramatically?
2. What would you most want the earth to know or understand about God?
3. What would you most want the families of the earth to know or understand about God?

PRAY

Begin by asking God to lead you in your prayer. Wait for Him. Once you get started, you may wish to say something like, "O God, I'm so glad you are . . ." and finish with ideas from this psalm.

LIVE

If you could shout this psalm from anywhere in the world, where would that be? (It might be on a specific mountaintop or by a certain waterfall or even before an international group, such as the United Nations.) Picture yourself saying these verses from your heart in that setting, without embarrassment or any other reservation. Rest in your boldness.

OUR DAYS ARE LIKE A SHADOW

1 CHRONICLES 29:12-19

¹² Riches and honor come from You, and You are the ruler of everything. Power and might are in Your hand, and it is in Your hand to make great and to give strength to all. ¹³ Now therefore, our God, we give You thanks and praise Your glorious name.

¹⁴ But who am I, and who are my people, that we should be able to give as generously as this? For everything comes from You, and we have given You only what comes from Your own hand. ¹⁵ For we live before You as foreigners and temporary residents in Your presence as were all our ancestors. Our days on earth are like a shadow, without hope. ¹⁶ Yahweh our God, all this wealth that we've provided for building You a house for Your holy name comes from Your hand; everything belongs to You. ¹⁷ I know, my God, that You test the heart and that You are pleased with what is right. I have willingly given all these things with an upright heart, and now I have seen Your people who are present here giving joyfully and willingly to You. ¹⁸ LORD God of Abraham, Isaac, and Israel, our ancestors, keep this desire forever in the thoughts of the hearts of Your people, and confirm their hearts toward You. ¹⁹ Give my son Solomon a whole heart to keep and to carry out all Your commands, Your decrees, and Your statutes, and to build the temple for which I have made provision.

READ

David is blessing God in this passage. To see his entire prayer, read the expanded passage, seeing how he dedicates to God the money and materials generously given by him and all the Israelites for building the temple.

THINK

When David talks about days on earth "like a shadow" — that everything we have is actually only being borrowed from God — how does that strike you? What item do you own, or what relationship do you have, that you hold more tightly than you would a shadow? Be honest.

PRAY

As you approach God in prayer, picture yourself bringing with you the item that is hard to hold loosely. Talk to God about what keeps you attached to it. Don't try to navigate the prayer so that by the end you are letting go of your treasured thing. Don't try to force yourself to be less attached to it than you actually are. Simply talk to God while you imaginatively hold it tightly in your hands, and tell Him about why it's so important to you. Keep in mind that if you are still in the same position internally at the end of your prayer time, that's okay.

LIVE

Take a few more minutes to reflect on what talking to God was like as you held on to the item you're unwilling to give up — at least not easily. Did you feel guilty or uncomfortable, or do you have trouble being honest with Him? Why might that be?

DEDICATION CEREMONIES

2 CHRONICLES 6:12-18

¹² Then Solomon stood before the altar of the LORD in front of the entire congregation of Israel and spread out his hands. ¹³ For Solomon had made a bronze platform 7½ feet long, 7½ feet wide, and 4½ feet high and put it in the court. He stood on it, knelt down in front of the entire congregation of Israel, and spread out his hands toward heaven. ¹⁴ He said:

> LORD God of Israel,
> there is no God like You
> in heaven or on earth,
> keeping His gracious covenant
> with Your servants who walk before You
> with their whole heart.
> ¹⁵ You have kept what You promised
> to Your servant, my father David.
> You spoke directly to him,
> and You fulfilled Your promise by Your power,
> as it is today.
> ¹⁶ Therefore, LORD God of Israel,
> keep what You promised
> to Your servant, my father David:
> "You will never fail to have a man
> to sit before Me on the throne of Israel,
> if only your sons guard their way to walk in My Law
> as you have walked before Me."
> ¹⁷ Now, LORD God of Israel, please confirm
> what You promised to Your servant David.
>
> ¹⁸ But will God indeed live on earth with man?
> Even heaven, the highest heaven, cannot contain You,
> much less this temple I have built.

READ

Read the passage, underlining words that stand out to you.

THINK

King Solomon, son of King David, built the famous temple to the Lord on Mount Zion in Jerusalem as a gathering place for the Jews to worship Yahweh. It took him years to build this temple, and at its completion he assembled all the people for a public dedication. To dedicate something is to set it aside for a special purpose. As you read the dedication prayer of Solomon, notice the gratitude and the humility of the king as he prays.

What precious aspects of your life (for example, people, positions, locations, important events, yourself) do you need to set solely aside for the Lord as a public reminder that all you have belongs to God? What would it take for you to do that . . . and with the attitude of Solomon?

PRAY

Write out a prayer of dedication to God for an individual, situation, event, or position.

LIVE

Keep your dedication prayer so you can occasionally refer to it. In fact, if you wish, make a note on your calendar a few weeks from today to reread your prayer. At that time, think about what's different in your life due to your dedication.

FROG:
FULLY RELY ON GOD

2 CHRONICLES 16:7-9

[7] At that time, Hanani the seer came to King Asa of Judah and said to him, "Because you depended on the king of Aram and have not depended on the LORD your God, the army of the king of Aram has escaped from your hand. [8] Were not the Cushites and Libyans a vast army with many chariots and horsemen? When you depended on Yahweh, He handed them over to you. [9] For the eyes of Yahweh roam throughout the earth to show Himself strong for those whose hearts are completely His. You have been foolish in this matter. Therefore, you will have wars from now on."

READ

Read the passage aloud slowly.

THINK

Read the passage again slowly. Previously Asa had been a good king. After hearing convicting prophecy, he "took courage and removed the detestable idols from the whole land," cleaning out the temples (15:8).

1. Which phrase or idea sticks with you?

   ☐ that Asa depended on the king of Aram and not on the Lord
   ☐ that "the eyes of Yahweh roam throughout the earth to show Himself strong for those whose hearts are completely His"
   ☐ that not relying on God results in "wars from now on"
   ☐ other:

2. Why does that idea stick with you?
3. The theme of this passage could be summed up in the acronym FROG, standing for Fully Rely On God. Consider your life — for what large or small issues might you FROG that you have not thought of before? (Don't use this passage to beat yourself up; that's not profitable. Use it instead as a springboard to ask God for guidance.)

PRAY

Thank God that you can fully rely on Him. Admire God for His divine alertness and for how relying on Him keeps you out of trouble. Take your time so that you fully explore your gratitude and admiration.

LIVE

Take some deep breaths and ponder what it would feel like in your gut to rely on God all the time, every day. Taste the sweetness of reliance so it's not a chore but the absolute best way to live.

OPEN ARMS

2 CHRONICLES 30:1,5-9

¹ Then Hezekiah sent word throughout all Israel and Judah, and he also wrote letters to Ephraim and Manasseh to come to the LORD's temple in Jerusalem to observe the Passover of Yahweh, the God of Israel. . . . ⁵ So they affirmed the proposal and spread the message throughout all Israel, from Beer-sheba to Dan, to come to observe the Passover of Yahweh, the God of Israel in Jerusalem, for they hadn't observed it often, as prescribed.

⁶ So the couriers went throughout Israel and Judah with letters from the hand of the king and his officials, and according to the king's command, saying, "Israelites, return to Yahweh, the God of Abraham, Isaac, and Israel so that He may return to those of you who remain, who have escaped from the grasp of the kings of Assyria. ⁷ Don't be like your fathers and your brothers who were unfaithful to Yahweh, the God of their ancestors so that He made them an object of horror as you yourselves see. ⁸ Don't become obstinate now like your fathers did. Give your allegiance to Yahweh, and come to His sanctuary that He has consecrated forever. Serve the LORD your God so that He may turn His burning anger away from you, ⁹ for when you return to Yahweh, your brothers and your sons will receive mercy in the presence of their captors and will return to this land. For Yahweh your God is gracious and merciful; He will not turn His face away from you if you return to Him."

READ

Read the passage several times.

THINK

As you read, listen for a new perspective on the way life is, or the way God is, that stands out to you today. Perhaps you will notice that God can have dangerously "burning anger," yet under other circumstances He is tender and open to a people who have walked far from intimacy with Him. Maybe you'll be struck by the pigheadedness that kept some Israelites from returning to Yahweh.

PRAY

Study the perspective you've absorbed, looking at it from different angles and holding it up against different experiences you've had. Do you ever fear approaching God because you worry He might snub you? Have you ever refused grace? Consider a specific situation. Then become aware of God's presence with you. Tell Him what was going on during that time. How does the God of this passage (offering His mercy to the Israelites) compare to your image of God in that situation?

LIVE

Close your time today by saying the Lord's Prayer. Speak the words aloud very slowly. Picture the righteous but compassionate God described in this passage, the One who is hearing your prayer now: "Our Father in heaven, Your name be honored as holy. Your kingdom come. Your will be done on earth as it is in heaven. Give us today our daily bread. And forgive us our debts, as we also have forgiven our debtors. And do not bring us into temptation, but deliver us from the evil one. [For Yours is the kingdom and the power and the glory forever. Amen]" (Matthew 6:9-13).

54

WHAT CAN WE SAY IN LIGHT OF THIS?

EZRA 9:10-15

[10] Now, our God, what can we say in light of this? For we have abandoned the commands [11] You gave through Your servants the prophets, saying: "The land you are entering to possess is an impure land. The surrounding peoples have filled it from end to end with their uncleanness by their impurity and detestable practices. [12] So do not give your daughters to their sons in marriage or take their daughters for your sons. Never seek their peace or prosperity, so that you will be strong, eat the good things of the land, and leave it as an inheritance to your sons forever." [13] After all that has happened to us because of our evil deeds and terrible guilt — though You, our God, have punished us less than our sins deserve and have allowed us to survive — [14] should we break Your commands again and intermarry with the peoples who commit these detestable practices? Wouldn't You become so angry with us that You would destroy us, leaving no survivors? [15] LORD God of Israel, You are righteous, for we survive as a remnant today. Here we are before You with our guilt, though no one can stand in Your presence because of this.

READ

Read this prayer, spoken by Ezra on behalf of all the exiled Israelites.

THINK

Think about how you relate to this prayer. Have you ever felt similar remorse to what Ezra expresses here? Maybe you feel frustration with the injustices of your community or nation, or maybe you experience guilt on a deep level — not for anything in particular, but just a general sense of not getting it right, ever. What have you done with that feeling? Stuffed it? Allowed it to constantly criticize what you do and say? Have you ever thought of sharing it with God?

PRAY

Ezra's raw confession of messing up before God indicates that he feels very secure in God's merciful love; otherwise, being this defenseless before anyone is hard.

Read Ezra's prayer again, looking for a word, a phrase, or even something about his tone that resonates with you. Take several minutes to mull this over, and listen for what it gives voice to in your heart. Allow yourself to make Ezra's prayer your own, repeating it and following him in prayer to God. Or perhaps you don't identify with what he says, yet beyond your words is a pain you want to share with God. Sit with Him in this.

LIVE

When you mess up today, remember Ezra, and remember God's merciful love.

DAY 56

GOD ENCOUNTERS

On this seventh day, review and reflect on all you have read this week. Take the time to revel in the ways you've encountered God in the past six days.

BURDEN FOR THE POOR

NEHEMIAH 5:6-11

⁶ I became extremely angry when I heard their outcry and these complaints. ⁷ After seriously considering the matter, I accused the nobles and officials, saying to them, "Each of you is charging his countrymen interest." So I called a large assembly against them ⁸ and said, "We have done our best to buy back our Jewish countrymen who were sold to foreigners, but now you sell your own countrymen, and we have to buy them back." They remained silent and could not say a word. ⁹ Then I said, "What you are doing isn't right. Shouldn't you walk in the fear of our God and not invite the reproach of our foreign enemies? ¹⁰ Even I, as well as my brothers and my servants, have been lending them money and grain. Please, let us stop charging this interest. ¹¹ Return their fields, vineyards, olive groves, and houses to them immediately, along with the percentage of the money, grain, new wine, and olive oil that you have been assessing them."

LIVE

In preparation for this lesson, fast from one meal. (Use discernment regarding fasting; check with your doctor before doing it. If you can't do it for whatever reason, that's okay.) When you feel the pangs of hunger, use that discomfort as a catalyst for this devotion.

READ

Read the passage slowly.

THINK

While in Babylonian exile as a cupbearer to a foreign king, Nehemiah has a God-given burden: to rebuild the ransacked walls of the forgotten city of Jerusalem and, in the process, to restore the hope of his people. But in the midst of this massive architectural restoration project, the people are being abused by their own countrymen.

Nehemiah's burden grows larger. His burden now includes poverty and injustice. Imagine yourself in Nehemiah's shoes today. What does this burden feel like? Consider your empty stomach and write down how you feel.

PRAY

Begin praying by listening for God's heart regarding justice. Ask Him to show you people who need your prayers. Then ask Him to point out when you need to speak up on their behalf, and ask for the courage to actually follow through with it.

ZEAL FOR RIGHTEOUSNESS

NEHEMIAH 13:7-13

[7] Then I discovered the evil that Eliashib had done on behalf of Tobiah by providing him a room in the courts of God's house. [8] I was greatly displeased and threw all of Tobiah's household possessions out of the room. [9] I ordered that the rooms be purified, and I had the articles of the house of God restored there, along with the grain offering and frankincense. [10] I also found out that because the portions for the Levites had not been given, each of the Levites and the singers performing the service had gone back to his own field. [11] Therefore, I rebuked the officials, saying, "Why has the house of God been neglected?" I gathered the Levites and singers together and stationed them at their posts. [12] Then all Judah brought a tenth of the grain, new wine, and oil into the storehouses. [13] I appointed as treasurers over the storehouses Shelemiah the priest, Zadok the scribe, and Pedaiah of the Levites, with Hanan son of Zaccur, son of Mattaniah to assist them, because they were considered trustworthy. They were responsible for the distribution to their colleagues.

READ

Read the passage, including the expanded portion for background, if you can.

THINK

In these earlier days, what do you notice about the way of life God required His people to abide by? Why do you think this was important to Him? What do you think their relationship with God was like? How might it be different from your relationship with Him?

PRAY

Become aware of God's presence with you now. Share your thoughts with Him, including what you noticed about your own relationship with Him. Let this lead you into silent prayer, pondering what's happened in your life since you last talked with Him and whether there is anything you need to clear up. Listen for what He might be saying in response to you. If you don't sense Him saying anything directly, be open to other ways He might try to communicate with you (such as through other people or recent experiences).

LIVE

Think about the passion Nehemiah demonstrates for honoring God. What would your life look like with more passion? How might you honor God with your lifestyle the way Nehemiah desires to honor God? Jesus said, "Love the Lord your God with all your heart, with all your soul, and with all your mind. . . . Love your neighbor as yourself" (Matthew 22:37,39). With this command in mind, think of one small new habit you could cultivate that would honor God in a particular area of your life.

SUCH A TIME AS THIS

ESTHER 4:7-14

⁷ Mordecai told him everything that had happened as well as the exact amount of money Haman had promised to pay the royal treasury for the slaughter of the Jews.

⁸ Mordecai also gave him a copy of the written decree issued in Susa ordering their destruction, so that Hathach might show it to Esther, explain it to her, and command her to approach the king, implore his favor, and plead with him personally for her people. ⁹ Hathach came and repeated Mordecai's response to Esther.

¹⁰ Esther spoke to Hathach and commanded him to tell Mordecai, ¹¹ "All the royal officials and the people of the royal provinces know that one law applies to every man or woman who approaches the king in the inner courtyard and who has not been summoned — the death penalty. Only if the king extends the gold scepter will that person live. I have not been summoned to appear before the king for the last 30 days." ¹² Esther's response was reported to Mordecai.

¹³ Mordecai told the messenger to reply to Esther, "Don't think that you will escape the fate of all the Jews because you are in the king's palace. ¹⁴ If you keep silent at this time, liberation and deliverance will come to the Jewish people from another place, but you and your father's house will be destroyed. Who knows, perhaps you have come to your royal position for such a time as this."

READ

As you read this story, imagine how you might feel if you were Esther: You were chosen to be queen by a king who doesn't know of your ethnicity, and now you're hearing word of a political plot that will wipe out your people and your family.

THINK

Focus your attention on either Esther's fear of putting her life on the line for her people or Mordecai's challenge to her in the face of her fear. Meditatively read that part of the passage again. Picture the speaker, including the situation from which the words are spoken. Select one word or phrase to contemplate during your prayer time.

PRAY

Prayerfully ponder a word or phrase from Mordecai or Esther and identify a memory that relates. Maybe at one time you were called on to do something courageous — big or small — but couldn't bring yourself to do it. Or maybe you wonder why God would allow Esther to bear such a heavy responsibility. Or perhaps you were recently helped because someone took a stand for you.

Invite God the Father into your meditation. Try not to analyze or push toward solutions. Just notice what comes up and show it to Him, as a child might show Daddy a favorite toy that's broken or tell Him about a fascinating discovery.

LIVE

Take some time now to rest with the Father. If you have more to say in your conversation with Him about Esther's dilemma, continue it. If you have other subjects you'd like to talk to Him about, do so. But if you want to just sit in the presence of your loving Father, go ahead.

PREOCCUPATIONS

ESTHER 5:9-13

[9] That day Haman left full of joy and in good spirits. But when Haman saw Mordecai at the King's Gate, and Mordecai didn't rise or tremble in fear at his presence, Haman was filled with rage toward Mordecai. [10] Yet Haman controlled himself and went home. He sent for his friends and his wife Zeresh to join him. [11] Then Haman described for them his glorious wealth and his many sons. He told them all how the king had honored him and promoted him in rank over the other officials and the royal staff. [12] "What's more," Haman added, "Queen Esther invited no one but me to join the king at the banquet she had prepared. I am invited again tomorrow to join her with the king. [13] Still, none of this satisfies me since I see Mordecai the Jew sitting at the King's Gate all the time."

READ

Read the passage aloud slowly. Haman is upset because the king ordered all those at the King's Gate to bow to him, and Mordecai the Jew does not (see Esther 3:2-6).

THINK

Read the passage again slowly.

1. How did Haman's preoccupations affect him? What did those pre-occupations reveal about the kind of person he was inside?
2. What preoccupations have filled your mind for the past twenty-four hours? What do these preoccupations reveal about who you are inside?
3. What things would you like to be preoccupied with?

PRAY

Pray this verse in your own words: "Set your minds on what is above" (Colossians 3:2). Ask God for guidance in what kind of person you want to be and what to focus on.

LIVE

Dream about becoming the kind of person whose mind is preoccupied with God. Contemplation is a time for receiving from God. Receive an image of yourself from Him. Embrace the future you.

JUSTICE SERVED

ESTHER 7:3-10

[3] Queen Esther answered, "If I have obtained your approval, my king, and if the king is pleased, spare my life — this is my request; and spare my people — this is my desire. [4] For my people and I have been sold out to destruction, death, and extermination. If we had merely been sold as male and female slaves, I would have kept silent. Indeed, the trouble wouldn't be worth burdening the king."

[5] King Ahasuerus spoke up and asked Queen Esther, "Who is this, and where is the one who would devise such a scheme?"

[6] Esther answered, "The adversary and enemy is this evil Haman."

Haman stood terrified before the king and queen. [7] Angered by this, the king arose from where they were drinking wine and went to the palace garden. Haman remained to beg Queen Esther for his life because he realized the king was planning something terrible for him. [8] Just as the king returned from the palace garden to the house of wine drinking, Haman was falling on the couch where Esther was reclining. The king exclaimed, "Would he actually violate the queen while I am in the palace?" As soon as the statement left the king's mouth, Haman's face was covered.

[9] Harbona, one of the royal eunuchs, said: "There is a gallows 75 feet tall at Haman's house that he made for Mordecai, who gave the report that saved the king."

The king commanded, "Hang him on it."

[10] They hanged Haman on the gallows he had prepared for Mordecai. Then the king's anger subsided.

READ

Take some time before you begin to sit in silence. Let your thoughts settle. Now read the passage once silently.

THINK

Read this story of justice being served again, this time aloud. Listen specifically for a word or a phrase that touches your heart in some way. When you finish reading, close your eyes. Recall the word and sit quietly, mulling it over. After a few moments, write the word down. Don't explain it or say more about it; just note it.

PRAY

Read the passage aloud again, this time looking for a person or an action that accentuates your internal picture of God's justice or heightens your understanding of how He governs the world. Perhaps it will be Haman's response to his fate or King Xerxes' authoritative command. How is this depiction of God's justice meaningful to you today? Again sit in silence. Briefly note what comes to you.

LIVE

Read the text one final time. This time, listen for what God, through the text, is inviting you to do or become. Perhaps He is offering a new perspective on how He cares when unjust things happen to you, just as King Xerxes was outraged to discover the threat to Esther's people. Or maybe you sense that God is calling you to take a stand for justice in a particular situation, like Esther did. Write down what you are being invited to do.

GOD GIVES, GOD TAKES

JOB 1:1,8-11,20-21

¹ There was a man in the country of Uz named Job. He was a man of perfect integrity, who feared God and turned away from evil. . . .

⁸ Then the LORD said to Satan, "Have you considered My servant Job? No one else on earth is like him, a man of perfect integrity, who fears God and turns away from evil."

⁹ Satan answered the LORD, "Does Job fear God for nothing? ¹⁰ Haven't You placed a hedge around him, his household, and everything he owns? You have blessed the work of his hands, and his possessions have increased in the land. ¹¹ But stretch out Your hand and strike everything he owns, and he will surely curse You to Your face." . . .

²⁰ Then Job stood up, tore his robe, and shaved his head. He fell to the ground and worshiped, ²¹ saying:

> Naked I came from my mother's womb,
> and naked I will leave this life.
> The LORD gives, and the LORD takes away.
> Praise the name of Yahweh.

READ

Read the passage, noticing God's involvement in the story and circling *God* each time He is mentioned.

THINK

Notice the interaction between God and Satan. Does it bother you that God is bartering with Satan for Job's life? Is this the God you know?

Notice the words of Job, "Naked I came from my mother's womb, and naked I will leave this life. The LORD gives, and the LORD takes away. Praise the name of Yahweh." If you lost everything — family, fortune, and eventually your health — would you be able to say such a thing? Why or why not? What would have to happen for you to utter similar words — and actually mean them?

PRAY

Spend time meditating on the gut-honest yet God-honoring words of Job. Let your emotions serve as a backdrop to your prayers. Invite the Holy Spirit to speak to you in the silence.

LIVE

Today as you use different objects (your car, computer, TV, and so on) and as you enter different places (your home, school, workplace, and so on), consider how you might respond if God instantly removed an item without explanation.

DAY 63

GOD ENCOUNTERS

On this seventh day, review and reflect on all you have read this week. Take the time to revel in the ways you've encountered God in the past six days.

GIVING COMFORT

JOB 5:17-21

17 See how happy the man is God corrects;
   so do not reject the discipline of the Almighty.
18 For He crushes but also binds up;
   He strikes, but His hands also heal.
19 He will rescue you from six calamities;
   no harm will touch you in seven.
20 In famine He will redeem you from death,
   and in battle, from the power of the sword.
21 You will be safe from slander
   and not fear destruction when it comes.

READ

Read the passage aloud slowly, keeping in mind that Eliphaz from Teman is speaking to his friend Job, who has just experienced the death of his children and the loss of all he had.

THINK

Read the passage again and put yourself in the place of Job, who listened to these words. How do they fall on your ear?

Read the passage again and put yourself in the place of Eliphaz. What feelings and attitudes fill you as you speak these words?

1. What makes a comforter really helpful? Is telling the truth enough?
2. What did Job need from Eliphaz?
3. What might be in the heart of a person who preaches at someone who is so far down?

PRAY

Ask the Comforter, the Holy Spirit, to give you what is needed to truly comfort despairing people. If you want guidance for your prayer, ask the Comforter to give you tools to help people in trouble go to Him. Ask Him to give you tools to draw them out to say to Him whatever they need to express. Plead with the Comforter to make you His messenger, to prevent you from moralizing and giving advice.

LIVE

Rest your mind on someone who is in deep trouble. Pray only the word *peace* for them — no suggestions, no fixing, no rescuing. Just trusting.

THE MYSTERY OF A MIGHTY GOD

JOB 9:2-4,14-23

2 Yes, I know what you've said is true,
but how can a person be justified before God?

3 If one wanted to take Him to court,
he could not answer God once in a thousand times.

4 God is wise and all-powerful.
Who has opposed Him and come out unharmed? . . .

14 How then can I answer Him
or choose my arguments against Him?

15 Even if I were in the right, I could not answer.
I could only beg my Judge for mercy.

16 If I summoned Him and He answered me,
I do not believe He would pay attention to what I said.

17 He batters me with a whirlwind
and multiplies my wounds without cause.

18 He doesn't let me catch my breath
but soaks me with bitter experiences.

19 If it is a matter of strength, look, He is the Mighty One!
If it is a matter of justice, who can summon Him?

20 Even if I were in the right, my own mouth would condemn me;
if I were blameless, my mouth would declare me guilty.

21 Though I am blameless,
I no longer care about myself;
I renounce my life.

22 It is all the same. Therefore I say,
"He destroys both the blameless and the wicked."

23 When disaster brings sudden death,
He mocks the despair of the innocent.

READ

Read the passage. In Job's response to his recent tragedy, notice the powerful feelings that underlie his words: fear, anger, grief, and hope.

THINK

What phrase in Job's lament stands out to you? Spend time meditating on it. Mentally chew it the way you would chew a piece of gum — repeat it to yourself, pausing each time to see where it leads your mind and emotions.

PRAY

Keeping your phrase in mind, picture God in the room with you. How do you relate to His presence? Maybe you sit in reverence at His power, wisdom, and justice, realizing you've forgotten or minimized those qualities lately. Maybe you feel anguish like Job. Maybe you open up to your desire for a rescuer, for Christ's mercy.

At the end of this time, recall what this experience held for you. Write down for future reference anything that seemed significant.

LIVE

During the next week, before you begin your times of prayerful reading, recall your picture of God in the room. Recollect who He was to you and retain this image of Him in your mind during each prayer time. Let that aspect of God mingle with the God you relate to during the week.

TALKING TRANSPARENTLY WITH GOD

JOB 19:13-27

13 He has removed my brothers from me;
my acquaintances have abandoned me.
14 My relatives stop coming by,
and my close friends have forgotten me.
15 My house guests and female servants regard me as a stranger;
I am a foreigner in their sight.
16 I call for my servant, but he does not answer,
even if I beg him with my own mouth.
17 My breath is offensive to my wife,
and my own family finds me repulsive.
18 Even young boys scorn me.
When I stand up, they mock me.
19 All of my best friends despise me,
and those I love have turned against me.
20 My skin and my flesh cling to my bones;
I have escaped by the skin of my teeth.

21 Have mercy on me, my friends, have mercy,
for God's hand has struck me.
22 Why do you persecute me as God does?
Will you never get enough of my flesh?

23 I wish that my words were written down,
that they were recorded on a scroll
24 or were inscribed in stone forever
by an iron stylus and lead!
25 But I know my living Redeemer,
and He will stand on the dust at last.
26 Even after my skin has been destroyed,
yet I will see God in my flesh.
27 I will see Him myself;
my eyes will look at Him, and not as a stranger.
My heart longs within me.

READ

Read the passage slowly, noticing the raw way Job communicates about God.

THINK

As you read Job's honest description of his situation — what it's really like — what word or phrase gives voice to some of your own thoughts, feelings, and desires? Perhaps one of Job's statements brings to mind something in your life that's weighing on you or confuses you.

PRAY

Talk to God about the feelings and thoughts that surface. Be as open as Job as you share them with Him. You might write them out to Him or just talk to Him like a friend — one you're in conflict with, but one who wants to work through that conflict with you.

LIVE

As you go through the rest of your day, pay close attention to thoughts and feelings (similar to or different from those in your prayer time) that arise in relation to events, conversations, and experiences. Tell God about them as they come up, so you're carrying on an extended dialogue with Him all day long.

At the end of the day, take a few moments to remember what happened, in particular what it was like to talk to God throughout the day's circumstances.

EMPTY COMFORT

JOB 22:1-11

¹ Then Eliphaz the Temanite replied:

2   Can a man be of any use to God?
     Can even a wise man be of use to Him?
3   Does it delight the Almighty if you are righteous?
     Does He profit if you perfect your behavior?

4   Does He correct you and take you to court
     because of your piety?
5   Isn't your wickedness abundant
     and aren't your iniquities endless?
6   For you took collateral from your brothers without cause,
     stripping off their clothes and leaving them naked.
7   You gave no water to the thirsty
     and withheld food from the famished,
8   while the land belonged to a powerful man
     and an influential man lived on it.
9   You sent widows away empty-handed,
     and the strength of the fatherless was crushed.
10   Therefore snares surround you,
     and sudden dread terrifies you,
11   or darkness, so you cannot see,
     and a flood of water covers you.

READ

As you read the passage, consider what might have been comforting for Job and what might have left him more hurt than before.

THINK

Have there been times when you wished people would refrain from giving you perfectly packaged Christian clichés in an attempt to console you? "Pray harder." "You'll have to persevere." "Oh, God's just working on you." "Search for the sin in your life and get rid of it." "Obey God." Maybe you didn't know what you wanted in your suffering, but that definitely wasn't it. Sometimes true comfort comes through silence and a hug.

Eliphaz, Bildad, and Zophar don't offer comfort, but instead attempt to convince Job of his sins. This time it's the social sin of neglecting the poor, the hungry, and the naked — none of which Job is guilty of.

Who are the people you interact with on a regular basis who are suffering emotional, mental, spiritual, or physical pain?

What are some ways you can appropriately comfort them in their pain?

PRAY

Who are hurting people in your life? Pray for them, submitting to God's guidance for how to best serve and minister to them.

LIVE

Consider a friend or acquaintance who needs comfort. Prayerfully approach the suffering individual, asking God to use you as a healing agent of comfort and hope. Also ask God to keep you from being someone who merely offers trite words that fall short.

THIRSTING FOR JUSTICE

JOB 24:1-10

1   Why does the Almighty not reserve times for judgment?
    Why do those who know Him never see His days?

2   The wicked displace boundary markers.
    They steal a flock and provide pasture for it.

3   They drive away the donkeys owned by the fatherless
    and take the widow's ox as collateral.

4   They push the needy off the road;
    the poor of the land are forced into hiding.

5   Like wild donkeys in the desert,
    the poor go out to their task of foraging for food;
    the wilderness provides nourishment for their children.

6   They gather their fodder in the field
    and glean the vineyards of the wicked.

7   Without clothing, they spend the night naked,
    having no covering against the cold.

8   Drenched by mountain rains,
    they huddle against the rocks, shelterless.

9   The fatherless infant is snatched from the breast;
    the nursing child of the poor is seized as collateral.

10 Without clothing, they wander about naked.
    They carry sheaves but go hungry.

READ

Read the passage aloud slowly.

THINK

Read the passage again, noting the words or phrases that touch you.

1. Why do these phrases touch you?
2. What is the heart of God like for these situations?

Though God stays hidden in order to let human beings be the autonomous beings He created them to be, He delights in bringing justice. Slowly read aloud Isaiah 51:5 twice:

> My righteousness is near,
> My salvation appears,
> and My arms will bring justice to the nations.
> The coastlands will put their hope in Me,
> and they will look to My strength.

Ponder your heart's response to this.

PRAY

Ask God to intervene in situations you think are unjust, small or big. If nothing comes to you, look at a newspaper or watch a newscast. Then come before God and ask for people to be treated with fairness and goodness and kindness.

LIVE

While you pray, hold in front of you a symbol of the world's troubles, perhaps a newspaper or newsmagazine, a globe or map. Hold it up for God's light to permeate.

GOD'S SILENCE

JOB 30:15-20

15   Terrors are turned loose against me;
        they chase my dignity away like the wind,
        and my prosperity has passed by like a cloud.

16   Now my life is poured out before my eyes,
        and days of suffering have seized me.

17   Night pierces my bones,
        but my gnawing pains never rest.

18   My clothing is distorted with great force;
        He chokes me by the neck of my garment.

19   He throws me into the mud,
        and I have become like dust and ashes.

20   I cry out to You for help, but You do not answer me;
        when I stand up, You merely look at me.

READ

Read the passage, attempting to identify in your own heart and mind with the expressions of the speaker.

THINK

Read the passage slowly again — until the words sink into your consciousness, becoming familiar to you and resonating with your present state of mind. Don't try to analyze Job's response or determine its validity. Simply open yourself to his experience.

PRAY

What goes on inside you when you hear Job talk about God's silence? Perhaps you feel irritated, or maybe you relate because you've experienced times when God seemed inaccessible. Talk to God about your reaction to this passage. To help clarify your reaction, write about it. Give yourself permission to be completely open and honest.

LIVE

Right now, practice resting in the knowledge that God is with you in both words and silence — whether you're doing things right or doing nothing at all, whether you feel He's near or you feel nothing. If this is especially tough for you to do, pray the prayer "Lord, I believe a little; help me believe more."

DAY 70

GOD ENCOUNTERS

On this seventh day, review and reflect on all you have read this week. Take the time to revel in the ways you've encountered God in the past six days.

CREATION MOVIE

JOB 38:4-11,24-27

⁴ Where were you when I established the earth?
Tell Me, if you have understanding.
⁵ Who fixed its dimensions? Certainly you know!
Who stretched a measuring line across it?
⁶ What supports its foundations?
Or who laid its cornerstone
⁷ while the morning stars sang together
and all the sons of God shouted for joy?

⁸ Who enclosed the sea behind doors
when it burst from the womb,
⁹ when I made the clouds its garment
and thick darkness its blanket,
¹⁰ when I determined its boundaries
and put its bars and doors in place,
¹¹ when I declared: "You may come this far, but no farther;
your proud waves stop here"? . . .

²⁴ What road leads to the place where light is dispersed?
Where is the source of the east wind that spreads across the earth?

²⁵ Who cuts a channel for the flooding rain
or clears the way for lightning,
²⁶ to bring rain on an uninhabited land,
on a desert with no human life,
²⁷ to satisfy the parched wasteland
and cause the grass to sprout?

READ

Read the passage aloud slowly.

THINK

Read the passage again aloud, noticing that this is a poetic account of the Creation of the world in contrast to Genesis 1, which is a narrative account. Think about the following questions, remembering to consider the "why" behind each one.

1. What is your favorite moment in this Creation story?
2. Are you more fascinated by God for His meticulous measurements or for His ability to tame the sea?
3. How do you respond to God as one who "clears the way for lightning" and "cuts a channel" in the canyon for the rain?
4. For what part of God's creation would you have wanted a front-row seat (for example, a daisy, a zebra, or a waterfall)?

PRAY

Tell God your responses to these questions. What do you think might be God's response to you?

LIVE

Go for a walk or hike or run in a beautiful place. Notice every single detail of nature that you can, and take pleasure in thinking about how God created it.

GOD CAN HANDLE YOU

JOB 42:7-13

⁷ After the LORD had finished speaking to Job, He said to Eliphaz the Temanite: "I am angry with you and your two friends, for you have not spoken the truth about Me, as My servant Job has. ⁸ Now take seven bulls and seven rams, go to My servant Job, and offer a burnt offering for yourselves. Then My servant Job will pray for you. I will surely accept his prayer and not deal with you as your folly deserves. For you have not spoken the truth about Me, as My servant Job has." ⁹ Then Eliphaz the Temanite, Bildad the Shuhite, and Zophar the Naamathite went and did as the LORD had told them, and the LORD accepted Job's prayer.

¹⁰ After Job had prayed for his friends, the LORD restored his prosperity and doubled his previous possessions. ¹¹ All his brothers, sisters, and former acquaintances came to his house and dined with him in his house. They sympathized with him and comforted him concerning all the adversity the LORD had brought on him. Each one gave him a *qesitah* and a gold earring.

¹² So the LORD blessed the last part of Job's life more than the first. He owned 14,000 sheep, 6,000 camels, 1,000 yoke of oxen, and 1,000 female donkeys. ¹³ He also had seven sons and three daughters.

READ

As you read this passage aloud, picture the events taking place.

THINK

In the silence that follows your reading, continue to mentally engage with the scene. Focus on the part of the story that affects you most, the one that provokes an internal response. How do you relate to God as He appears in this passage? Share that with Him.

PRAY

What do you feel or think when you see God affirming Job's honesty, even though that included sharing strong negative feelings like anger and grief? Is it surprising? Are you apprehensive? Is it a relief? Tell God about what you find inside.

LIVE

Peter Kreeft writes, "[Job] is in a true relationship to God, as the three friends are not: a relationship of heart and soul, life-or-death passion. . . . God is infinite love, and the opposite of love is not hate but indifference. Job's love for God is infected with hate, but the three friends' love for God is infected with indifference. Job stays married to God and throws dishes at him; the three friends have a polite nonmarriage, with separate bedrooms and separate vacations. The family that fights together stays together."[6]

Ponder the idea that God can handle you, all of you, even your negative emotions. Do you really believe that God desires this honest intimacy with you? What would it look like for you to go one level deeper in intimacy with God?

72

A TREE PLANTED BESIDE STREAMS

PSALM 1

1   How happy is the man
     who does not follow the advice of the wicked
     or take the path of sinners
     or join a group of mockers!
2   Instead, his delight is in the LORD's instruction,
     and he meditates on it day and night.
3   He is like a tree planted beside streams of water
     that bears its fruit in season
     and whose leaf does not wither.
     Whatever he does prospers.

4   The wicked are not like this;
     instead, they are like chaff that the wind blows away.
5   Therefore the wicked will not survive the judgment,
     and sinners will not be in the community of the righteous.

6   For the LORD watches over the way of the righteous,
     but the way of the wicked leads to ruin.

READ

Go outside to your yard or a park. Once you find a healthy-looking tree, sit down and focus on it for a few moments. Look at the trunk and consider its strength. Focus on the leaves and admire their intricacies. Examine the roots that are above ground and consider the roots that are below ground.

After you do this, read the passage.

THINK

Contemplate the correlation between being in God's Word and the strength of a tree. Notice the difference between the wicked and the righteous in this psalm. What are the equivalents of "advice of the wicked," "path of sinners," and "group of mockers" in your life that should be avoided? Be specific. What would your life look like if it "bears its fruit in season"?

PRAY

With your eyes open and looking at the tree, ask God to guide you in such a way that you will always be in blossom and bearing fruit. Pray that your roots will go down deep and find their place in the healthy soil of God's Word.

LIVE

Thank God for the gift of His Word. Let the metaphor of a healthy tree guide your decisions today. Plan a time later to spend some additional minutes in His Word, living out the words of this psalm.

MAGNIFICENT IS YOUR NAME

PSALM 8

1   Yahweh, our Lord,
    how magnificent is Your name throughout the earth!

    You have covered the heavens with Your majesty.
2   Because of Your adversaries,
    You have established a stronghold
    from the mouths of children and nursing infants
    to silence the enemy and the avenger.

3   When I observe Your heavens,
    the work of Your fingers,
    the moon and the stars,
    which You set in place,
4   what is man that You remember him,
    the son of man that You look after him?
5   You made him little less than God
    and crowned him with glory and honor.
6   You made him lord over the works of Your hands;
    You put everything under his feet:
7   all the sheep and oxen,
    as well as the animals in the wild,
8   the birds of the sky,
    and the fish of the sea
    that pass through the currents of the seas.

9   Yahweh, our Lord,
    how magnificent is Your name throughout the earth!

READ

Read the passage aloud slowly.

THINK

Read the passage aloud again, letting your mouth play with the phrases, connections, and comparisons that appeal to you. Perhaps one of these does:

- "established a stronghold" and "silence the enemy"
- "Your heavens" and "what is man"
- "works of Your hands" and "under his feet"
- "Your name throughout the earth" and "Yahweh, our Lord"

One by one, hold in your mind the words that stood out to you. Imagine their physical representation, how they relate to each other. For example, hear the sounds of children silencing the enemy, see God's name (and presence and power) as known by all yet so brilliantly magnificent throughout the earth. What do these comparisons have to do with your life?

PRAY

Consider the exercise you just did. What does it make you want to say to God? Words of admiration? Requests to be a good caretaker of the earth? Offer it to Him.

LIVE

In the evening or early morning when the sky is dark, take this book and a flashlight outside and read this psalm to God. Even if you have to whisper to avoid being heard, put your heart into it. Revel in the moment and enjoy God.

TELL GOD YOUR DESIRE

PSALM 13

¹ LORD, how long will You forget me?
   Forever?
   How long will You hide Your face from me?
² How long will I store up anxious concerns within me,
   agony in my mind every day?
   How long will my enemy dominate me?

³ Consider me and answer, LORD my God.
   Restore brightness to my eyes;
   otherwise, I will sleep in death.
⁴ My enemy will say, "I have triumphed over him,"
   and my foes will rejoice because I am shaken.

⁵ But I have trusted in Your faithful love;
   my heart will rejoice in Your deliverance.
⁶ I will sing to the LORD
   because He has treated me generously.

READ

Read the passage with passion, experiencing for yourself the shift in emotion.

THINK

As you hear the psalmist's desire for God's attention, be aware of how you feel similarly. Search your awareness of what you want or need from God until you have a name for that desire. Desiring something practical, like a good grade on an exam, is fine. But pause to see what deeper desire might be behind it — perhaps a single word like *significance* or a phrase like "to know that you love me no matter what."

Now think about what name for God is most meaningful to you in light of the desire you just pinpointed. For example, if you desire a God who will radically alter a difficult circumstance, perhaps you will think of Him as Powerful One. If you desire a God who will soothe your hurts and hold you close, perhaps you will think of Him as Daddy.

PRAY

Consider that God is inviting you to express what you want. Tell Him honestly and plainly. Combine your deeper desire with the name you chose for God. End up with a prayer that is six to nine syllables long, such as "Powerful One, give me justice." Use the next several minutes to pray this prayer to God, repeating it with each breath.

LIVE

Throughout the day, pray your phrase as often as possible — as you drive, as you wait in line, as you exercise. At times your prayer may be in the foreground of your thoughts; at others, in the background. At the end of the day, think about how God responded to your desire.

STAYING WITH GOD

PSALM 27:4-6

⁴ I have asked one thing from the L<small>ORD</small>;
   it is what I desire:
   to dwell in the house of the L<small>ORD</small>
   all the days of my life,
   gazing on the beauty of the L<small>ORD</small>
   and seeking Him in His temple.
⁵ For He will conceal me in His shelter
   in the day of adversity;
   He will hide me under the cover of His tent;
   He will set me high on a rock.
⁶ Then my head will be high
   above my enemies around me;
   I will offer sacrifices in His tent with shouts of joy.
   I will sing and make music to the L<small>ORD</small>.

READ

Read the passage rhythmically. Sing it, if you wish. See if you can find a pattern to the words. Pay attention to the syllables of the words in each line.

THINK

The psalms are some of the most honest words to God ever put on paper. David's expression, though raw, shows his confidence that God will protect him when his enemies are trying to harm or kill him. What would have to happen for you to speak to God in the same honest way?

David's desire is that God will be his guiding light and life source. He wrote, "The LORD is the stronghold of my life — of whom should I be afraid?" (verse 1). What would have to happen for you to say this same line . . . and mean it?

David sang, "I am certain that I will see the LORD's goodness in the land of the living. Wait for the LORD; be strong and courageous. Wait for the LORD" (verses 13-14). When are you tempted to quit on God? What keeps you from running from Him?

PRAY/LIVE

Find an atlas or compass. Look at it and ponder the words of this psalm: "Show me Your way, LORD, and lead me on a level path" (verse 11).

Ask God to guide you down His highway and help you live the life He wants you to live.

DAY 77

GOD ENCOUNTERS

On this seventh day, review and reflect on all you have read this week. Take the time to revel in the ways you've encountered God in the past six days.

RESCUED FROM THE PIT

PSALM 28:1-2,6-9

1   Lord, I call to You;
     my rock, do not be deaf to me.
     If You remain silent to me,
     I will be like those going down to the Pit.
2   Listen to the sound of my pleading
     when I cry to You for help,
     when I lift up my hands
     toward Your holy sanctuary. . . .

6   May the Lord be praised,
     for He has heard the sound of my pleading.
7   The Lord is my strength and my shield;
     my heart trusts in Him, and I am helped.
     Therefore my heart rejoices,
     and I praise Him with my song.

8   The Lord is the strength of His people;
     He is a stronghold of salvation for His anointed.
9   Save Your people, bless Your possession,
     shepherd them, and carry them forever.

READ

Read the passage aloud slowly.

THINK

Read the passage again, whispering verses 1-2 as if in fear and then reading verses 6-9 in a louder, confident voice.

Put yourself in the "Pit," a cold, tar-black hole, silent except for the dripping of water. You call out to God and lift your arms to Him, but at first there is no answer. Stay in this place for a few minutes. Imagine what you would do and think. What would you think about God? What would you say to Him?

Feel in your body the moment when God shows up, when He takes your arms and pulls you out of the hole into the warm, bright light. You shiver and blink. Stay in this moment for a few minutes.

PRAY

Speak to God about what is most powerful for you in these verses. You might ask God to help you call out to Him, to count on Him, whenever you're close to the Pit of life. If you are in a pit right now, ask God to help you raise your hands in prayer and bless Him. If you are not now in a pit, offer a prayer that someone with a joyful heart might pray.

LIVE

Try it. Jump for joy and shout and sing.

CELEBRATING GOD

PSALM 34:1-9

1 I will praise the LORD at all times;
His praise will always be on my lips.
2 I will boast in the LORD;
the humble will hear and be glad.
3 Proclaim Yahweh's greatness with me;
let us exalt His name together.

4 I sought the LORD, and He answered me
and delivered me from all my fears.
5 Those who look to Him are radiant with joy;
their faces will never be ashamed.
6 This poor man cried, and the LORD heard him
and saved him from all his troubles.
7 The Angel of the LORD encamps
around those who fear Him, and rescues them.

8 Taste and see that the LORD is good.
How happy is the man who takes refuge in Him!
9 You who are His holy ones, fear Yahweh,
for those who fear Him lack nothing.

READ

Read the passage aloud as many times as it takes for the words and thoughts to become familiar to you.

THINK/PRAY

Imagine the face and posture of the psalmist expressing this worship. Maybe you'd like to join him, or maybe you're annoyed. What posture does your body take on when you hear the speaker's enthusiasm? When you imagine the God he's speaking about? Move your body into this posture — be it bowing on the floor, clenching your fists, hugging your knees, folding your arms across your chest, dancing, or something else.

Now set aside your physical response and return to the text. Mull over the words until you can determine your mental reaction to them. Can you put clear words to your thoughts? Tell God, and write them down.

Now return to the text one last time. Read it silently, listening for God's response to your posture and your words.

LIVE

In his book *Prayer*, Richard Foster speaks of stepping-stones along the path of learning to adore God. Ultimately, adoring God involves gratitude, magnifying Him, and "foot-stomping celebration," but these must be grown into, and our hearts must be taught. A good first step is simply to make a habit of watching small things in nature: ducks, butterflies, fluttering leaves. This does not mean analyzing but rather discovering the pleasure in simply observing and participating in nature.[7]

Find a small part of God's creation and spend a few minutes enjoying and engaging with it.

A SAFE PLACE TO HIDE

PSALM 46:4-11

4   There is a river —
     its streams delight the city of God,
     the holy dwelling place of the Most High.
5   God is within her; she will not be toppled.
     God will help her when the morning dawns.
6   Nations rage, kingdoms topple;
     the earth melts when He lifts His voice.
7   The LORD of Hosts is with us;
     the God of Jacob is our stronghold.   *Selah*

8   Come, see the works of the LORD,
     who brings devastation on the earth.
9   He makes wars cease throughout the earth.
     He shatters bows and cuts spears to pieces;
     He burns up the chariots.
10   "Stop your fighting — and know that I am God,
     exalted among the nations, exalted on the earth."
11   Yahweh of Hosts is with us;
     the God of Jacob is our stronghold.   *Selah*

READ

Read the passage aloud.

THINK

When have you felt the safest in your lifetime? Why? Circle or underline every word in this passage that deals with the concept of safety and security. Consider your emotions that rise up in response to the words of this passage.

Why do you think the psalmist repeats this phrase: "the God of Jacob is our stronghold"?

What would your life look like if you lived this out: "Stop your fighting—and know that I am God, exalted among the nations, exalted on the earth"?

PRAY

Take several minutes to free your mind of every anxious thought, concern, or stress that you have. Ask God to release you from these thoughts that hold you captive and paralyze you.

After this time, ask God to fill you with the promises from this psalm concerning the safety and security found only in Him.

LIVE

In the midst of your busy schedule today, live in the safety of God.

CLEANSE ME FROM MY SIN

PSALM 51:1-12

1   Be gracious to me, God,
     according to Your faithful love;
     according to Your abundant compassion,
     blot out my rebellion.
2   Wash away my guilt
     and cleanse me from my sin.
3   For I am conscious of my rebellion,
     and my sin is always before me.
4   Against You — You alone — I have sinned
     and done this evil in Your sight.
     So You are right when You pass sentence;
     You are blameless when You judge.
5   Indeed, I was guilty when I was born;
     I was sinful when my mother conceived me.

6   Surely You desire integrity in the inner self,
     and You teach me wisdom deep within.
7   Purify me with hyssop, and I will be clean;
     wash me, and I will be whiter than snow.
8   Let me hear joy and gladness;
     let the bones You have crushed rejoice.
9   Turn Your face away from my sins
     and blot out all my guilt.

10 God, create a clean heart for me
     and renew a steadfast spirit within me.
11 Do not banish me from Your presence
     or take Your Holy Spirit from me.
12 Restore the joy of Your salvation to me,
     and give me a willing spirit.

READ

Read the passage aloud slowly.

THINK

Read the passage again, noting these items:

- the wrongs the psalmist confesses
- what the psalmist asks for from God

1. This psalm is an ideal psalm of confession because the psalmist not only confesses sins but also focuses on the way forward, noting the next positive steps to take. He asks for good things from God and does not get stuck in the past. Find where he does that.
2. The psalmist also understands that his sin is not just something he did, but a sin against God personally. Find the words *You* and *Your.*
3. The biggest issue is not that he sinned but that he loves God. Why do you think we often make our sin the biggest issue instead?

PRAY

Pray the passage aloud, paraphrasing and embellishing the lines that fit your life today.

LIVE

Sit with your hands open in front of you with palms turned upward as a way of letting your confession bring you healing, cleansing, and renewal.

GOD RESTORES

PSALM 53:1-6

1   The fool says in his heart, "God does not exist."
They are corrupt, and they do vile deeds.
There is no one who does good.

2   God looks down from heaven on the human race
to see if there is one who is wise,
one who seeks God.

3   All have turned away;
all alike have become corrupt.
There is no one who does good,
not even one.

4   Will evildoers never understand?
They consume My people as they consume bread;
they do not call on God.

5   Then they will be filled with terror —
terror like no other —
because God will scatter
the bones of those who besiege you.
You will put them to shame,
for God has rejected them.

6   Oh, that Israel's deliverance would come from Zion!
When God restores the fortunes of His people,
Jacob will rejoice; Israel will be glad.

PRAY

Spend several minutes in silence, examining your heart. What's in it today? Note what you find, but don't get too engrossed or sidetracked by any single thought or feeling. Simply acknowledge each item, as though you're gathering all your concerns and feelings into a basket.

READ

When you finish examining your heart, temporarily set aside the basket. Read the passage slowly and thoroughly, taking in the psalmist's experience. His energy is rising in response to a tough situation, and he is letting it drive him toward God.

THINK

What one aspect of the passage draws your attention? Maybe it is the psalmist's desire for justice, rather than a passive tolerance of wrongs. Or maybe it is his deep belief in God's concern for his welfare. Spend time pondering this.

Now return to your basket. Pick up each item and look at it through the filter of this passage. Again, don't get too absorbed in any one concern, but stay attuned to the psalm's message to you. How does it meet up with the items in your basket?

LIVE

Read the passage slowly again. To what action — whether emotional, mental, or physical — might God be calling you through these verses?

HE IS MY ROCK

PSALM 62:1-2

1 I am at rest in God alone;
   my salvation comes from Him.
2 He alone is my rock and my salvation,
   my stronghold; I will never be shaken.

READ

Take this book outside and read the passage.

THINK

In our Western mind-set, we describe God with intangible ideas, such as God is love, God is peace, or God is compassionate. But in the Eastern mind-set, thoughts are described in vivid imagery and word pictures. The Psalms in particular describe God with tangible ideas: God is Father, God is the wind, God is an eagle. In this psalm David describes God as a rock.

Outdoors, find a few rocks and look at them. Take a few moments to reflect on the specific characteristics of rocks and how they describe God's character. Write down your reflections.

PRAY

Thank God that He is like a rock, referring to your list to offer specific details. Thank Him for what each of these aspects of His character means to you.

LIVE

Find a small stone and carry it with you today in your pocket or purse. Every time your hand closes on it, reflect on the fact that God is your rock.

DAY 84

GOD ENCOUNTERS

On this seventh day, review and reflect on all you have read this week. Take the time to revel in the ways you've encountered God in the past six days.

I THIRST FOR YOU

PSALM 63:1-8

¹ God, You are my God; I eagerly seek You.
I thirst for You;
my body faints for You
in a land that is dry, desolate, and without water.
² So I gaze on You in the sanctuary
to see Your strength and Your glory.

³ My lips will glorify You
because Your faithful love is better than life.
⁴ So I will praise You as long as I live;
at Your name, I will lift up my hands.
⁵ You satisfy me as with rich food;
my mouth will praise You with joyful lips.

⁶ When I think of You as I lie on my bed,
I meditate on You during the night watches
⁷ because You are my helper;
I will rejoice in the shadow of Your wings.
⁸ I follow close to You;
Your right hand holds on to me.

READ

Read the passage silently and slowly.

PRAY

Tell God how you honestly respond to this psalm.

Perhaps you don't have this drooling, lip-smacking desire for God. Maybe the idea even embarrasses you. Or maybe you'd like to be this way, but it sounds far too spiritual. Reveal your honest feelings to God.

Perhaps you do have these intense feelings for God. If so, which words in the psalm best describe that?

THINK

Read the passage again.

If one word or phrase describes your present state, say it aloud.

If one word or phrase describes how you would like to be, say it aloud.

LIVE

Consider this quotation from *The Cloud of Unknowing*: "Nourish in your heart a lively longing for God."[8] Bask in that idea, and try to see yourself doing it.

THE POSTURE OF GRATITUDE

PSALM 75:1-4

1   We give thanks to You, God;
     we give thanks to You, for Your name is near.
     People tell about Your wonderful works.

2   "When I choose a time,
     I will judge fairly.
3   When the earth and all its inhabitants shake,
     I am the One who steadies its pillars.   *Selah*
4   I say to the boastful, 'Do not boast,'
     and to the wicked, 'Do not lift up your horn.'"

LIVE

Take a clean sheet of paper and fill the page with all the things you are thankful for, big and small. Include items like names of people, elements of creation, God-orchestrated events and timing, and small things you often overlook. When you're finished, thank God for those blessings He is giving you today as well as those blessings He gave you months or even years ago.

READ/THINK

Now read the expanded passage. Notice the psalmist's reasons for thanking God. Make a list of these reasons on the back of your sheet of paper. This psalm highlights the fact that God is in complete and total control of the entire earth. Stop and ponder: Does that make you thankful or anxious or . . . ? Why?

PRAY

Based on the general outline of the expanded passage, take the list you made and prayerfully write your own psalm (poem) to God. Be creative and personal. (Nobody has to read what you write.) When you are finished, use your psalm to worship God. Read it aloud at least once.

I'LL WORSHIP YOU UNDIVIDED

PSALM 86:14-17

¹⁴ God, arrogant people have attacked me;
a gang of ruthless men seeks my life.
They have no regard for You.

¹⁵ But You, Lord, are a compassionate and gracious God,
slow to anger and rich in faithful love and truth.

¹⁶ Turn to me and be gracious to me.
Give Your strength to Your servant;
save the son of Your female servant.

¹⁷ Show me a sign of Your goodness;
my enemies will see and be put to shame
because You, LORD, have helped and comforted me.

READ

Stand up and read aloud the psalmist's proclamation of God's trust-worthiness. As you read the phrase "God, arrogant people have attacked me," kneel. Remain on your knees until you finish the passage, as the psalmist expresses the depth of his trust in God amid danger. Repeat slowly and attentively three times.

THINK

What do you notice about yourself as you do this exercise? In what ways do you experience the passage differently than you normally would? Perhaps your body's position helps your mind focus. Or perhaps you protest the position because it doesn't fit your mood or energy level. Meditate on the reasons for your reaction.

PRAY

Now read the passage again, this time silently, keeping in mind what you just learned about yourself. Let the Holy Spirit show you a word or phrase that touches what has arisen in you. Spend a few minutes repeating the word or phrase prayerfully. How is God speaking to you?

LIVE

Consider what it was like for you to let your body take the lead in prayer. In what ways did your body help or hinder you in engaging with God?

WHEN THE ROCKS CRY OUT

PSALM 96:7-10

⁷ Ascribe to the LORD, you families of the peoples,
ascribe to the LORD glory and strength.
⁸ Ascribe to Yahweh the glory of His name;
bring an offering and enter His courts.
⁹ Worship the LORD in the splendor of His holiness;
tremble before Him, all the earth.

¹⁰ Say among the nations: "The LORD reigns.
The world is firmly established; it cannot be shaken.
He judges the peoples fairly."

READ

Get in a comfortable position on your knees. As you are in this posture of submission, ask God to help your body be a symbolic expression of your heart during the next few moments. Admit to God that you want to be submissive to Him — even if doing so is difficult — as you engage with His Word.

Keeping this position, read the passage.

THINK

The psalmist invites other people to join him in the praise of God. "Say among the nations: 'The LORD reigns.'" In what specific ways can we get the message out in our praise of God?

Consider this picture of worship: "Ascribe to Yahweh the glory of His name; bring an offering and enter His courts." Is it hard to imagine that God likes it when His people celebrate? Why or why not?

What is one attribute of God that you could celebrate right now? Why do you think that attribute comes to mind?

PRAY

While still on your knees, invite the Holy Spirit to come in and guide your prayers. Praise Him for whatever comes to mind. If you feel comfortable, speak your praise aloud.

LIVE

Find a worship album or Christian radio station and spend the next several minutes listening to worship music. If you know the words to a song, join in and sing along, or invite friends to join you. If you know how to play an instrument, spend a few minutes playing it while singing praises to God.

PRAISING GOD

PSALM 103:1-14

1   My soul, praise Yahweh,
    and all that is within me, praise His holy name.
2   My soul, praise the LORD,
    and do not forget all His benefits.

3   He forgives all your sin;
    He heals all your diseases.
4   He redeems your life from the Pit;
    He crowns you with faithful love and compassion.
5   He satisfies you with goodness;
    your youth is renewed like the eagle.

6   The LORD executes acts of righteousness
    and justice for all the oppressed.
7   He revealed His ways to Moses,
    His deeds to the people of Israel.
8   The LORD is compassionate and gracious,
    slow to anger and rich in faithful love.
9   He will not always accuse us
    or be angry forever.
10 He has not dealt with us as our sins deserve
    or repaid us according to our offenses.

11 For as high as the heavens are above the earth,
    so great is His faithful love
    toward those who fear Him.
12 As far as the east is from the west,
    so far has He removed
    our transgressions from us.
13 As a father has compassion on his children,
    so the LORD has compassion on those who fear Him.
14 For He knows what we are made of,
    remembering that we are dust.

READ

Read the passage quietly to yourself.

THINK

The idea of our soul praising God may sound foreign. We might think, *How can my praise bless God? Does God really need my praise?* But the literal meaning of the Hebrew word *bless* is "to kneel."[9] When we praise, or bless, God, our souls kneel to Him, usually in worship or gratitude.

Read the passage again with your heart kneeling before God. If possible, physically kneel where you are and read aloud. As you do, notice the phrases that reflect what you are most eager to praise God for — perhaps that He is "slow to anger" or "will not always accuse."

PRAY

Stay kneeling and pray aloud those phrases about God that touched you most. As you pray, add to them other ideas about God that come to mind. Raise your hands if you wish.

LIVE

Quietly kneel before God in whatever posture and mood this psalm has brought you:

- resting peacefully on your heels with your hands in your lap
- rising onto your knees with your hands raised
- kneeling before a chair or bed and bringing your whole self forward onto it

Be with God this way for a few minutes.

89

SPIRITUAL HISTORY LESSONS

PSALM 106:1-4,6-12

1 Hallelujah!
Give thanks to the LORD, for He is good;
His faithful love endures forever.

2 Who can declare the LORD's mighty acts
or proclaim all the praise due Him?

3 How happy are those who uphold justice,
who practice righteousness at all times.

4 Remember me, LORD,
when You show favor to Your people.
Come to me with Your salvation. . . .

6 Both we and our fathers have sinned;
we have done wrong and have acted wickedly.

7 Our fathers in Egypt did not grasp
the significance of Your wonderful works
or remember Your many acts of faithful love;
instead, they rebelled by the sea — the Red Sea.

8 Yet He saved them because of His name,
to make His power known.

9 He rebuked the Red Sea, and it dried up;
He led them through the depths as through a desert.

10 He saved them from the hand of the adversary;
He redeemed them from the hand of the enemy.

11 Water covered their foes;
not one of them remained.

12 Then they believed His promises
and sang His praise.

READ

As you read this passage, listen for a word or phrase that says in some small way, "I am for you today."

THINK/PRAY

Let this word or phrase sink deeply into you by repeating it slowly to yourself several times. Bring your worries, thoughts, and memories to it, and see how it casts light on them. Talk to God about what's going through your mind and heart. Do you feel like He is "for you"?

LIVE

Ebenezer literally means "stone of help" in Hebrew. It can be used to refer to anything that reminds us of something spiritually significant. Today, create an Ebenezer for yourself.

First, think about how God spoke to you or what He did for you through today's passage. Second, write one sentence or a few words on a small piece of paper to describe that. Third, pick a symbol for it: Find a pebble from your yard, buy an inexpensive cross, or cut out a picture from a magazine. Fourth, fold up your note and attach it to the object. Fifth, put your Ebenezer somewhere you will see it often, as a visible reminder of what God said and did.

In the future, periodically reflect on your life (maybe two to four times a year) and create more Ebenezers, keeping them in a box, bowl, or bucket. Whenever you see them, recall who God has been to you.

DAY 91

GOD ENCOUNTERS

On this seventh day, review and reflect on all you have read this week. Take the time to revel in the ways you've encountered God in the past six days.

THE GIFT OF SCRIPTURE

PSALM 119:89-101,105

89 LORD, Your word is forever;
   it is firmly fixed in heaven.
90 Your faithfulness is for all generations;
   You established the earth, and it stands firm.
91 They stand today in accordance with Your judgments,
   for all things are Your servants.
92 If Your instruction had not been my delight,
   I would have died in my affliction.
93 I will never forget Your precepts,
   for You have given me life through them.
94 I am Yours; save me,
   for I have sought Your precepts.
95 The wicked hope to destroy me,
   but I contemplate Your decrees.
96 I have seen a limit to all perfection,
   but Your command is without limit.

מ *Mem*

97 How I love Your instruction!
   It is my meditation all day long.
98 Your commands make me wiser than my enemies,
   for they are always with me.
99 I have more insight than all my teachers
   because Your decrees are my meditation.
100 I understand more than the elders
    because I obey Your precepts.
101 I have kept my feet from every evil path
    to follow Your word. . . .

נ *Nun*

105 Your word is a lamp for my feet
    and a light on my path.

READ

Read the passage very slowly. Then read it again, this time even slower.

THINK

You've probably heard people say, "The Lord spoke to me" or "God told me x-y-z," and then been left feeling disbelief, confusion, frustration, or guilt. God does speak to us but not in a booming voice that sounds like actor James Earl Jones. God speaks to us through different means: creation, other people's words of guidance, promptings of the Holy Spirit, and "a soft whisper" (1 Kings 19:12). But He also speaks to us through His Word.

Explore your attitudes or preconceived ideas about God's Word. Be brutally honest with yourself and God. Think of ways you could value His Word more and find yourself more attentive to what it has to say.

Spend several minutes considering how God might be speaking to you through this passage concerning His Word.

PRAY

Pray through this passage of Scripture. Simply make the passage your very own, turning the words back to God (rephrased in your own words, if you wish) as a way to converse with Him. Be assured that He is listening to you.

LIVE

Invite God to reveal general and specific elements of Scripture to guide your words, thoughts, and actions today.

CONFIDENCE IN GOD

PSALM 121

1   I lift my eyes toward the mountains.
Where will my help come from?

2   My help comes from the LORD,
the Maker of heaven and earth.

3   _____, He will not allow your foot to slip;
your Protector will not slumber.

4   Indeed, the Protector of Israel
does not slumber or sleep.

5   The LORD protects you, _____;
the LORD is a shelter right by your side.

6   The sun will not strike you by day, _____,
or the moon by night.

7   The LORD will protect you, _____, from all harm;
He will protect your life.

8   The LORD will protect your coming and going, _____,
both now and forever.

READ

Read the passage aloud slowly.

THINK

This psalm ranks as one of the greatest psalms of trust and confidence. As you read it aloud a second time, do something different from verse 3 on. Address yourself by name in the places where a blank appears.

As you read the passage a third time, notice the word or phrase that stands out most to you. Use that to create a mind-picture of yourself in a situation where you need to remember to trust. For example, picture yourself desperate for protection, and reread a phrase from verse 7 or 8. Or picture yourself in a situation where you need to know that God doesn't overlook or forget you, and reread a phrase from verse 3 or 4.

PRAY

Speak with God about how much you do or don't trust Him. Tell Him about your confidence level and ask Him to give you grace to grow in it.

LIVE

Have a little fun here. Keep these ideas about confidence in mind and stand as confidently as you can. You might even want to gesture — put your hands on your hips or hold out your fists in front of you. Stay in this pose for several seconds, going over your selected phrase.

Now do this in front of a mirror. Imagine God standing next to you, protecting you in some way. For example, He could be shielding you from the side or standing behind you with arms wrapped around you.

LIKE A WEANED CHILD

PSALM 131

1 Lord, my heart is not proud;
   my eyes are not haughty.
   I do not get involved with things
   too great or too difficult for me.
2 Instead, I have calmed and quieted myself
   like a little weaned child with its mother;
   I am like a little child.

3 Israel, put your hope in the Lord,
   both now and forever.

READ

After you read this psalm, wait patiently for your response to the material.

THINK/PRAY

How does the message of the psalm resonate with you? Maybe the reality of your life is different from the speaker's, but he gives voice to your desire. Or maybe his message challenges your attitude or perspective.

Read it a second time, then share your response with God through prayer. At first it will feel natural to pray in your own words, responding to what you're reading, but as you keep going, stretch beyond this and pray using the words of the passage. Although doing so might feel awkward at first, give yourself time to get used to it. You'll likely hear yourself praying statements you don't genuinely mean and then feel your heart protesting. But stay honest with God by acknowledging this to Him. Don't be hard on yourself. Just recall that God accepts you and loves you, then continue.

When you read this psalm one more time, let your meditation go a bit deeper. Wait for deeper memories and thoughts. These mirror more about you and your life. Bring these insights into your prayer.

LIVE

Spend time in silence. Imagine your soul as "a little weaned child with its mother." Even if you find your thoughts continuously running, practice silence. Achieving silence doesn't mean you have to focus on stopping your thoughts. Just let them pass through, then bring your mind back to the image of resting. Just enjoy being in the presence of God.

CHEWING THE CUD

PSALM 139:1-12

1 LORD, You have searched me and known me.
2 You know when I sit down and when I stand up;
You understand my thoughts from far away.
3 You observe my travels and my rest;
You are aware of all my ways.
4 Before a word is on my tongue,
You know all about it, LORD.
5 You have encircled me;
You have placed Your hand on me.
6 This extraordinary knowledge is beyond me.
It is lofty; I am unable to reach it.

7 Where can I go to escape Your Spirit?
Where can I flee from Your presence?
8 If I go up to heaven, You are there;
if I make my bed in Sheol, You are there.
9 If I live at the eastern horizon
or settle at the western limits,
10 even there Your hand will lead me;
Your right hand will hold on to me.
11 If I say, "Surely the darkness will hide me,
and the light around me will be night" —
12 even the darkness is not dark to You.
The night shines like the day;
darkness and light are alike to You.

THINK

To ruminate literally means "to chew the cud." A cow will chew on one particular wad of cud for hours at a time, over and over again, swallowing it and bringing it back up from its stomach. Consider the metaphor of the cud as you think about the phrases "searched me and known me," "You understand my thoughts," and "You have encircled me."

READ

Read the passage three times slowly, ruminating on it. Don't skim or speed-read; chew on each word. Hold the words in your mind until you feel you've considered every aspect of them.

PRAY

Spend time in silence, meditating on these phrases. Let them bounce around in your brain. Look at them from every direction. As you do that, explore the emotions and thoughts you are having. Specifically ask God, "Why am I feeling this way, God?" and put your heart in a posture of listening. Expect to hear from God.

LIVE

Spend a few more minutes listening to God and ask Him, "What do you want me to do with what You have given to me?"

NO ONE IS LEFT OUT

PSALM 145:7-9,15-21

7   They will give a testimony of Your great goodness
    and will joyfully sing of Your righteousness.

8   The LORD is gracious and compassionate,
    slow to anger and great in faithful love.
9   The LORD is good to everyone;
    His compassion rests on all He has made. . . .

15 All eyes look to You,
    and You give them their food at the proper time.
16 You open Your hand
    and satisfy the desire of every living thing.

17 The LORD is righteous in all His ways
    and gracious in all His acts.
18 The LORD is near all who call out to Him,
    all who call out to Him with integrity.
19 He fulfills the desires of those who fear Him;
    He hears their cry for help and saves them.
20 The LORD guards all those who love Him,
    but He destroys all the wicked.
21 My mouth will declare Yahweh's praise;
    let every living thing
    praise His holy name forever and ever.

READ

Read the passage aloud slowly.

THINK

This psalm celebrates God's goodness to all and His goodness through everything. Notice how often the words *all* and *every* appear. While many psalms emphasize God as "my God," this one shows God's mercy to all.

Read it again, either emphasizing or pausing after the words *all* and *every*.

1. Who might *all* include that you may not have thought about before? Maybe people you know, people far away, or objects foreign to you. As you do this, what pictures come to mind?
2. Notice the many phrases about God's goodness. Which ones resonate most with you?

PRAY

Thank God for His deep goodness toward all. Use phrases from the psalm that best express this theme from your point of view.

LIVE

Go for a walk or hike, taking this book with you. As you walk, stop at certain points and read a verse or two aloud. Listen to the echo of your voice. Enjoy God, who is enjoying hearing you pour forth these words.

PRAISE HIM, SUN AND MOON

PSALM 148:2-12

2 Praise Him, all His angels;
praise Him, all His hosts.

3 Praise Him, sun and moon;
praise Him, all you shining stars.

4 Praise Him, highest heavens,
and you waters above the heavens.

5 Let them praise the name of Yahweh,
for He commanded, and they were created.

6 He set them in position forever and ever;
He gave an order that will never pass away.

7 Praise the LORD from the earth,
all sea monsters and ocean depths,

8 lightning and hail, snow and cloud,
powerful wind that executes His command,

9 mountains and all hills,
fruit trees and all cedars,

10 wild animals and all cattle,
creatures that crawl and flying birds,

11 kings of the earth and all peoples,
princes and all judges of the earth,

12 young men as well as young women,
old and young together.

READ

Read the passage a few times aloud, zeroing in on each image. Allow the words to wash over you in their vividness: See specific birds or wild animals, sense the chill of the snowstorm, hear the roaring of the ocean. Watch every action of the characters. Compare the way each created thing uniquely praises its Maker.

THINK

In the silence that follows the reading, meditate on what you've seen and heard. With all these pieces of creation in the background, praising God, how do you see Him? What is He like? Spend time thinking about Him.

PRAY

Pick the character attribute of God that seems the most powerful after your meditation. Envision God in this role, then see yourself entering His presence. How do you respond to Him? How does He treat you? Rest in God's presence or talk to Him or adore Him — whatever fits the scene.

LIVE

As you go through your day, pay special attention to natural objects around you (rocks, trees, animals, hills) as well as people (individuals, crowds). Observe how they glorify their Creator by their existence. Don't be overcritical or get caught up in evaluating — just notice.

DAY 98

GOD ENCOUNTERS

On this seventh day, review and reflect on all you have read this week. Take the time to revel in the ways you've encountered God in the past six days.

SEEK WISDOM

PROVERBS 2:1-5

1 My son, if you accept my words
   and store up my commands within you,
2 listening closely to wisdom
   and directing your heart to understanding;
3 furthermore, if you call out to insight
   and lift your voice to understanding,
4 if you seek it like silver
   and search for it like hidden treasure,
5 then you will understand the fear of the LORD
   and discover the knowledge of God.

READ

Read the passage, imagining a grandparent or an older, wiser friend saying these words to you.

THINK

Our culture rarely considers or values wisdom. People want many things, but wisdom isn't usually one of them, or it's not high on the priority list. And there seems to be a widespread assumption that a person simply grows into wisdom as he or she gets older. This is a passive approach to obtaining wisdom. But the writer of this proverb tells us not only that wisdom is worth pursuing but also that it should be pursued with much time and energy. This is a proactive approach to obtaining wisdom.

Read the passage again. What would pursuing wisdom with all your might look like? Do you believe that wisdom is "more profitable than silver" (3:14)? Is that hard to believe? Why or why not?

PRAY

Pause and ask God to give you wisdom. Ask Him to help you raise the value and preciousness of wisdom in your life. Ask Him to show you how to actively pursue wisdom. Listen for anything He might say now in response to your requests.

LIVE

Live wisely today, asking God to give you a spirit of discernment as you work, play, rest, eat, read, and sleep.

GUARD YOUR HEART

PROVERBS 4:20-23; 5:8-14

20 My son, pay attention to my words;
    listen closely to my sayings.
21 Don't lose sight of them;
    keep them within your heart.
22 For they are life to those who find them,
    and health to one's whole body.
23 Guard your heart above all else,
    for it is the source of life. . . .

8   Keep your way far from her.
    Don't go near the door of her house.
9   Otherwise, you will give up your vitality to others
    and your years to someone cruel;
10 strangers will drain your resources,
    and your earnings will end up in a foreigner's house.
11 At the end of your life, you will lament
    when your physical body has been consumed,
12 and you will say, "How I hated discipline,
    and how my heart despised correction.
13 I didn't obey my teachers
    or listen closely to my mentors.
14 I am on the verge of complete ruin
    before the entire community."

READ

Read the passage aloud slowly, keeping in mind that "her" refers to the things in your life that seduce you, meaning anything that sucks you in, lures you, misleads you, or even corrupts you.

THINK

1. Consider what has caused you to squander days of your life and left you full of regret. It might be patterns of relating to people, patterns of spending your time, or patterns of making decisions. Then read 5:8-14 again and wait for thoughts to rise to the surface of your mind.
2. Read 4:20-23 and see what comes to you about the ways you need to avoid such patterns. Do you need to listen? Keep God's message in plain view? Keep a vigilant heart?
3. What would guarding your heart look like? Guarding might be different for you than for others. Avoid grabbing at the first thing that comes to mind. Wait in that.

PRAY

Begin by confessing your regrets about time and energy you've squandered. Don't rush through this. Allow enough time to fully describe these things and let them go. Then ask God to help you listen to Him and keep a watchful heart.

LIVE

Leave this book open to this passage and underline the phrase in 4:20-23 that stands out to you. As you move through your day, allow this to remind you to listen and keep an alert heart.

LURED INTO AMBUSH

PROVERBS 7:7-8,13-23

⁷ I saw among the inexperienced,
I noticed among the youths,
a young man lacking sense.

⁸ Crossing the street near her corner,
he strolled down the road to her house. . . .

¹³ She grabs him and kisses him;
she brazenly says to him,

¹⁴ "I've made fellowship offerings;
today I've fulfilled my vows.

¹⁵ So I came out to meet you,
to search for you, and I've found you.

¹⁶ I've spread coverings on my bed —
richly colored linen from Egypt.

¹⁷ I've perfumed my bed
with myrrh, aloes, and cinnamon.

¹⁸ Come, let's drink deeply of lovemaking until morning.
Let's feast on each other's love!

¹⁹ My husband isn't home;
he went on a long journey.

²⁰ He took a bag of money with him
and will come home at the time of the full moon."

²¹ She seduces him with her persistent pleading;
she lures with her flattering talk.

²² He follows her impulsively
like an ox going to the slaughter,
like a deer bounding toward a trap

²³ until an arrow pierces its liver,
like a bird darting into a snare —
he doesn't know it will cost him his life.

PRAY

Before you begin, ask the Holy Spirit to make His presence palpable as you pray. Ask Him to make you open to whatever He gives, rather than taking charge of this time or trying to fix yourself. Even if a part of you disagrees, present yourself with the truth that opening to Him is all you can really do.

READ/THINK

Read the passage once, slowly. Allow the story of the foolish man and the seductress to sink in until you understand its message. How do the words relate to your life? In what areas are you tempted to live foolishly? What are some things you know are right to do, but you drag your feet and don't do them? Don't try to fix yourself or be down on yourself. Instead, just let the reality settle in that this is who you are: someone very much in need of God's grace and mercy.

LIVE

Finish your devotion today by picturing God sitting with you. Tell Him, "God, this is who I am." Remain open to whatever this might be, and if necessary, remind yourself that you don't want to fix yourself. If this seems difficult or if relaxing in His presence is challenging, take a few minutes to consider this truth: "The Lord is very compassionate and merciful" (James 5:11). Then return to relaxing in God's presence. Write down anything significant from this time that you can refer to.

SELF-EXAMINATION

PROVERBS 10:22-32

22 The LORD's blessing enriches,
and struggle adds nothing to it.

23 As shameful conduct is pleasure for a fool,
so wisdom is for a man of understanding.

24 What the wicked dreads will come to him,
but what the righteous desire will be given to them.

25 When the whirlwind passes,
the wicked are no more,
but the righteous are secure forever.

26 Like vinegar to the teeth and smoke to the eyes,
so the slacker is to the one who sends him on an errand.

27 The fear of the LORD prolongs life,
but the years of the wicked are cut short.

28 The hope of the righteous is joy,
but the expectation of the wicked comes to nothing.

29 The way of the LORD is a stronghold for the honorable,
but destruction awaits the malicious.

30 The righteous will never be shaken,
but the wicked will not remain on the earth.

31 The mouth of the righteous produces wisdom,
but a perverse tongue will be cut out.

32 The lips of the righteous know what is appropriate,
but the mouth of the wicked, only what is perverse.

READ

Stand in front of a mirror and read the passage. When you're finished, stand motionless. Stare at yourself in the mirror.

THINK

When we read passages of God's Word that speak about the unrighteous or the evil or foolish person, we are often reminded of other individuals and think to ourselves, *That certainly isn't talking about me.* But we must be careful not to be blinded by the sin and pride in our own lives. Take a few minutes to perform a thorough self-examination. (This might be a difficult exercise for you; being willing to see our true selves is not easy.)

PRAY

Reread the passage. After each verse, pause, look in the mirror, and whisper, "God, is this me?" Allow time for God to prompt truths in your heart. Some of these thoughts may be hard to hear. If God brings to mind specific areas where you have failed, ask Him to forgive you. If God brings to mind areas where you can grow, ask Him to help you mature as you follow Him. If God brings to mind ways in which you are living faithfully, thank Him for His grace in your life.

LIVE

Whatever God-honoring quality was revealed to you today as you asked the question, "God, is this me?" go and live in that manner.

WISDOM AND INTEGRITY

PROVERBS 14:2-13

2   Whoever lives with integrity fears the LORD,
but the one who is devious in his ways despises Him.

3   The proud speech of a fool brings a rod of discipline,
but the lips of the wise protect them.

4   Where there are no oxen, the feeding trough is empty,
but an abundant harvest comes
through the strength of an ox.

5   An honest witness does not deceive,
but a dishonest witness utters lies.

6   A mocker seeks wisdom and doesn't find it,
but knowledge comes easily to the perceptive.

7   Stay away from a foolish man;
you will gain no knowledge from his speech.

8   The sensible man's wisdom is to consider his way,
but the stupidity of fools deceives them.

9   Fools mock at making restitution,
but there is goodwill among the upright.

10   The heart knows its own bitterness,
and no outsider shares in its joy.

11   The house of the wicked will be destroyed,
but the tent of the upright will stand.

12   There is a way that seems right to a man,
but its end is the way to death.

13   Even in laughter a heart may be sad,
and joy may end in grief.

READ

Read through these wise observations about life, pausing after each to consider what it says. Pick the statement that seems particularly vivid to you today, and read through it several more times, silently and aloud, until you become familiar with its message.

THINK

Where do you see yourself and the way you act fitting into this observation about life's realities? Maybe the image of the ox makes you recognize the laziness you've been lounging in, or perhaps you're struck by how much energy you expend trying to fit in with people. As you absorb this reality check, what are you feeling?

PRAY

Allow your inner exploration to take you into dialogue with God. Tell Him about your discoveries. Let yourself be led into thankfulness, humility, or need. Maybe you're grateful to see the danger of your laziness before you get burned, or maybe you want to tell God how much you desire validation, even when you understand the folly of measuring your worth by the acceptance of others. Whatever this passage offers you personally, continue exploring it with God. Return to the passage if you find yourself stuck.

LIVE

Maybe the words "integrity," "lips of the wise," or "wisdom" mean something new to you after pondering this passage. In what area is God inviting you to turn your life around — with His help? Write down in a short statement what you sense God inviting you to do.

THE IMPORTANCE OF WORDS

PROVERBS 16:21-32

21   Anyone with a wise heart is called discerning,
and pleasant speech increases learning.

22   Insight is a fountain of life for its possessor,
but the discipline of fools is folly.

23   A wise heart instructs its mouth
and increases learning with its speech.

24   Pleasant words are a honeycomb:
sweet to the taste and health to the body.

25   There is a way that seems right to a man,
but its end is the way to death.

26   A worker's appetite works for him
because his hunger urges him on.

27   A worthless man digs up evil,
and his speech is like a scorching fire.

28   A contrary man spreads conflict,
and a gossip separates close friends.

29   A violent man lures his neighbor,
leading him in a way that is not good.

30   The one who narrows his eyes is planning deceptions;
the one who compresses his lips brings about evil.

31   Gray hair is a glorious crown;
it is found in the way of righteousness.

32   Patience is better than power,
and controlling one's temper, than capturing a city.

READ

Read the passage. Underline the word or phrase that stands out to you the most. Read the passage again. Underline a different word or phrase that stands out to you.

THINK

You may have heard the saying that only two things cannot be taken back: time and our words. Think back over all the words you have said in conversation over the past twenty-four hours (conversations you have had with friends, comments you have made in passing, phone calls, jokes you have told, and so on). What percentage of your conversation would you say was positive, encouraging, and uplifting? What percentage was negative, discouraging, and sarcastic?

Consider the words you are glad you said. Consider the words you regret saying.

PRAY

For the words you regret, ask for forgiveness. For the positive words you spoke, thank God they were words that built up rather than tore down.

Ask God to bring to mind words of truth and healing that you could speak to others. Ask Him to bring to mind specific people to whom you could speak these words in the next few days.

LIVE

Have the courage to seek out opportunities to speak words of truth and healing to people who need to hear them. Hold your tongue when you are upset or frustrated — when you are about to speak words you'll regret. Above all else, ask God to help you guard your mouth by thinking before speaking.

104
105

DAY 105

GOD ENCOUNTERS

On this seventh day, review and reflect on all you have read this week. Take the time to revel in the ways you've encountered God in the past six days.

HUMILITY

PROVERBS 18:10-15

¹⁰ The name of Yahweh is a strong tower;
the righteous run to it and are protected.

¹¹ A rich man's wealth is his fortified city;
in his imagination it is like a high wall.

¹² Before his downfall a man's heart is proud,
but humility comes before honor.

¹³ The one who gives an answer before he listens —
this is foolishness and disgrace for him.

¹⁴ A man's spirit can endure sickness,
but who can survive a broken spirit?

¹⁵ The mind of the discerning acquires knowledge,
and the ear of the wise seeks it.

READ

Read the passage aloud slowly.

THINK

Read the passage again slowly. Notice the different ways humility is expressed.

1. Which phrases describe who you have been and who you'd like to be?
2. What fears do you have about what might happen to you if you were humble? How might these fears be addressed by living in God's name, God's power, and God's presence as your place of protection?

Read the passage again.

3. What touches you most about this passage?
4. What is occurring in your life right now that this passage addresses?

PRAY

Ask God to show you more about living a richly humble life. Tell God what you need to learn from Him about being His devoted, constant, listening student.

LIVE

Soak in the protection of God's name, presence, and power. Notice how this makes being humble easier.

WAIT FOR GOD

PROVERBS 20:22-30

²² Don't say, "I will avenge this evil!"
Wait on the LORD, and He will rescue you.

²³ Differing weights are detestable to the LORD,
and dishonest scales are unfair.

²⁴ A man's steps are determined by the LORD,
so how can anyone understand his own way?

²⁵ It is a trap for anyone to dedicate something rashly
and later to reconsider his vows.

²⁶ A wise king separates out the wicked
and drives the threshing wheel over them.

²⁷ The LORD's lamp sheds light on a person's life,
searching the innermost parts.

²⁸ Loyalty and faithfulness deliver a king;
through loyalty he maintains his throne.

²⁹ The glory of young men is their strength,
and the splendor of old men is gray hair.

³⁰ Lashes and wounds purge away evil,
and beatings cleanse the innermost parts.

READ

Read this list of statements and instructions, pausing after each one to consider what it says. Does one stand out to you? Memorize it.

THINK

Why does this stand out to you? Let it lead you to ponder your own life. Try to avoid thinking about other people's actions or motives; think instead about only your own. Maybe you'll be reminded of making an impulsive promise, or perhaps you'll check your attitude toward the "splendor of . . . gray hair" versus "the glory of young men."

PRAY

Invite God into your thoughts. Tell Him what you have been discovering. Be aware of your feelings while you pray — maybe fear of emptiness at the thought of getting older, joy that God will "rescue you" someday, or sadness over a foolish decision and its consequences. Be yourself in God's presence.

LIVE

Explore your overall experience with this text so far. Why did you respond the way you did to the wise instruction God is communicating in this passage? If you didn't care much, this might tell you that you don't care much about doing the right thing. If you anxiously tried to think of ways to improve yourself, perhaps you feel uncomfortable exposing your weakness to God. Honestly recognize what's in your heart today — and what that tells you about how you see yourself and how you see God.

Remember that God knows all about you — even the parts of you that are rebellious and don't care about what's right — and yet He loves you deeply. If you struggle to believe this, read Isaiah 43:1-7.

DOLLARS AND CENTS

PROVERBS 22:22-23,26-27; 23:4-8

22 Don't rob a poor man because he is poor,
    and don't crush the oppressed at the gate,
23 for the LORD will take up their case
    and will plunder those who plunder them. . . .

26 Don't be one of those who enter agreements,
    who put up security for loans.
27 If you have no money to pay,
    even your bed will be taken from under you. . . .

4 Don't wear yourself out to get rich;
    stop giving your attention to it.
5 As soon as your eyes fly to it, it disappears,
    for it makes wings for itself
    and flies like an eagle to the sky.

6 Don't eat a stingy person's bread,
    and don't desire his choice food,
7 for it's like someone calculating inwardly.
    "Eat and drink," he says to you,
    but his heart is not with you.
8 You will vomit the little you've eaten
    and waste your pleasant words.

READ

Read the passage. Make a note of every implication to finances and wealth that you find.

THINK

Scripture has a lot to say about how we deal with our finances. Wisdom will determine a lot about how we deal with money, and money will determine a lot about how we deal with wisdom. Proverbs speaks often of the importance of dealing with money, because it's not simply about dollars and cents. It's a deeper issue that involves what our heart is attached to.

Think back over the purchases you have made in the past week, big and small. What was your motive in making those purchases (practical purposes, reputation, comfort and pleasure, necessity)?

Which of those would you categorize as being wise purchases? Which would you categorize as being unwise?

As you think about the purchases you have made in the past week, what emotions are you feeling? Are they positive or negative? Full of freedom and joy or guilt and frustration? Why do you think you are feeling that way?

PRAY

Take out your wallet, purse, money clip, credit cards, checkbook, and key chain, and hold them in your hands. As you look at the pile in your hands, keep your eyes open and pray. Ask your heavenly Father to help you be a wise steward of all the money and possessions He has entrusted to you.

LIVE

Every time you pull out your wallet or purse to make a purchase, ask yourself the question, *Will this purchase be a wise one, and will it honor God?*

WISDOM WITH FEET ON IT

PROVERBS 24:3-4,15-21,28-29

³ A house is built by wisdom,
and it is established by understanding;
⁴ by knowledge the rooms are filled
with every precious and beautiful treasure. . . .

¹⁵ Wicked man, don't set an ambush,
at the camp of the righteous man;
don't destroy his dwelling.
¹⁶ Though a righteous man falls seven times,
he will get up,
but the wicked will stumble into ruin.

¹⁷ Don't gloat when your enemy falls,
and don't let your heart rejoice when he stumbles,
¹⁸ or the LORD will see, be displeased,
and turn His wrath away from him.

¹⁹ Don't be agitated by evildoers,
and don't envy the wicked.
²⁰ For the evil have no future;
the lamp of the wicked will be put out.

²¹ My son, fear the LORD, as well as the king,
and don't associate with rebels. . . .

²⁸ Don't testify against your neighbor without cause.
Don't deceive with your lips.
²⁹ Don't say, "I'll do to him what he did to me;
I'll repay the man for what he has done."

READ

Read the passage slowly. Now read the expanded passage.

THINK

Read the passage again, noticing that the first two verses introduce the importance of wisdom.

1. If you're wondering what wisdom is, notice the way the other verses describe how you can live out wisdom. Underline the practical descriptions of wisdom you find there.
2. Now read aloud the phrases you underlined. Which one resonates with you? Which one sounds like guidance you've been hearing God say to you for a while?
3. How does that phrase connect with you?

PRAY

Talk to God about what's been going on in your life and how the wise ideas in this passage shed light on your situation. Tell God why you would find it difficult or easy to do the wise thing. Thank God that He never finds it difficult — and that He can help you.

LIVE

Play with the idea that you're a truly wise person. Doodle a little in a journal, drawing a representation of yourself as wise. Consider why you drew what you did. Being wise doesn't mean you're a know-it-all or superior to other people so they don't want to hang out with you. Jesus was wise, but plenty of people liked to hang out with Him.

WORD TO THE WISE

PROVERBS 28:4-12

4   Those who reject the law praise the wicked,
    but those who keep the law battle against them.

5   Evil men do not understand justice,
    but those who seek the LORD understand everything.

6   Better a poor man who lives with integrity
    than a rich man who distorts right and wrong.

7   A discerning son keeps the law,
    but a companion of gluttons humiliates his father.

8   Whoever increases his wealth through excessive interest
    collects it for one who is kind to the poor.

9   Anyone who turns his ear away from hearing the law —
    even his prayer is detestable.

10 The one who leads the upright into an evil way
    will fall into his own pit,
    but the blameless will inherit what is good.

11 A rich man is wise in his own eyes,
    but a poor man who has discernment sees through him.

12 When the righteous triumph,
    there is great rejoicing,
    but when the wicked come to power,
    people hide themselves.

READ

Read the passage slowly, pausing for about thirty seconds after each verse to think about it.

THINK

There are many parts of Proverbs that carry a specific theme. But other parts of Proverbs deliver wise advice like machine-gun fire into the sky — wise sayings about various subjects in no particular order. Chapter 28 is one of these machine-gun-into-the-sky chapters. Yet no matter how they're fired, every bullet is precious.

This time, read the expanded passage, inviting the Holy Spirit to help you pick out two proverbs that speak to your specific condition this week.

PRAY

Ask the Holy Spirit to mold you and shape you so you become more and more like the two verses you have written down, so your life shows evidence of the change. Share these two verses with a close friend or family member, and invite him or her to help you work on these areas of your life.

LIVE

Write on an index card these verses the Holy Spirit brought to your attention. Carry the card with you. When you're sitting in traffic or have a few minutes between meetings or classes, pull out the card and consider the wise ways in which to live.

NOTICING THE NEEDY

PROVERBS 29:7,13-14,23,27

7   The righteous person knows the rights of the poor,
    but the wicked one does not understand these concerns. . . .

13   The poor and the oppressor have this in common:
    the LORD gives light to the eyes of both.

14   A king who judges the poor with fairness —
    his throne will be established forever. . . .

23   A person's pride will humble him,
    but a humble spirit will gain honor. . . .

27   An unjust man is detestable to the righteous,
    and one whose way is upright
    is detestable to the wicked.

READ

Read the verses aloud slowly.

THINK

God is the strong Reedemer of the needy (see Proverbs 23:11). The biblical categories of the needy (the widow, the fatherless, and the alien or stranger) are "voiceless." Because their voices are not valued or heard, God commissions His people to become modern-day public defenders, so to speak, defending the causes of the needy, maintaining their rights, and pleading their cases (see Deuteronomy 27:19; Psalm 82:3; Proverbs 23:10-11; Isaiah 1:17).

1. Read the verses again, noticing what God asks of you regarding the poor.
2. Read the verses one more time, asking God to show you what you need to know about your relationship to the have-nots in your society and neighborhood.

PRAY

Ask God to help you find ways to understand what it's like to be poor, to treat fairly those who are overlooked, and to participate in fairness toward the needy.

LIVE

Start seeing the have-nots in your world. You might find them riding buses, standing outside convenience stores, or riding their bikes. These people are present, but we usually overlook them. Really look at each person, especially in his or her face. Acknowledge the person with a nod or a smile. Breathe in the deep good-heartedness of God, who asks you to understand what it's like to be poor.

DAY 112

GOD ENCOUNTERS

On this seventh day, review and reflect on all you have read this week. Take the time to revel in the ways you've encountered God in the past six days.

THE SKEPTIC AND THE BELIEVER

PROVERBS 30:1-9

¹ The words of Agur son of Jakeh. The oracle.

The man's oration to Ithiel, to Ithiel and Ucal:

²   I am more stupid than any other man,
    and I lack man's ability to understand.
³   I have not gained wisdom,
    and I have no knowledge of the Holy One.
⁴   Who has gone up to heaven and come down?
    Who has gathered the wind in His hands?
    Who has bound up the waters in a cloak?
    Who has established all the ends of the earth?
    What is His name,
    and what is the name of His Son —
    if you know?
⁵   Every word of God is pure;
    He is a shield to those who take refuge in Him.
⁶   Don't add to His words,
    or He will rebuke you, and you will be proved a liar.

⁷   Two things I ask of You;
    don't deny them to me before I die:
⁸   Keep falsehood and deceitful words far from me.
    Give me neither poverty nor wealth;
    feed me with the food I need.
⁹   Otherwise, I might have too much
    and deny You, saying, "Who is the LORD?"
    or I might have nothing and steal,
    profaning the name of my God.

READ

As you read the words of this passage, be aware of the parts of your heart that are represented by the words. Perhaps under certain circumstances, you have intentionally ignored God's rules, while at other times you have run to God for protection, knowing He would help you.

THINK/PRAY

Read the passage a few more times. Each time you read, narrow your focus to the part that most deeply touches the reality of your life. Mull that over. Explore with God what He is saying to you through it, how He may want to lead, challenge, or refresh you.

LIVE

The prayer of verses 7-9 acknowledges the relationship between our physical and spiritual selves: When full of food, we may feel a false sense of security and disregard our need for God. When hungry, we may feel our need yet doubt that God will meet it.

Consider fasting today, for part or all of the day. Give up food or drink, or perhaps something you enjoy, such as reading or watching television. (Be sure to do this when you'll have time to replace your fasted activity with prayer. Also, check with your doctor before fasting from food or drink.) Let your fast help you get in touch with your heart's reaction to God.

When you would normally engage in the activity you're fasting from or when you feel an emptiness that you normally wouldn't notice, prayerfully read verse 9. In what ways does your fasting experience show you your need for God? Can you trust Him to provide for your needs, or is your impulse to try to provide for yourself?

ALL THAT MY EYES DESIRED

ECCLESIASTES 2:4-10

[4] I increased my achievements. I built houses and planted vineyards for myself. [5] I made gardens and parks for myself and planted every kind of fruit tree in them. [6] I constructed reservoirs of water for myself from which to irrigate a grove of flourishing trees. [7] I acquired male and female servants and had slaves who were born in my house. I also owned many herds of cattle and flocks, more than all who were before me in Jerusalem. [8] I also amassed silver and gold for myself, and the treasure of kings and provinces. I gathered male and female singers for myself, and many concubines, the delights of men. [9] So I became great and surpassed all who were before me in Jerusalem; my wisdom also remained with me. [10] All that my eyes desired, I did not deny them. I did not refuse myself any pleasure, for I took pleasure in all my struggles. This was my reward for all my struggles.

READ

Read the passage.

THINK

Nobody knows for certain who wrote Ecclesiastes — some have suggested King Solomon — but one thing is certain: The writer communicates with piercing honesty and urgent desperation about the condition of life. The writer has pursued every possible pleasure and has still come away empty.

Write down your prayerful answers to these questions:

1. What pleasures — big and small, evil and seemingly innocent — have you pursued in the past week?
2. What were your motives — good or bad — for pursuing and engaging in those things? Dig deep and be honest: What meaning were you attempting to get?
3. What does it mean that you pursue pleasure? In other words, what lies does pleasure whisper in your ear?

PRAY

Choose the one pleasure you sought with the most effort. Write out a prayer to God that involves this pursuit and the pleasure itself. Maybe you need to ask God to forgive you because you sought it ultimately for meaning and significance. Now pray about the bigger picture. Take a hard look at the lifestyle you lead and the amount of pleasure you engage in on a regular basis. Lay everything before God and ask, "God, are these worth pursuing?"

LIVE

This week, with every pleasure you pursue, big and miniscule, consider what your motive is in approaching it.

DON'T GO IT ALONE

ECCLESIASTES 4:9-12

[9] Two are better than one because they have a good reward for their efforts. [10] For if either falls, his companion can lift him up; but pity the one who falls without another to lift him up. [11] Also, if two lie down together, they can keep warm; but how can one person alone keep warm? [12] And if someone overpowers one person, two can resist him. A cord of three strands is not easily broken.

READ

Read the passage aloud slowly.

THINK

Community is an important spiritual practice. The Trinity itself is a community of love. Here on earth we get to try that out! We were built for relationship — to help others and be helped by them. Read the passage again aloud, remembering that it's poetry and trying to read it with rhythm, emphasis, and pauses.

1. What words or phrases speak to you? Why?
2. What do these words or phrases tell you about how you've been helped? About how you're built to help others?

PRAY

Ask God to show you clearly how people have shared their work and their wealth with you, how they've picked you up when you've fallen down, how they've warmed you when you were alone, how they've protected you when you faced the worst. Take as long as you need.

LIVE

Hold a rope or anything braided in your hand. (If you don't have something braided, you can do this in a hardware store or by sketching a braid on a piece of paper.) Run your finger along one of the strands and identify that strand as yourself. Ponder who the other two strands might be in your life — perhaps people you have overlooked. Keep your eyes open for your other two strands today.

WHAT'S THE POINT?

ECCLESIASTES 6:1-9

[1] Here is a tragedy I have observed under the sun, and it weighs heavily on humanity: [2] God gives a man riches, wealth, and honor so that he lacks nothing of all he desires for himself, but God does not allow him to enjoy them. Instead, a stranger will enjoy them. This is futile and a sickening tragedy. [3] A man may father a hundred children and live many years. No matter how long he lives, if he is not satisfied by good things and does not even have a proper burial, I say that a stillborn child is better off than he. [4] For he comes in futility and he goes in darkness, and his name is shrouded in darkness. [5] Though a stillborn child does not see the sun and is not conscious, it has more rest than he. [6] And if he lives a thousand years twice, but does not experience happiness, do not both go to the same place?

> [7] All man's labor is for his stomach,
> yet the appetite is never satisfied.

[8] What advantage then does the wise man have over the fool? What advantage is there for the poor person who knows how to conduct himself before others? [9] Better what the eyes see than wandering desire. This too is futile and a pursuit of the wind.

READ

Read the passage slowly.

THINK

In what ways do you relate to this point of view? Maybe you feel disillusioned with the promises of happiness made by each "new and improved" object, program, or adventure. Maybe you've felt so much pain you wish you'd never been born. Maybe you've been showered with good stuff that leaves you secure and comfortable, and you're left unsettled by the reality check in this passage. Look deep inside yourself and find out what's being stirred up there. What one image in the passage best encapsulates your thoughts?

PRAY

Sit with that image in your mind, and become aware of Jesus in the room with you now. Allow yourself to think more deeply about what He is saying through this passage about you and your life. Respond to Him with an honest heart. Share with Him exactly what you're feeling — the discontent and longing, the pain, the unsettling doubt, whatever it is. If you feel uncomfortable because you wish you could be doing something else, tell Him that.

LIVE

Were you able to connect with Jesus in this time? If so, what was it like for you to relate to Him? How would you describe the way Jesus was toward you during this time? If you weren't able to connect with Him, what was that like for you? What would you have wanted from this time? Share your thoughts and feelings with Jesus.

PAIN

ECCLESIASTES 7:2-3

2   It is better to go to a house of mourning
than to go to a house of feasting,
since that is the end of all mankind,
and the living should take it to heart.
3   Grief is better than laughter,
for when a face is sad, a heart may be glad.

READ

Spend five minutes slowly reading and rereading these two verses.

THINK

Why would the author of these words say such things? Do you relate to these verses? What feelings arise in response to them? Do you agree or disagree that "it is better to go to a house of mourning"? Why?

Consider a time when you experienced extreme sorrow. Looking back, what did you learn?

"Grief is better than laughter, for when a face is sad, a heart may be glad." Do you agree or disagree with this statement? Why?

PRAY

If you are currently experiencing sorrow, request that the Lord give you a teachable spirit to learn valuable lessons during this time. If you are not experiencing sorrow, invite the Lord to prepare your heart for those times when you will.

LIVE

C. S. Lewis wrote, "God whispers to us in our joy and shouts to us in our pain."[10] Next time you hear about the death of someone you know or attend a funeral, journal your thoughts or process with a friend what you observed and what you learned. In the meantime, live a life that is teachable and moldable, especially during difficult times.

DO ALL TO THE GLORY OF GOD

ECCLESIASTES 9:7-10

⁷ Go, eat your bread with pleasure, and drink your wine with a cheerful heart, for God has already accepted your works. ⁸ Let your clothes be white all the time, and never let oil be lacking on your head. ⁹ Enjoy life with the wife you love all the days of your fleeting life, which has been given to you under the sun, all your fleeting days. For that is your portion in life and in your struggle under the sun. ¹⁰ Whatever your hands find to do, do with all your strength, because there is no work, planning, knowledge, or wisdom in Sheol where you are going.

READ

Read the passage aloud slowly.

THINK

This passage pictures what it looks like to do everything to the glory of God: "Whatever you do, in word or in deed, do everything in the name of the Lord Jesus, giving thanks to God the Father through Him" (Colossians 3:17).

1. In what ways does God "drink" or "enjoy"?
2. What pleasures do you enjoy that you think God might enjoy with you?

Read the passage aloud slowly again, noting the words or phrases that stand out to you.

3. What about life do you need to drink or enjoy?

PRAY

Respond to God regarding this idea of drinking and enjoying. Tell God if you're surprised to think of Him this way. Talk to God about whether you need to do what this text says or cut back on doing too much of it. Be willing to hear from God about these things rather than coming up with your own answers, which might be based on what others have told you.

LIVE

Take a walk, preferably a hike. Move mentally and physically in the style of this passage. Enjoy every view open to you. Drink in the colors you see, the sounds you hear, and the aromas you smell. Relish a leaf or flower by rubbing it against your cheek.

DAY 119

GOD ENCOUNTERS

On this seventh day, review and reflect on all you have read this week. Take the time to revel in the ways you've encountered God in the past six days.

REJOICE WHILE YOU ARE YOUNG

ECCLESIASTES 11:9; 12:1-7

⁹   Rejoice, young man, while you are young,
and let your heart be glad in the days of your youth.
And walk in the ways of your heart
and in the sight of your eyes;
but know that for all of these things God will bring you to
judgment. . . .

¹   So remember your Creator in the days of your youth:

Before the days of adversity come,
and the years approach when you will say,
"I have no delight in them";
²   before the sun and the light are darkened,
and the moon and the stars,
and the clouds return after the rain;
³   on the day when the guardians of the house tremble,
and the strong men stoop,
the women who grind cease because they are few,
and the ones who watch through the windows see dimly,
⁴   the doors at the street are shut
while the sound of the mill fades;
when one rises at the sound of a bird,
and all the daughters of song grow faint.
⁵   Also, they are afraid of heights and dangers on the road;
the almond tree blossoms,
the grasshopper loses its spring,
and the caper berry has no effect;
for man is headed to his eternal home,
and mourners will walk around in the street;
⁶   before the silver cord is snapped,
and the gold bowl is broken,
and the jar is shattered at the spring,
and the wheel is broken into the well;
⁷   and the dust returns to the earth as it once was,
and the spirit returns to God who gave it.

READ

Read the passage.

THINK/LIVE

You are likely young, strong, healthy, and full of potential. But as you read this passage again, look deeply at the perspective it presents: old age. Mull over the images, putting yourself in that place as best you can. Think of the contact you've had with elderly people: the physical aspects, such as sights, sounds, textures, and smells; and the mental aspects, such as attitude, knowledge, and experience.

Now return to the present. Look down at your body. Examine your hands; feel your legs and stretch them out. Touch your hair and some of the muscles in your body. Look in a mirror at your eyes and face. Forget your standard checklist when you evaluate yourself. Instead see your youth, health, and strength. What does that feel like? What do you notice?

PRAY

Now read the first few lines of the passage again. When you are told to "rejoice . . . while you are young" and "be glad in" it, what does that mean to you? What would being present to your life and enjoying it right now mean? Does being aware that you won't always be young change your view? Talk with God about what you think of youth and old age, and write down anything significant from this time.

ACCEPTED JUST AS YOU ARE

SONG OF SONGS 1:5-10

W

⁵ Daughters of Jerusalem,
   I am dark like the tents of Kedar,
   yet lovely like the curtains of Solomon.
⁶ Do not stare at me because I am dark,
   for the sun has gazed on me.
   My mother's sons were angry with me;
   they made me a keeper of the vineyards.
   I have not kept my own vineyard.

⁷ Tell me, you, the one I love:
   Where do you pasture your sheep?
   Where do you let them rest at noon?
   Why should I be like one who veils herself
   beside the flocks of your companions?

M

⁸ If you do not know,
   most beautiful of women,
   follow the tracks of the flock,
   and pasture your young goats
   near the shepherds' tents.

⁹ I compare you, my darling,
   to a mare among Pharaoh's chariots.
¹⁰ Your cheeks are beautiful with jewelry,
   your neck with its necklace.

READ

Read the passage slowly.

THINK

Ask some questions of the text. Who are the speakers? What is the situation? What do you notice about the woman's fears? Do you have similar insecurities about your appearance or about what others think of you? Consider these questions, but don't let information gathering steal too much time from prayer.

PRAY

Read the passage again. As you listen to this couple's dialogue, watch for the quiet voice of a word or the subtle quality of an image through which God seems to be expressing His acceptance of you today. Mull over this word or image, letting it interplay with your concerns, ideas, and feelings. Remember not to be afraid of distracting memories or thoughts; they're part of the "you" that you bring to this experience.

Allow your mulling to turn into a conversation with this accepting God. If deeper memories or feelings arise, share them with Him. Be open to how He may want to use the word or image He's given you as a means of blessing in the midst of your insecurities and fears.

LIVE

Take a while to let yourself relax in God's acceptance. If thoughts or feelings come, share them. If they do not, just enjoy the quietness, and experience what it's like to be accepted by God just as you are, without having to do anything or be anyone else.

GOD HAS EYES FOR YOU

SONG OF SONGS 4:9-15

M

9   You have captured my heart, my sister, my bride.
   You have captured my heart with one glance of your eyes,
   with one jewel of your necklace.

10   How delightful your love is, my sister, my bride.
   Your love is much better than wine,
   and the fragrance of your perfume than any balsam.

11   Your lips drip sweetness like the honeycomb, my bride.
   Honey and milk are under your tongue.
   The fragrance of your garments is like the fragrance of Lebanon.

12   My sister, my bride, you are a locked garden —
   a locked garden and a sealed spring.

13   Your branches are a paradise of pomegranates
   with choicest fruits,
   henna with nard —

14   nard and saffron, calamus and cinnamon,
   with all the trees of frankincense,
   myrrh and aloes,
   with all the best spices.

15   You are a garden spring,
   a well of flowing water
   streaming from Lebanon.

READ

Read the passage slowly.

THINK

Read the passage again, but aloud this time. Consider this as God's love poem to you. Song of Songs illustrates how God treasures us — He can't take His eyes off us.

Which image do you prefer to be in God's sight?

☐ a bride
☐ one who captured God's heart
☐ better than wine
☐ as fragrant as an exotic spice
☐ one with kisses like honey
☐ one whose clothes have a pleasing fragrance
☐ a lover and friend
☐ a garden and spring
☐ a well of flowing water

PRAY

Pray what you most need to pray — perhaps that:

- you would grasp how loved and treasured you are by God
- you would define your relationship with God in the way of this passage rather than seeing yourself as _____ (maybe "God's slave")
- you would begin to grasp what it means to treasure God

LIVE

Put yourself near one of the objects mentioned in this poem: a pleasing drink, a fragrant spice, a garden, a spring. Gaze at it and smell it, cherishing the idea that this is how God cherishes you.

LOVE IS INVINCIBLE

SONG OF SONGS 8:6-7,11-12

W

⁶ Set me as a seal on your heart,
as a seal on your arm.
For love is as strong as death;
ardent love is as unrelenting as Sheol.
Love's flames are fiery flames—
the fiercest of all.

⁷ Mighty waters cannot extinguish love;
rivers cannot sweep it away.
If a man were to give all his wealth for love,
it would be utterly scorned. . . .

¹¹ Solomon owned a vineyard in Baal-hamon.
He leased the vineyard to tenants.
Each was to bring for his fruit
1,000 pieces of silver.

¹² I have my own vineyard.
The 1,000 are for you, Solomon,
but 200 for those who guard its fruits.

READ

Read the passage twice.

THINK

Direct your attention to the part of the text where you have the strongest reaction, either positive or negative. Maybe you'll consider the woman's statements about love. Do you agree or disagree with them? Or as you read the expanded passage, maybe you'll consider the man's promise to protect what is his. How do you respond to that promise?

PRAY

Start your prayer time by examining your feelings and beliefs about love — and not necessarily *romantic* love. Sift through these to see what in you is truly feeling and what is belief. For example, a feeling might be "I feel rejected." And a related belief might be "I believe no one could truly love me." Ask God what He thinks about your feelings and beliefs.

LIVE

Read the passage again, this time asking the Holy Spirit to show you a word or concept summing up something God is saying about love that you don't fully grasp or believe or that you don't yet accept or live out naturally. Ask God to teach you in the coming days and weeks, perhaps through further meditation, more about what He created love to be like.

BURNING OFF SIN

ISAIAH 6:1-8

¹ In the year that King Uzziah died, I saw the Lord seated on a high and lofty throne, and His robe filled the temple. ² Seraphim were standing above Him; each one had six wings: with two he covered his face, with two he covered his feet, and with two he flew. ³ And one called to another:

> Holy, holy, holy is the LORD of Hosts;
> His glory fills the whole earth.

⁴ The foundations of the doorways shook at the sound of their voices, and the temple was filled with smoke.
⁵ Then I said:

> Woe is me for I am ruined
> because I am a man of unclean lips
> and live among a people of unclean lips,
> and because my eyes have seen the King,
> the LORD of Hosts.

⁶ Then one of the seraphim flew to me, and in his hand was a glowing coal that he had taken from the altar with tongs. ⁷ He touched my mouth with it and said:

> Now that this has touched your lips,
> your wickedness is removed
> and your sin is atoned for.

⁸ Then I heard the voice of the Lord saying:

> Who should I send?
> Who will go for Us?

I said:

> Here I am. Send me.

READ

Read the passage, making special note of the dialogue between the angels and Isaiah.

THINK

As the Lord God's mouthpiece to the nations, Isaiah experiences this unforgettable encounter with the Master at the outset of his ministry. An angel-seraph flies down to Isaiah and touches his mouth with a burning coal.

The mouth is one of the most sensitive parts of the body. Explore your spiritual life to identify sensitive areas that would hurt deeply at God's touch. Why are these areas the most sensitive? Consider what your relationship with God might look like, now and in the long term, if He purified these areas of your life.

PRAY

Invite God to burn these sensitive areas of your life so you can serve Him more effectively. This is a scary prayer when offered sincerely and earnestly, but be encouraged by what happened in Isaiah's life as a result of his burned lips.

LIVE

Ask two people who are close to you what they believe to be areas of your life in need of refining by God's touch. Be prepared to consider answers that may be hard to hear but are beneficial.

THE PEACEABLE KINGDOM OF GOD

ISAIAH 11:6-9

⁶ The wolf will live with the lamb,
and the leopard will lie down with the goat.
The calf, the young lion, and the fatling will be together,
and a child will lead them.
⁷ The cow and the bear will graze,
their young ones will lie down together,
and the lion will eat straw like the ox.
⁸ An infant will play beside the cobra's pit,
and a toddler will put his hand into a snake's den.
⁹ None will harm or destroy another
on My entire holy mountain,
for the land will be as full
of the knowledge of the LORD
as the sea is filled with water.

READ

Read the passage aloud slowly, noting how natural enemies are coexisting side by side (wolf and lamb, cow and bear, toddler and snake).

THINK

Read the passage again, noting which images are most powerful or amazing to you.

This passage gives us a vivid picture of the kingdom of God as it will exist in the future. What a different place it will be! Interact with this passage in one of these ways, depending on what stood out to you:

- Ponder what you would like best about such a peaceable world — one that is "as full of the knowledge of the LORD as the sea is filled with water."
- Ponder what feelings would be present for these creatures to exist this way (for example, serenity).
- Name your own natural enemies and imagine them standing beside you, with you, for you. You might choose political enemies (for example, parties, opponents, countries, regions); family members, coworkers, or acquaintances you're at odds with; or an animal or a natural element that's difficult for you (for example, spiders, if you hate spiders).

PRAY

Share with God how you feel about such a peaceable world. Share with Him what you think such a world shows you about Him.

LIVE

Ponder the idea that this passage describes your future reality. You *will* experience this. This is what God is creating for you.

DAY 126

GOD ENCOUNTERS

On this seventh day, review and reflect on all you have read this week. Take the time to revel in the ways you've encountered God in the past six days.

A STRONG GOD

ISAIAH 27:1-5

¹ On that day the LORD with His harsh, great, and strong sword, will bring judgment on Leviathan, the fleeing serpent — Leviathan, the twisting serpent. He will slay the monster that is in the sea.

² On that day
sing about a desirable vineyard:
³ I, Yahweh, watch over it;
I water it regularly.
I guard it night and day
so that no one disturbs it.
⁴ I am not angry,
but if it produces thorns and briers for Me,
I will fight against it, trample it,
and burn it to the ground.
⁵ Or let it take hold of My strength;
let it make peace with Me —
make peace with Me.

READ

Read the passage slowly, letting your imagination play with the imagery. Picture everything vividly, as if you were a child reading a story with beautiful, lifelike illustrations.

THINK

Read the passage again. What do you notice about the way God interacts with "the monster"? With the "vineyard"? What is He like? Now put yourself in the scene. What part do you play? How do you feel?

PRAY

Picture God turning to you and inviting you to talk with Him about what you are feeling and thinking. Does He ever seem angry to you, or uncaring? What's it like for you to hear Him say otherwise? Share with Him your thoughts and feelings, and allow the conversation to unfold.

LIVE

Write about your experience of encountering the God who mercilessly kills the sea monster, meanwhile mercifully letting the vineyard hold to His strength as it grows. Be sure to include what dialoguing with Him was like for you. What will you take away from this time?

DEPENDING ON HORSES

ISAIAH 31:1-3

¹ Woe to those who go down to Egypt for help
and who depend on horses!
They trust in the abundance of chariots
and in the large number of horsemen.
They do not look to the Holy One of Israel
and they do not seek the LORD's help.

² But He also is wise and brings disaster.
He does not go back on what He says;
He will rise up against the house of wicked men
and against the allies of evildoers.

³ Egyptians are men, not God;
their horses are flesh, not spirit.
When the LORD raises His hand to strike,
the helper will stumble
and the one who is helped will fall;
both will perish together.

READ

Read the passage at least six times. Don't rush through it. Get familiar with it.

THINK

In ancient times, Egypt was a prosperous and powerful nation. Horses and chariots were crucial for ensuring security, especially in times of war. We don't rely on horses and chariots to protect us today, but there are countless things we put our trust in.

Consider the circumstances in your life when you have depended on something or someone other than God. If God and God alone provides ultimate security and comfort, why do you think we turn to Him for help only as a last resort? If we truly understood God's power and control — His sovereignty — how might that change how we live?

PRAY

Spend a few minutes in quiet and solitude. Use the time to seek out the dark corners of your life. Whisper, "What do I put my trust in?" Allow the Spirit to do His work. Don't rush the process, but simply wait for Him to reveal the horses and chariots you depend on. When you see them clearly, confess them to God immediately. Be assured that He hears your prayers and forgives you graciously.

LIVE

Be constantly aware of the horses and chariots that seek your trust. Remind yourself of their lies — that they offer complete security and comfort — and the futility in believing those lies.

PICTURES OF RESTORATION

ISAIAH 35:4-9

4   Say to the cowardly:
"Be strong; do not fear!
Here is your God; vengeance is coming.
God's retribution is coming; He will save you."

5   Then the eyes of the blind will be opened,
and the ears of the deaf unstopped.

6   Then the lame will leap like a deer,
and the tongue of the mute will sing for joy,
for water will gush in the wilderness,
and streams in the desert;

7   the parched ground will become a pool of water,
and the thirsty land springs of water.
In the haunt of jackals, in their lairs,
there will be grass, reeds, and papyrus.

8   A road will be there and a way;
it will be called the Holy Way.
The unclean will not travel on it,
but it will be for the one who walks the path.
Even the fool will not go astray.

9   There will be no lion there,
and no vicious beast will go up on it;
they will not be found there.
But the redeemed will walk on it.

READ

Read the first verse aloud and then read the rest silently.

THINK

Read the passage again, watching for its emphasis on restoration and healing.

1. What pictures of healing speak to you?

   ☐ God bringing vengeance
   ☐ blind eyes opening
   ☐ deaf ears hearing
   ☐ disabled people leaping
   ☐ mute people singing
   ☐ water gushing in the desert
   ☐ parched ground becoming a pool of water

2. What do you like best about the "Holy Way"?

   ☐ only for the one who walks the path
   ☐ you can't go astray
   ☐ no dangerous animals

3. What one phrase speaks to you most? Why do you think that is? What does your choice tell you about what you want from God?

PRAY

Tell God about the images you most resonate with. Tell Him why. Ask God for the restoration or healing that you or others need.

LIVE

Choose a color that symbolizes you as a fully restored or healed person. Why did you choose it? Pick up something of that color and be glad you're holding it.

YOU ARE GOD—
YOU ALONE

ISAIAH 37:9-11,14-20

⁹ The king had heard this about Tirhakah king of Cush: "He has set out to fight against you." So when he heard this, he sent messengers to Hezekiah, saying, ¹⁰ "Say this to Hezekiah king of Judah: 'Don't let your God, whom you trust, deceive you by promising that Jerusalem won't be handed over to the king of Assyria. ¹¹ Look, you have heard what the kings of Assyria have done to all the countries: they completely destroyed them. Will you be rescued?'" . . .

¹⁴ Hezekiah took the letter from the messengers, read it, then went up to the LORD's temple and spread it out before the LORD. ¹⁵ Then Hezekiah prayed to the LORD: ¹⁶ "LORD of Hosts, God of Israel, who is enthroned above the cherubim, You are God—You alone—of all the kingdoms of the earth. You made the heavens and the earth. ¹⁷ Listen closely, LORD, and hear; open Your eyes, LORD, and see. Hear all the words that Sennacherib has sent to mock the living God. ¹⁸ LORD, it is true that the kings of Assyria have devastated all these countries and their lands. ¹⁹ They have thrown their gods into the fire, for they were not gods but made by human hands—wood and stone. So they have destroyed them. ²⁰ Now, LORD our God, save us from his power so that all the kingdoms of the earth may know that You are the LORD—You alone."

READ

Read this passage a few times slowly. Picture what's going on, and imagine what Hezekiah, the king of Judah, might be feeling in this situation.

THINK

Notice the Assyrian king's reaction to the news that he's about to be attacked by an enemy: He tries to puff himself up by scoffing at Judah. What might have motivated him to do this at this specific time? In contrast, how does Hezekiah react to the message his enemy sends him? What stands out to you about these different attitudes? How do they relate to you?

PRAY

Think about an area in which you hold responsibility, such as being a group leader at school or a manager at work — or having responsibility to uphold your end of a friendship. What are some recent problems that you are responsible to help resolve? In what ways are you dealing (or not dealing) with them? Have a conversation with God about what it's like for you to have responsibility in this area; share your heart and mind with Him.

LIVE

Now read the passage again, keeping in mind the specific situation. Try to bring the problem to God the way Hezekiah did. For help, write a description of the dilemma on a piece of paper and then follow Hezekiah's example, spreading it out before God and asking for His help. Ask Him to guide you in how to resolve it. Be aware that God is your leader, even as you are a leader to others.

YOU ARE MINE

ISAIAH 43:1-4

1   Now this is what the LORD says —
the One who created you, Jacob,
and the One who formed you, Israel —
"Do not fear, for I have redeemed you;
I have called you by your name; you are Mine.

2   I will be with you
when you pass through the waters,
and when you pass through the rivers,
they will not overwhelm you.
You will not be scorched
when you walk through the fire,
and the flame will not burn you.

3   For I Yahweh your God,
the Holy One of Israel, and your Savior,
give Egypt as a ransom for you,
Cush and Seba in your place.

4   Because you are precious in My sight
and honored, and I love you,
I will give people in exchange for you
and nations instead of your life.

READ

Read the passage aloud slowly, keeping in mind that God is the speaker.

THINK

Read the passage aloud again even more slowly, pausing between verses. Read it with the idea that God is saying these words directly to you.

1. Of God's words to you in this passage, what is your favorite?
2. Which phrase do you most need to hear from God?

Read the passage one more time. Rest in silence. Wait on God and hear Him speaking directly to you.

PRAY

Respond to what God has said to you, perhaps with amazement or gratitude.

LIVE

Read the passage aloud one more time, and hear the echo of the words lingering in the air. Make up a song using a line from these verses. If you wish, use a tune you already know.

DEPENDABLE GODS?

ISAIAH 46:1-7

1   Bel crouches; Nebo cowers.
    Their idols are consigned to beasts and cattle.
    The images you carry are loaded,
    as a burden for the weary animal.

2   The gods cower; they crouch together;
    they are not able to rescue the burden,
    but they themselves go into captivity.

3   "Listen to Me, house of Jacob,
    all the remnant of the house of Israel,
    who have been sustained from the womb,
    carried along since birth.

4   I will be the same until your old age,
    and I will bear you up when you turn gray.
    I have made you, and I will carry you;
    I will bear and save you.

5   "Who will you compare Me or make Me equal to?
    Who will you measure Me with,
    so that we should be like each other?

6   Those who pour out their bags of gold
    and weigh out silver on scales —
    they hire a goldsmith and he makes it into a god.
    Then they kneel and bow down to it.

7   They lift it to their shoulder and bear it along;
    they set it in its place, and there it stands;
    it does not budge from its place.
    They cry out to it but it doesn't answer;
    it saves no one from his trouble."

READ

Read the passage. Bel and Nebo were ancient false gods of the Israelites' neighbors. People would orient their lives around what they believed these gods were demanding or promising.

THINK

After you read how God addresses Israel's tendency to act like its neighbors — rather than trusting and obeying Him — consider what gods might be in your culture and in your life. These don't have to be people or objects. They could be principles or beliefs that shape how we live, think, and feel every day. For example, "Having more money makes a person secure," or "If people just lost weight and worked out more, the opposite sex would be attracted to them."

Identify a god that tempts you personally. Are there aspects of the true God that you find difficult to accept (such as His holiness or the facts that He is invisible and sometimes silent)? In what ways do these idols capitalize on those doubts and make themselves appear more appealing than God? What do they promise you? Now consider: What do they really bring you?

PRAY/LIVE

Read God's plea to Israel once more. Tell Him what you see in yourself and in this god you've identified. Be real. Now hear Him ask you, "Who will you compare Me or make Me equal to?" Don't answer immediately, but ponder the question. Ask Him to help you stay committed to Him and to working through the struggles you have with Him. Watch today for when your idols or images are the most appealing to you, for when you are most likely to "bow down" to them or believe their message.

DAY 133

GOD ENCOUNTERS

On this seventh day, review and reflect on all you have read this week. Take the time to revel in the ways you've encountered God in the past six days.

THE GOD WHO REMEMBERS

ISAIAH 49:13-18

¹³ Shout for joy, you heavens!
Earth, rejoice!
Mountains break into joyful shouts!
For the LORD has comforted His people,
and will have compassion on His afflicted ones.

¹⁴ Zion says, "The LORD has abandoned me;
The Lord has forgotten me!"

¹⁵ "Can a woman forget her nursing child,
or lack compassion for the child of her womb?
Even if these forget,
yet I will not forget you.

¹⁶ Look, I have inscribed you on the palms of My hands;
your walls are continually before Me.

¹⁷ Your builders hurry;
those who destroy and devastate you will leave you.

¹⁸ Look up, and look around.
They all gather together; they come to you.
As I live" —

this is the LORD's declaration —

"you will wear all your children as jewelry,
and put them on as a bride does."

READ

Read the passage, underlining or mentally noting each time the word *forget* is present.

THINK

Can you think of a specific moment when you were forgotten — either intentionally or unintentionally? How did that make you feel? Why?

What times in your life do you most desire to be remembered? Be specific. How does it feel for you to know that there is a God who will never forget you under any circumstance?

PRAY

Pour out your heart in gratitude before God for the fact that he will "not forget you."

LIVE

"Look, I have inscribed you on the palms of My hands." Take a pen and make a small mark on the palm of each of your hands. Every time you glance at one of the marks, remember God's character and rejoice in knowing that you are His child who will never be forgotten. If someone asks you about the marks, tell them about The God Who Remembers.

THE SUFFERING SERVANT

ISAIAH 53:2-5,11-12

2 He grew up before Him like a young plant
and like a root out of dry ground.
He didn't have an impressive form
or majesty that we should look at Him,
no appearance that we should desire Him.

3 He was despised and rejected by men,
a man of suffering who knew what sickness was.
He was like someone people turned away from;
He was despised, and we didn't value Him.

4 Yet He Himself bore our sicknesses,
and He carried our pains;
but we in turn regarded Him stricken,
struck down by God, and afflicted.

5 But He was pierced because of our transgressions,
crushed because of our iniquities;
punishment for our peace was on Him,
and we are healed by His wounds. . . .

11 He will see it out of His anguish,
and He will be satisfied with His knowledge.
My righteous Servant will justify many,
and He will carry their iniquities.

12 Therefore I will give Him the many as a portion,
and He will receive the mighty as spoil,
because He submitted Himself to death,
and was counted among the rebels;
yet He bore the sin of many
and interceded for the rebels.

READ

Read the passage aloud slowly, knowing that this "suffering servant" passage is a prophecy about Jesus. If possible, read the expanded passage as well.

THINK

Read the passage again. This time, consider who is speaking.

1. *We, our,* and *us* (verses 2-5) indicate that the speaker is Israel as a nation or a prophet of Israel (Isaiah). In this section, what words, phrases, or ideas are most personal for you?
2. *I* and *My* (verses 11-12) indicate God is the speaker. In this section, what most touches you about God's words about Jesus?
3. How will Jesus "justify many"?

   ☐ His sacrifice of His life
   ☐ His actions inspiring others
   ☐ His person calling you
   ☐ His praying for you (see Romans 8:34)
   ☐ other:

PRAY

Respond to God about the words that touched you most. Talk also to God about how Jesus can make you righteous.

LIVE

Move through your day with this idea: Jesus died without a thought for His own welfare. If He died that way, how much more must He have lived that way? Try living that selflessly a few minutes at a time.

MY LOVE WILL NOT BE REMOVED

ISAIAH 54:4-10

4 "Do not be afraid, for you will not be put to shame;
don't be humiliated, for you will not be disgraced.
For you will forget the shame of your youth,
and you will no longer remember
the disgrace of your widowhood.

5 Indeed, your husband is your Maker —
His name is Yahweh of Hosts —
and the Holy One of Israel is your Redeemer;
He is called the God of all the earth.

6 For the LORD has called you,
like a wife deserted and wounded in spirit,
a wife of one's youth when she is rejected,"
says your God.

7 "I deserted you for a brief moment,
but I will take you back with great compassion.

8 In a surge of anger
I hid My face from you for a moment,
but I will have compassion on you
with everlasting love,"
says the LORD your Redeemer.

9 "For this is like the days of Noah to Me:
when I swore that the waters of Noah
would never flood the earth again,
so I have sworn that I will not be angry with you
or rebuke you.

10 Though the mountains move
and the hills shake,
My love will not be removed from you
and My covenant of peace will not be shaken,"
says your compassionate LORD.

READ

Read this passage picturing God speaking to Israel after yet another problem in their relationship.

THINK/PRAY

When you hear God saying that He hid His face in anger only for a moment but was not giving up on the relationship, what is your reaction? When you try to picture a commitment that won't fall apart, what does this evoke in you? Share your response with God. Maybe you've never experienced a relationship like that, so you don't know what it would look like. Maybe you've had similar promises made to you but were betrayed. If this reminds you of someone in your life (past or present), talk with God about what you might be incorrectly assuming to be true of God based on your experience with that person. Recognize that God knows your past, and He knows the baggage you bring into your relationship with Him. Trust that He is caring for you with compassion and will help you deal with that baggage.

LIVE

Make a note of the themes that emerged during your prayer time. Ask God to help you grow in trust that He is completely committed to you as one whose "love will not be removed" and one who will "have compassion on you." Spend a few minutes sitting quietly in His presence, enjoying the tranquillity of that space before you move on to the rest of your day.

OUR TRANSGRESSION

ISAIAH 59:9-15

⁹ Therefore justice is far from us,
   and righteousness does not reach us.
   We hope for light, but there is darkness;
   for brightness, but we live in the night.
¹⁰ We grope along a wall like the blind;
   we grope like those without eyes.
   We stumble at noon as though it were twilight;
   we are like the dead among those who are healthy.
¹¹ We all growl like bears
   and moan like doves.
   We hope for justice, but there is none;
   for salvation, but it is far from us.
¹² For our transgressions have multiplied before You,
   and our sins testify against us.
   For our transgressions are with us,
   and we know our iniquities:
¹³ transgression and deception against the LORD,
   turning away from following our God,
   speaking oppression and revolt,
   conceiving and uttering lying words from the heart.
¹⁴ Justice is turned back,
   and righteousness stands far off.
   For truth has stumbled in the public square,
   and honesty cannot enter.
¹⁵ Truth is missing,
   and whoever turns from evil is plundered.

   The LORD saw that there was no justice,
   and He was offended.

READ

Read the passage aloud. Reflect the nature of the words by your tone and inflection. (That is, if these were your words, how might you sound if you said them?)

THINK

The subject of this passage may seem like a depressing one to explore. But so is our sin. We often attempt to live our lives with God while forgetting to acknowledge our transgressions before Him. Yet confession of wrongdoing is a normal and expected part of life for followers of God. We regularly fall short of God's desires for us, and He wants to hear us acknowledge this and depend on Him in every area of our lives.

Read the passage again aloud, but make it more personal. When you come to the word *we,* replace it with *I,* and when you come to the word *our,* replace it with *my.* What might God be thinking as He hears you read this?

PRAY

Now, make a list of sins — big and small — that you've committed in the past seven days. Perhaps include things you felt you were supposed to do but did not. In prayer, go through your list and, with each item, admit to God that you should not have participated in such wrongdoing. Do this with a humble and repentant heart.

LIVE

As you walk to class or drive to work or whenever you are between tasks, confess your sins to God. As you do this, be as specific as you can about your sins, acknowledging your desperation and futility in attempting to live apart from Him.

137

RESCUE AND RELEASE

ISAIAH 61:1-3,10-11

¹ The Spirit of the Lord GOD is on Me,
because the LORD has anointed Me
to bring good news to the poor.
He has sent Me to heal the brokenhearted,
to proclaim liberty to the captives
and freedom to the prisoners;

² to proclaim the year of the LORD's favor,
and the day of our God's vengeance;
to comfort all who mourn,

³ to provide for those who mourn in Zion;
to give them a crown of beauty instead of ashes,
festive oil instead of mourning,
and splendid clothes instead of despair.
And they will be called righteous trees,
planted by the LORD
to glorify Him. . . .

¹⁰ I greatly rejoice in the LORD,
I exult in my God;
for He has clothed me with the garments of salvation
and wrapped me in a robe of righteousness,
as a groom wears a turban
and as a bride adorns herself with her jewels.

¹¹ For as the earth produces its growth,
and as a garden enables what is sown to spring up,
so the Lord GOD will cause righteousness and praise
to spring up before all the nations.

READ

Read the passage aloud slowly.

THINK

Read verses 1-3 aloud slowly.

1. What roles of deliverance, rescue, and release do you most admire in God (which Jesus also claimed)?
2. Consider what words or phrases in verses 1-3 stand out to you. What do they tell you about the work God is calling you to do alongside Him?

Read verses 10-11 aloud slowly, keeping in mind that those who rescue and release others this way find great joy in it. When they work alongside God, they do not burn out.

3. Consider what words or phrases in verses 10-11 stand out to you. What "rejoic[ing] in the LORD" are you being called to, especially as it comes through serving under God, partnering with Him in what He is doing on this earth?

PRAY

Ask God for guidance in how you serve. You might pray about the avenues of service you are choosing. Or pray about serving with great joy in God instead of serving with joy in results or feelings of success.

LIVE

As you serve someone today, be present to the reality that you are doing this with God's hand, under His power. This is His work and you get to be a part of it!

HE DELIGHTS IN YOU

ISAIAH 62:2-5

2   Nations will see your righteousness
and all kings, your glory.
You will be called by a new name
that the LORD's mouth will announce.

3   You will be a glorious crown in the LORD's hand,
and a royal diadem in the palm of your God.

4   You will no longer be called Deserted,
and your land will not be called Desolate;
instead, you will be called My Delight is in Her,
and your land Married;
for the LORD delights in you,
and your land will be married.

5   For as a young man marries a young woman,
so your sons will marry you;
and as a groom rejoices over his bride,
so your God will rejoice over you.

READ

Read the passage aloud slowly.

THINK

Read the passage again. This time reverse all the *you* pronouns to *I* and *me* pronouns. For example, change

- "you will be called by a new name" to "I will be called by a new name"
- "the LORD delights in you" to "the LORD delights in me"
- "so your God will rejoice over you" to "so my God will rejoice over me"

Have fun reading it this way a few times.

1. If you were to ask God for a new name, what would it be?
2. Set aside the idea that these verses are fantasy, and ponder the idea that they describe reality — a reality of our universe that most people don't understand.

PRAY

Tell God how it makes you feel to know that He delights in you and is happy with you. Tell God what you would like your new name to be. Wait in this moment and see if other names come to you.

LIVE

Rest for a few minutes in the truth that God delights in you. If you wish, imagine situations in which you feel anything but special (for example, when you are hard on yourself, when someone puts you down, or when you get back a test, paper, or work review that isn't so great). See yourself responding to the situation by saying, "Yes, this is true, but God delights in me."

DAY 140

GOD ENCOUNTERS

On this seventh day, review and reflect on all you have read this week. Take the time to revel in the ways you've encountered God in the past six days.

ANTICIPATING THE WORKINGS OF GOD

ISAIAH 65:17-22

17 "For I will create a new heaven and a new earth;
the past events will not be remembered or come to mind.
18 Then be glad and rejoice forever
in what I am creating;
for I will create Jerusalem to be a joy
and its people to be a delight.
19 I will rejoice in Jerusalem
and be glad in My people.
The sound of weeping and crying
will no longer be heard in her.
20 In her, a nursing infant will no longer live
only a few days,
or an old man not live out his days.
Indeed, the youth will die at a hundred years,
and the one who misses a hundred years will be cursed.
21 People will build houses and live in them;
they will plant vineyards and eat their fruit.
22 They will not build and others live in them;
they will not plant and others eat.
For My people's lives will be
like the lifetime of a tree.
My chosen ones will fully enjoy
the work of their hands."

READ

Read the passage.

THINK

In this passage God speaks with great joy, and the people feel great excitement. Here we find, in the midst of judgment and sorrow, the promise of a bright future for those who love and trust the Lord. God makes statements about the future peace that will be among His people. He is sending out the old and bringing in the new. For followers of God, there is intense anticipation.

Think about your own future. What are those things, general and specific, that you believe God will use to bring hope into your life? Joy? Peace? How does God promise this will happen? How does the promise of hope and joy and peace influence the way you live?

PRAY

Pick some specific elements of how God will bring hope and joy and peace into your life. Share the details with Him, including your excitement and anticipation.

LIVE

Live with the deep assurance of God's desire for you to possess hope and joy and peace today.

GOD'S KNOWLEDGE OF US

JEREMIAH 1:5

5   I chose you before I formed you in the womb;
     I set you apart before you were born.
     I appointed you a prophet to the nations.

READ

Write out Jeremiah 1:5 on an index card. Meditate on this verse.

THINK

God told Jeremiah that He had plans for Jeremiah's life before Jeremiah was even given his name. What a claim from God! Can you believe that God had plans for your life and knew everything about you before you were even conceived? Why or why not?

What emotions bubble to the surface when you consider that God knows you intimately? Are you excited? Comforted? Scared? Anxious? Indifferent? Why?

If God already knows everything about us, why does He desire that we pray to Him?

PRAY

Meditate on this thought: The Creator of the universe, the living God, knows every possible thing about you. As you do so, tell God what you are feeling and why.

LIVE

Take the index card and put it where you will see it often (for example, on your bedside table, taped to the mirror in the bathroom, taped to the dashboard of your car, or in your purse or wallet). Whenever you look at it, read it and be reminded that God marked out a plan for your life long before you were born.

A TIME TO GRIEVE

JEREMIAH 8:18-21; 9:1-3

18 My joy has flown away;
grief has settled on me.
My heart is sick.

19 Listen — the cry of my dear people
from a far away land,
"Is the Lord no longer in Zion,
her King not within her?"
Why have they provoked me to anger
with their carved images,
with their worthless foreign idols?

20 Harvest has passed, summer has ended,
but we have not been saved.

21 I am broken by the brokenness
of my dear people.
I mourn; horror has taken hold of me. . . .

1 If my head were a spring of water,
my eyes a fountain of tears,
I would weep day and night
over the slain of my dear people.

2 If only I had a traveler's lodging place
in the wilderness,
I would abandon my people
and depart from them,
for they are all adulterers,
a solemn assembly of treacherous people.

3 They bent their tongues like their bows;
lies and not faithfulness prevail in the land,
for they proceed from one evil to another,
and they do not take Me into account.
This is the Lord's declaration.

READ

Read the passage aloud slowly. Most of it describes Jeremiah's grieving over the way Judah ignores God. In 9:3, God interrupts and agrees.

THINK

What makes God grieve that also makes you grieve? What breaks your heart that breaks the heart of God? Perhaps it resembles the following: the wickedness of people (such as genocide or sex trafficking in the world), the lack of desire — even among professed believers — to know God, the diseases that terrorize people's bodies.

Read the passage aloud again, reflecting on the tragic circumstance that breaks your heart and also breaks the heart of God. What words or phrases in the passage best express your grief? What does it feel like to grieve over the things that grieve God? How do you respond to the idea that God often weeps throughout the prophetic portion of the Bible and that we need to honor that grief and join Him?

PRAY

Grieve with God in prayer as a prophet (like Jeremiah), using the phrases in the passage that stood out to you. Don't feel that you have to tidy up your prayer with a positive ending, although "God, help!" would be appropriate.

LIVE

Watch the news, listening for the evil and suffering in the world that God surely grieves over. Notice how different such listening is from detached curiosity. Hear about these events with the listening ears of God.

ROTTEN AS OLD UNDERWEAR

JEREMIAH 13:1-11

¹ This is what the LORD said to me: "Go and buy yourself a linen under-garment and put it on, but do not put it in water." ² So I bought underwear as the LORD instructed me and put it on.

³ Then the word of the LORD came to me a second time: ⁴ "Take the underwear that you bought and are wearing, and go at once to the Euphrates and hide it in a rocky crevice." ⁵ So I went and hid it by the Euphrates, as the LORD commanded me.

⁶ A long time later the LORD said to me, "Go at once to the Euphrates and get the underwear that I commanded you to hide there." ⁷ So I went to the Euphrates and dug up the underwear and got it from the place where I had hidden it, but it was ruined — of no use at all.

⁸ Then the word of the LORD came to me: ⁹ "This is what the LORD says: Just like this I will ruin the great pride of both Judah and Jerusalem. ¹⁰ These evil people, who refuse to listen to Me, who follow the stubbornness of their own hearts, and who have followed other gods to serve and worship — they will be like this underwear, of no use at all. ¹¹ Just as underwear clings to one's waist, so I fastened the whole house of Israel and of Judah to Me" — this is the LORD's declaration — "so that they might be My people for My fame, praise, and glory, but they would not obey."

READ

As you read the passage, imaginatively put yourself in Jeremiah's place.

THINK

In your mind's eye, look down and see the linen underwear you've been wearing for days or weeks. Set out on the journey to the Euphrates. Discover the crack in the rock. Envision the long time that passes — what you do in the meantime, any particular events, the seasons that pass.

Now return to the rock and feel your own sweat as you dig out the underwear again. How do you first detect them? By touch? Smell? Sight? As you unearth them, what thoughts go through your head? What is the smell like? What do they look like?

Next think about God's metaphor. Listen to His explanation of the Israelites' rotted hearts illustrated by this decaying underwear. As you hear God's words, what are you thinking? What are you feeling?

PRAY

Set the text aside and explore your own heart honestly with God. When you think of God the Father rebuking you for something, what is your internal reaction? Do you perceive it as a positive thing, done in love? Or does His rebuke seem to say He is against you, doesn't care for you, or wants you to fix yourself? Talk this over with Him.

LIVE

Read the passage again, listening for what God might be saying to you through Jeremiah. In what way is your Father challenging you? Make note of any action you feel He is leading you to.

TELLING GOD WHAT WE REALLY THINK

JEREMIAH 20:7-10

7   You deceived me, LORD, and I was deceived.
    You seized me and prevailed.
    I am a laughingstock all the time;
    everyone ridicules me.
8   For whenever I speak, I cry out,
    I proclaim, "Violence and destruction!"
    because the word of the LORD has become for me
    constant disgrace and derision.
9   If I say, "I won't mention Him
    or speak any longer in His name,"
    His message becomes a fire burning in my heart,
    shut up in my bones.
    I become tired of holding it in,
    and I cannot prevail.
10 For I have heard the gossip of many people,
    "Terror is on every side!
    Report him; let's report him!"
    Everyone I trusted watches for my fall.
    "Perhaps he will be deceived
    so that we might prevail against him
    and take our vengeance on him."

READ

Read the passage twice very slowly.

THINK

Jeremiah was called by God to be a mouthpiece to the nation of Israel, but they rejected his message, scorning and mocking him. They even made death threats against him. And in this passage we read Jeremiah's complaint. He is not shy about telling God exactly what he feels. In fact, he has some choice words for the Creator concerning his situation.

Is it easy or hard for you to tell God exactly what you're thinking? Why? Do you think it's hard for God to hear our prayers when we are completely and blatantly honest with Him?

LIVE

Write a letter to God, telling Him what you think about Him and how He is operating in the world. Include the good, the bad, and the ugly. Be thoughtful and honest and even raw if you need to be.

PRAY

After you finish writing the letter, find a room where you can shut the door and be alone. Read the letter aloud to God, speaking confidently because you know He hears your prayers.

CONSEQUENCES THAT BURN

JEREMIAH 28:10-17

[10] The prophet Hananiah then took the yoke bar from the neck of Jeremiah the prophet and broke it. [11] In the presence of all the people Hananiah proclaimed, "This is what the LORD says: 'In this way, within two years I will break the yoke of King Nebuchadnezzar of Babylon from the neck of all the nations.'" Jeremiah the prophet then went on his way.

[12] The word of the LORD came to Jeremiah after Hananiah the prophet had broken the yoke bar from the neck of Jeremiah the prophet: [13] "Go say to Hananiah: This is what the LORD says: 'You broke a wooden yoke bar, but in its place you will make an iron yoke bar.' [14] For this is what the LORD of Hosts, the God of Israel, says: 'I have put an iron yoke on the neck of all these nations that they might serve King Nebuchadnezzar of Babylon, and they will serve him. I have also put the wild animals under him.'"

[15] The prophet Jeremiah said to the prophet Hananiah, "Listen, Hananiah! The LORD did not send you, but you have led these people to trust in a lie. [16] Therefore, this is what the LORD says: 'I am about to send you off the face of the earth. You will die this year because you have spoken rebellion against the LORD.'" [17] And the prophet Hananiah died that year in the seventh month.

READ

Read the passage twice. (For more background, include the expanded passage.)

THINK

What does God seem to be addressing in Hananiah's underlying message or motive? Summarize in a sentence what you notice. What do you think about how God dealt with him? What do you, having read this story, feel toward God?

PRAY/LIVE

Take several minutes to think through your current situation. Where is God allowing you to feel the ache and consequence for something you've recently done (or not done)? Bring this openly before God and tell Him how you feel about it. Ask Him to help you see your heart clearly, to understand what drew you toward that action (or nonaction).

If you haven't let go of what you're doing wrong — despite the burning consequences — think about what rejecting this path might look like for you. What really keeps you from turning around? God is inviting you to live in a certain way in this area of your life. What are some small steps you could take toward receiving that invitation?

Take them.

DAY 147

GOD ENCOUNTERS

On this seventh day, review and reflect on all you have read this week. Take the time to revel in the ways you've encountered God in the past six days.

I WILL ANSWER YOU

JEREMIAH 33:2-3

[2] "The LORD who made the earth, the LORD who forms it to establish it, Yahweh is His name, says this: [3] Call to Me and I will answer you and tell you great and incomprehensible things you do not know."

READ

Find a quiet place and read this passage slowly. Pause in the silence. Let these words wash over you. Make them personal. Claim them as God speaking specifically to you.

THINK

What sticks out to you? What word or phrase settles deeply in your soul? Why?

Deep down, do you really believe that God will answer you when you call to Him? Why or why not? What does this passage say about His character?

As you hear God's personal message, spoken straight from His being, what do you feel? What words from this passage can you make your own?

PRAY

Ask God what He wants you to do with the word or phrase He has given you. Ask Him how you can best live out this gift that the Holy Spirit has placed before you. Listen patiently in the silence for the response. You may be tempted to move on to some other thought or task, but resist, simply resting in the silence yet listening actively.

LIVE

Go and live out the answer to what the Holy Spirit instructed you to do today.

148

BAD THINGS HAPPEN TO VERY GOOD PEOPLE

JEREMIAH 38:1-6

¹ Now Shephatiah son of Mattan, Gedaliah son of Pashhur, Jucal son of Shelemiah, and Pashhur son of Malchijah heard the words Jeremiah was speaking to all the people: ² "This is what the LORD says: 'Whoever stays in this city will die by the sword, famine, and plague, but whoever surrenders to the Chaldeans will live. He will keep his life like the spoils of war and will live.' ³ This is what the LORD says: 'This city will most certainly be handed over to the king of Babylon's army, and he will capture it.'"

⁴ The officials then said to the king, "This man ought to die, because he is weakening the morale of the warriors who remain in this city and of all the people by speaking to them in this way. This man is not seeking the well-being of this people, but disaster."

⁵ King Zedekiah said, "Here he is; he's in your hands since the king can't do anything against you." ⁶ So they took Jeremiah and dropped him into the cistern of Malchiah the king's son, which was in the guard's courtyard, lowering Jeremiah with ropes. There was no water in the cistern, only mud, and Jeremiah sank in the mud.

READ

Read the passage aloud slowly.

THINK

Even though Jeremiah was a faithful servant of God, circumstances weren't turning out well for him. Read the passage again and experience for yourself the feelings Jeremiah probably had. Feel yourself sinking in the mud.

1. How difficult is it for you to accept that bad things happen to people who love God and do good?
2. Pretend once again that you are Jeremiah sinking in the mud. All you have now is the companionship of God. How does that feel? How close is that to being enough for you? What do you (as Jeremiah) want to pray?
3. What does it mean to hope in God's own being instead of simply hoping God will rescue you?

PRAY

Talk to God about a situation in which you've been left behind in the mud. (This may be happening now or in the past, or it may be something you foresee happening in the future.)

LIVE

Sit with your palms open and turned upward toward God. Rest in the idea that some days we have the companionship of God when it appears we have nothing else. Is that enough?

Be on the lookout for people sinking in the mud whom you might be called to love and help.

GOD'S DEEP COMMITMENT

JEREMIAH 51:1-5

¹ This is what the LORD says:

> I am about to stir up a destructive wind against Babylon
> and against the population of Leb-qamai.
> ² I will send strangers to Babylon
> who will scatter her and strip her land bare,
> for they will come against her
> from every side in the day of disaster.
> ³ Don't let the archer string his bow;
> don't let him put on his armor.
> Don't spare her young men;
> completely destroy her entire army!
> ⁴ Those who were slain will fall in the land of the Chaldeans,
> those who were pierced through, in her streets.
> ⁵ For Israel and Judah are not left widowed
> by their God, the LORD of Hosts,
> though their land is full of guilt
> against the Holy One of Israel.

READ

Read the passage, including the expanded passage, if possible.

THINK

Sense for yourself God's vigor and aggression in going after His enemy Babylon. Take a few minutes to imagine the images God uses to describe how He will treat them. What is your reaction?

Now focus your attention on God's final statement, regarding His commitment to Israel. What does this tell you about God's motives for the destruction He's planning for Babylon? Think about His regard for Israel: What does He feel toward them? What does He feel about their sin?

PRAY

Look back on what you noticed about God — both His aggression and His commitment. Is there a phrase from the passage that stands out to you? As you think about this phrase and repeat it to yourself a few times, meditate on this picture of who God is. If in doing so you feel drawn into dialogue with Him, go ahead and enter in.

LIVE

Hold in your mind God's qualities of aggression and commitment, then consider your own life. Maybe you'll think about your relationships, your attitude at work or school, your hobbies, or what you enjoy doing on the weekends. What is God saying about an area of your life right now?

WHEN DISAPPOINTMENT COMES

LAMENTATIONS 3:19-30

ז Zayin
19 Remember my affliction and my homelessness,
   the wormwood and the poison.
20 I continually remember them
   and have become depressed.
21 Yet I call this to mind,
   and therefore I have hope:

ח Khet
22 Because of the LORD's faithful love
   we do not perish,
   for His mercies never end.
23 They are new every morning;
   great is Your faithfulness!
24 I say: The LORD is my portion,
   therefore I will put my hope in Him.

ט Tet
25 The LORD is good to those who wait for Him,
   to the person who seeks Him.
26 It is good to wait quietly
   for deliverance from the LORD.
27 It is good for a man to bear the yoke
   while he is still young.

י Yod
28 Let him sit alone and be silent,
   for God has disciplined him.
29 Let him put his mouth in the dust —
   perhaps there is still hope.
30 Let him offer his cheek
   to the one who would strike him;
   let him be filled with shame.

THINK

Lamentations is one of the saddest books in the Bible, but just because it's chock-full of disappointment doesn't mean it's absent of hope. Jeremiah, writing this book as he mourns the utter destruction of the famous and once-splendid city of Jerusalem, speaks of pain and sadness and disappointment. But he also reflects on the undying goodness and faithfulness of God.

READ

Read the passage carefully. As you do so, note Jeremiah's complete honesty before God. Also note the change in Jeremiah's attitude toward the end of the chapter from extreme disappointment to an embrace of hope because of God's faithfulness.

PRAY

Take a few minutes to consider the disappointments you have experienced or are experiencing. Then follow the guidance of Jeremiah's words, starting with "Let him sit alone and be silent." Just as he encourages, "Perhaps there is still hope."

LIVE

Don't ever forget that despite disappointment and pain, God always remains faithful.

IN THE PIT

LAMENTATIONS 3:52-58

צ *Tsade*

⁵² For no apparent reason, my enemies
hunted me like a bird.
⁵³ They dropped me alive into a pit
and threw stones at me.
⁵⁴ Water flooded over my head,
and I thought: I'm going to die!

ק *Qof*

⁵⁵ I called on Your name, Yahweh,
from the depths of the Pit.
⁵⁶ You hear my plea:
Do not ignore my cry for relief.
⁵⁷ You come near when I call on You;
You say: "Do not be afraid."

ר *Resh*

⁵⁸ You defend my cause, Lord;
You redeem my life.

READ

Read the passage aloud slowly. Jeremiah had been thrown into a cistern, where he sank in the mud (see Jeremiah 38:1-6). Here he may be telling us what he thought while he was down there.

THINK

Read verses 52-54 again and pause. Sit in that despair. Read verses 55-58. Grin with joy.

1. What words or phrases in each section resonate for you?
2. In what ways do you call out to God — or not? Do you numb out or shut yourself up instead? Why?
3. Have you ever sensed the closeness of God? If so, how? If not, what do you think it would be like?

PRAY

Talk to God about the times He has come close when you have called out. Or if this hasn't happened, talk with God about what you think it would be like.

LIVE

Be open to the closeness of God coming to you now — even if you're not in a pit. Store that closeness for the times when you'll need it.

REMEMBER WHAT HAS HAPPENED TO US

LAMENTATIONS 5:1-12,17

1   Yahweh, remember what has happened to us.
    Look, and see our disgrace!

2   Our inheritance has been turned over to strangers,
    our houses to foreigners.

3   We have become orphans, fatherless;
    our mothers are widows.

4   We must pay for the water we drink;
    our wood comes at a price.

5   We are closely pursued;
    we are tired, and no one offers us rest.

6   We made a treaty with Egypt
    and with Assyria, to get enough food.

7   Our fathers sinned; they no longer exist,
    but we bear their punishment.

8   Slaves rule over us;
    no one rescues us from their hands.

9   We secure our food at the risk of our lives
    because of the sword in the wilderness.

10   Our skin is as hot as an oven
    from the ravages of hunger.

11   Women are raped in Zion,
    girls in the cities of Judah.

12   Princes are hung up by their hands;
    elders are shown no respect. . . .

17   Because of this, our heart is sick;
    because of these, our eyes grow dim.

READ

Read the passage twice, keeping in mind other stories you've read about the Israelites' unreliable commitment to God and the times they walked away from Him.

THINK

When you hold side by side this expression of Israel's humility with stories of their pride and hardheartedness, what is your response to their prayer in this passage? If you were God, how would you respond to them? Jot down some words that summarize your reaction.

PRAY

Read and absorb the following words spoken by Jesus many years later to the same people, when He came to give His life for them: "Jerusalem, Jerusalem! She who kills the prophets and stones those who are sent to her. How often I wanted to gather your children together, as a hen gathers her chicks under her wings, but you were not willing!" (Luke 13:34). Set this book aside and sit with your eyes closed. Meditate on Jesus' words.

When you see this openhearted love that God continued to have for His people, despite their turning away, what do you feel? Ponder the reality that this is the God who rules the universe.

LIVE

What are the differences between your response to Israel and God's response? In what ways might your responses to yourself or others cloud your perception of how God responds? Ask Him to help you learn to distinguish your reaction from His, so that you might know more clearly what He's like.

153
154

DAY 154

GOD ENCOUNTERS

On this seventh day, review and reflect on all you have read this week. Take the time to revel in the ways you've encountered God in the past six days.

A MOUTHFUL

EZEKIEL 3:1-11

¹ He said to me: "Son of man, eat what you find here. Eat this scroll, then go and speak to the house of Israel." ² So I opened my mouth, and He fed me the scroll. ³ "Son of man," He said to me, "eat and fill your stomach with this scroll I am giving you." So I ate it, and it was as sweet as honey in my mouth.

⁴ Then He said to me: "Son of man, go to the house of Israel and speak My words to them. ⁵ For you are not being sent to a people of unintelligible speech or difficult language but to the house of Israel. ⁶ You are not being sent to many peoples of unintelligible speech or difficult language, whose words you cannot understand. No doubt, if I sent you to them, they would listen to you. ⁷ But the house of Israel will not want to listen to you because they do not want to listen to Me. For the whole house of Israel is hardheaded and hardhearted. ⁸ Look, I have made your face as hard as their faces and your forehead as hard as their foreheads. ⁹ I have made your forehead like a diamond, harder than flint. Don't be afraid of them or discouraged by the look on their faces, even though they are a rebellious house."

¹⁰ Next He said to me: "Son of man, listen carefully to all My words that I speak to you and take them to heart. ¹¹ Go to your people, the exiles, and speak to them. Tell them, 'This is what the Lord GOD says,' whether they listen or refuse to listen."

READ

Read the passage. Try to read as though you are far from God, have no understanding of who Jesus is, and have never read a Bible before.

THINK

In this book, God has many unique lessons to communicate to Ezekiel, which He desires Ezekiel to pass on to others. He gives him visions of spinning wheels, He has Ezekiel lie on his side for several days, He has him shave his beard and divide the hair into three parts — all in order to communicate an important message to others.

One of God's unique lessons has Ezekiel eating the sacred scroll of the Scriptures — literally eating the word-filled pages. And we read that Ezekiel says the Scriptures taste good, like honey.

Read the passage again, meditating particularly on the final portion that starts with "Listen carefully to all My words . . . and take them to heart." Metaphorically speaking, what is the taste of God's Word in your mouth?

PRAY/LIVE

What are two or three elements of Scripture that you are having a hard time digesting right now? Why? Tell God about it. Ask God to guide you in making the words your very own.

If you have honey, place a drop on your finger. Taste the honey slowly and attentively. Savor the sweetness in your mouth. As you do this, pray that God will give you such a desire for Scripture that it will taste like honey on your lips.

LEARN FROM THE WORST

EZEKIEL 18:14-17

[14] "Now suppose he has a son who sees all the sins his father has committed, and though he sees them, he does not do likewise. [15] He does not eat at the mountain shrines or raise his eyes to the idols of the house of Israel. He does not defile his neighbor's wife. [16] He doesn't oppress anyone, hold collateral, or commit robbery. He gives his bread to the hungry and covers the naked with clothing. [17] He keeps his hand from harming the poor, not taking interest or profit on a loan. He practices My ordinances and follows My statutes. Such a person will not die for his father's iniquity. He will certainly live."

READ

Read the passage aloud slowly.

THINK

Read the passage aloud again, noting all the things the child learned from the negative example of the parent.

1. What words or phases or ideas particularly speak to you?
2. When have you learned important truths from watching someone else's negative example and then chosen to do otherwise?
3. Consider whether there is someone in your life now whose negative example can teach you something. (This could be someone you are close to and love deeply.)

PRAY

Ask God for wisdom to learn from the negative examples of people around you. Also ask God to help you avoid feeling morally superior to them — but instead be grateful for what you can learn. Pray for that person who is or was a negative example.

LIVE

Look at yourself in a mirror. See yourself as wholly different from the person who is a negative example — particularly if this person is a parent. Thank God that being wholly different is possible through Him.

THE SHEPHERD AND ME

EZEKIEL 34:10-16

¹⁰ "This is what the Lord GOD says: Look, I am against the shepherds. I will demand My flock from them and prevent them from shepherding the flock. The shepherds will no longer feed themselves, for I will rescue My flock from their mouths so that they will not be food for them.

¹¹ "For this is what the Lord GOD says: See, I Myself will search for My flock and look for them. ¹² As a shepherd looks for his sheep on the day he is among his scattered flock, so I will look for My flock. I will rescue them from all the places where they have been scattered on a cloudy and dark day. ¹³ I will bring them out from the peoples, gather them from the countries, and bring them into their own land. I will shepherd them on the mountains of Israel, in the ravines, and in all the inhabited places of the land. ¹⁴ I will tend them with good pasture, and their grazing place will be on Israel's lofty mountains. There they will lie down in a good grazing place; they will feed in rich pasture on the mountains of Israel. ¹⁵ I will tend My flock and let them lie down." This is the declaration of the Lord GOD. ¹⁶ "I will seek the lost, bring back the strays, bandage the injured, and strengthen the weak, but I will destroy the fat and the strong. I will shepherd them with justice."

READ

Get a clean sheet of paper and something to draw with. Read the passage slowly, imagining the scene.

THINK

Read the passage again. As you do, let the images take vivid shape in your mind. You might read it a few times to get really familiar with the relationships, the experiences, the settings. In your mind, picture the pastures for grazing, the weak sheep and the strong, the way the shepherd interacts with them. Pick one thing that stands out to you and think about what it would look like or smell like or sound like and what it makes you feel.

PRAY

Consider whatever stood out to you and take several minutes to sketch whatever comes to mind. Avoid hurrying yourself or thinking that you can't draw. Just go with it. You might sketch many different things, or you might focus on one thing. As you draw, be aware of God's presence there with you. Don't force yourself to talk or think about anything in particular. Simply enjoy drawing with God.

LIVE

Think about approaching God as your Shepherd. What do you want to bring to Him today? Are you injured or struggling? Are you feeling strong? Are you needing rest? Bring Him your need and tell Him about it. Receive the comfort He gives.

NOT A HAIR SINGED

DANIEL 3:19-27

[19] Then Nebuchadnezzar was filled with rage, and the expression on his face changed toward Shadrach, Meshach, and Abednego. He gave orders to heat the furnace seven times more than was customary, [20] and he commanded some of the strongest soldiers in his army to tie up Shadrach, Meshach, and Abednego and throw them into the furnace of blazing fire. [21] So these men, in their trousers, robes, head coverings, and other clothes, were tied up and thrown into the furnace of blazing fire. [22] Since the king's command was so urgent and the furnace extremely hot, the raging flames killed those men who carried Shadrach, Meshach, and Abednego up. [23] And these three men, Shadrach, Meshach, and Abednego fell, bound, into the furnace of blazing fire.

[24] Then King Nebuchadnezzar jumped up in alarm. He said to his advisers, "Didn't we throw three men, bound, into the fire?"

"Yes, of course, Your Majesty," they replied to the king.

[25] He exclaimed, "Look! I see four men, not tied, walking around in the fire unharmed; and the fourth looks like a son of the gods."

[26] Nebuchadnezzar then approached the door of the furnace of blazing fire and called: "Shadrach, Meshach, and Abednego, you servants of the Most High God — come out!" So Shadrach, Meshach, and Abednego came out of the fire. [27] When the satraps, prefects, governors, and the king's advisers gathered around, they saw that the fire had no effect on the bodies of these men: not a hair of their heads was singed, their robes were unaffected, and there was no smell of fire on them.

READ

Read the passage aloud slowly.

THINK

Read the passage aloud again, but this time read the dialogue as theatrically as possible. Catch the incredulous tones of the king in verses 24-25. And in verse 26, call out loudly as the king did.

Now read the passage silently and let yourself become someone in the passage: a bystander watching it all, the king, one of the three men, or even the mysterious fourth man. Imagine the thoughts and feelings of the person whose role you have assumed. If you had been this person, how would this experience have affected your relationship with God?

PRAY

Respond to God from what has come to you in this passage, particularly about trusting in Him.

LIVE

Sit quietly before God with the palms of your hands open and turned upward. Receive from God. Be particularly open to receiving guidance, just as Shadrach, Meshach, and Abednego received from God. Receive the courage He gave them. Receive the power He gave them.

WHEN DOING THE RIGHT THING IS AGAINST THE LAW

DANIEL 6:6-10

[6] So the administrators and satraps went together to the king and said to him, "May King Darius live forever. [7] All the administrators of the kingdom, the prefects, satraps, advisers, and governors have agreed that the king should establish an ordinance and enforce an edict that for 30 days, anyone who petitions any god or man except you, the king, will be thrown into the lions' den. [8] Therefore, Your Majesty, establish the edict and sign the document so that, as a law of the Medes and Persians, it is irrevocable and cannot be changed." [9] So King Darius signed the document.

[10] When Daniel learned that the document had been signed, he went into his house. The windows in its upper room opened toward Jerusalem, and three times a day he got down on his knees, prayed, and gave thanks to his God, just as he had done before.

READ

The story of Daniel 6 is a familiar one, which means we often focus on Daniel inside the den of lions while missing what got him there in the first place. So before you read, pause and ask God to help you see this story with fresh eyes.

THINK

King Darius signs a deceptive decree that puts God-fearing Daniel in an interesting (to say the least) situation. But despite the new law and at great risk, Daniel maintains his routine of prayer. What does this story make you feel? Why?

Imagine yourself in the situation with Daniel. What do you see? What do you hear? If you were Daniel's friend, what would you say to him? What would you do? Would you kneel with him by the window? Would you kneel quietly in the corner so nobody could see you? Would you kneel at all? Would you stop praying to God?

Would these be difficult decisions for you? In what ways does this story speak to you about obedience?

PRAY

Allow the natural rhythm of your thoughts concerning Daniel's obedience to prompt you into conversation with God. (For example, you could pray after each category of thought or you could pray after your meditation is finished — whatever comes most naturally.)

Consider praying in a kneeling position by a window. As you pray, remember Daniel.

LIVE

Remember that God is worthy of your costly obedience.

KING OF THE UNIVERSE

DANIEL 7:11-14

[11] "I watched, then, because of the sound of the arrogant words the horn was speaking. As I continued watching, the beast was killed and its body destroyed and given over to the burning fire. [12] As for the rest of the beasts, their authority to rule was removed, but an extension of life was granted to them for a certain period of time. [13] I continued watching in the night visions,

> and I saw One like a son of man
> coming with the clouds of heaven.
> He approached the Ancient of Days
> and was escorted before Him.
> [14] He was given authority to rule,
> and glory, and a kingdom;
> so that those of every people,
> nation, and language
> should serve Him.
> His dominion is an everlasting dominion
> that will not pass away,
> and His kingdom is one
> that will not be destroyed."

READ

Read the passage as fast as you can. Then read it again at a normal pace. Finally read it aloud very slowly, focusing on and articulating each word.

THINK

The book of Daniel is full of radical stories of obedience, but it is also filled with strange and sensational dreams and visions. Chapter 7 includes a vision with four animals, plus the prophetic words found in verses 13-14.

Is God's kingly rule in the world evident to you? Do you believe He's really in charge? Think about God reigning as King over His people. Does that make you feel fear and dread or excitement and hope? Why?

If God is in control, we don't have to be. Does that thought induce anxiety or comfort? Why? Catastrophes, devastation, and suffering happen every day, yet God is ruling at this very moment. Do you believe that? How does believing that make you feel?

Not only is God in control today, but His reign lasts forever. In what ways does that fact impact your life?

PRAY

What are you worried about? Offer your concerns right now to the God who reigns over everything at this very moment and will continue to reign forever.

LIVE

Live freely and without worry as you focus on God's reign today.

DAY 161

GOD ENCOUNTERS

On this seventh day, review and reflect on all you have read this week. Take the time to revel in the ways you've encountered God in the past six days.

CONFESSING FOR YOUR GROUP

DANIEL 9:4-9,18

⁴ I prayed to the LORD my God and confessed:

> Ah, Lord — the great and awe-inspiring God who keeps His gracious covenant with those who love Him and keep His commands — ⁵ we have sinned, done wrong, acted wickedly, rebelled, and turned away from Your commands and ordinances. ⁶ We have not listened to Your servants the prophets, who spoke in Your name to our kings, leaders, fathers, and all the people of the land.

> ⁷ Lord, righteousness belongs to You, but this day public shame belongs to us: the men of Judah, the residents of Jerusalem, and all Israel — those who are near and those who are far, in all the countries where You have dispersed them because of the disloyalty they have shown toward You. ⁸ LORD, public shame belongs to us, our kings, our leaders, and our fathers, because we have sinned against You. ⁹ Compassion and forgiveness belong to the Lord our God, though we have rebelled against Him. . . .

> ¹⁸ Listen, my God, and hear. Open Your eyes and see our desolations and the city called by Your name. For we are not presenting our petitions before You based on our righteous acts, but based on Your abundant compassion.

READ

Read the passage aloud slowly.

THINK

Consider a group you belong to for which you could confess. This might be your family, your church, your nation, or a circle of friends or colleagues.

Read the passage again silently, noting if certain words or phrases apply to your group situation. Notice these phrases especially:

- "turned away from Your commands and ordinances"
- "this day public shame belongs to us"
- "have not listened to Your servants the prophets"

Read the passage again silently, noting the qualities of God that are mentioned. Which qualities does your group most need? Perhaps:

- keeping one's covenant, never giving up
- righteousness
- compassion and forgiveness

PRAY

Paraphrase verse 18 in a way that makes sense to your situation.

LIVE

Check your feelings regarding confession. Are you letting it be a time of release and rest in the presence of your Father or a time of beating yourself up? Rest in the release of it all.

LEAD MANY TO RIGHTEOUSNESS

DANIEL 12:1-3

¹ At that time
Michael the great prince
who stands watch over your people will rise up.
There will be a time of distress
such as never has occurred
since nations came into being until that time.
But at that time all your people
who are found written in the book will escape.

² Many of those who sleep in the dust
of the earth will awake,
some to eternal life,
and some to shame and eternal contempt.

³ Those who are wise will shine
like the bright expanse of the heavens,
and those who lead many to righteousness,
like the stars forever and ever.

READ

Read today's expanded passage, if possible. Lay your watch or a clock next to your Bible. As you read, consider how this passage affects time, both right now and in the future.

THINK

A great deal has been said and written about the end times — in radio talk shows, best-selling novels, Hollywood blockbusters, and conversations over coffee.

In light of these verses, what are you thinking about the end times? What are you feeling? Does talk like this about the future excite you or scare you?

Focus for a few minutes specifically on 12:1-3. How do we know if we are wise? What does it mean to "lead many to righteousness"? What are the implications of these words in your life? Who do you have the opportunity to help get on the path to righteousness?

Do you think it's fair that God gives some people eternal life and banishes others to eternal shame? Is He being just when He does that? Why or why not?

PRAY

Tell God how you feel about the future — both your immediate future and the end of the world. Ask Him to help you live wisely. Invite God to guide you in helping lead others to righteousness.

LIVE

Live with confidence today, knowing that God has already secured the future and will be victorious.

GOD AS LOVER

HOSEA 2:14-20

14 Therefore, I am going to persuade her,
lead her to the wilderness,
and speak tenderly to her.

15 There I will give her vineyards back to her
and make the Valley of Achor
into a gateway of hope.
There she will respond as she did
in the days of her youth,
as in the day she came out of the land of Egypt.

16 In that day —
this is the LORD's declaration —
you will call Me, "My husband,"
and no longer call Me, "My Baal."

17 For I will remove the names of the Baals
from her mouth;
they will no longer be remembered by their names.

18 On that day I will make a covenant for them
with the wild animals, the birds of the sky,
and the creatures that crawl on the ground.
I will shatter bow, sword,
and weapons of war in the land
and will enable the people to rest securely.

19 I will take you to be My wife forever.
I will take you to be My wife in righteousness,
justice, love, and compassion.

20 I will take you to be My wife in faithfulness,
and you will know Yahweh.

READ

Meditate on this passage.

THINK

When we think of love stories in the Bible, we usually think of the one narrated in Song of Songs, with all its steamy unpredictability. But Hosea offers us a love story too, one that's no less steamy, yet one that jolts us in a different way. In it Hosea actually lives out the heartbreaking metaphor of God's love for us . . . and our rejection of His love.

God commands Hosea to marry a prostitute named Gomer. Then God says that he is going to "persuade her" and "speak tenderly to her." Hosea had to pursue the woman again and again as a symbolic act of how God runs after us when we've been unfaithful.

We are the prostitute in this story. What does that feel like?

We are also God's beloved in this story. What does it feel like to be courted by such a lover, one who cares deeply about you despite your past? Is thinking of God as a lover — *your* lover — easy or difficult? Consider the possible reasons for your answer.

Read again the final words of this passage (starting with the line "I will take you to be My wife forever"). What is your reaction?

PRAY

Make these words your prayer as you desire to know God intimately: "You will know Yahweh."

LIVE

Carry the image of God as lover in your mind today.

LOVE AGAIN

HOSEA 3:1-3

¹ Then the LORD said to me, "Go again; show love to a woman who is loved by another man and is an adulteress, just as the LORD loves the Israelites though they turn to other gods and love raisin cakes."

² So I bought her for 15 shekels of silver and five bushels of barley. ³ I said to her, "You must live with me many days. Don't be promiscuous or belong to any man, and I will act the same way toward you."

READ

Read the passage slowly, whispering it.

THINK

Read the passage again slowly. Pause after verse 1 to consider how Hosea may have felt about doing what God instructed. Then read verses 2-3, noticing Hosea's firm resolution in restoring his wife.

1. What verses are most startling to you in this passage? Why?
2. How would you describe the way God loved the Israelite people (considering that they turned to other gods)?
3. Is there someone you need to love again? Reach out to? Simply stop criticizing and give that person a break?

PRAY

Ask God to help you love the person who came to mind in question 3 the way He loved the Israelites. If this seems too difficult, include in your prayer your paraphrase of Romans 5:5: "God's love has been poured out in our hearts through the Holy Spirit who was given to us."

Ask God what that love might look like; it may look different from what you might automatically assume. Consider what it might cost you to love this person the way God shows you.

LIVE

Sit quietly before God, trying to sense what it was like for Him to love the wayward Israelites no matter what.

LIP SERVICE

HOSEA 8:1-3

1   Put the horn to your mouth!
One like an eagle comes
against the house of the LORD,
because they transgress My covenant
and rebel against My law.
2   Israel cries out to Me,
"My God, we know You!"
3   Israel has rejected what is good;
an enemy will pursue him.

READ

Read the passage, focusing on the words *Me* and *My*.

THINK

Despite our lover God pursuing us tenderly, we continue to reject His love. We treat Him not with tenderness but with contempt, discarding all He has done for us. And we continue to live like adulterers.

Read the passage again. Israel claims to know God, but its actions don't match its words. When have you experienced a similar situation — family members, friends, significant others, or your spouse saying one thing to you but doing just the opposite? How does that feel?

Consider your actions over the past week, the times when you have been the one to say something and then do the opposite. Is your love for God displayed in your actions, or do your actions fly in the face of everything you say to Him?

PRAY

Tell God your desire to fall deeper and deeper in love with Him, praying and asking Him to help your actions communicate that to Him.

Confess recent circumstances when your actions toward God and people did not match your profession of love for God.

LIVE

Note whether your actions align with the love for God that you profess.

TIME TO SEEK THE LORD

HOSEA 10:11-12

¹¹ Ephraim is a well-trained calf
that loves to thresh,
but I will place a yoke on her fine neck.
I will harness Ephraim;
Judah will plow;
Jacob will do the final plowing.
¹² Sow righteousness for yourselves
and reap faithful love;
break up your unplowed ground.
It is time to seek the LORD
until He comes and sends righteousness
on you like the rain.

READ

Read the passage aloud slowly.

THINK

Read the passage aloud again. As you do, understand this to be God's dream for the northern tribes of Israel. Instead of doing these things, however, they rebelled.

Think of a time God used you to love someone or do something special for someone. In doing so, you were a well-trained calf!

1. What does this passage tell you about what a well-trained calf does?
2. Why is it a joy for a well-trained calf to "seek the LORD"?

Read the passage one more time. What words are attractive to your ears?

PRAY

Thank God for the times He has used you to do kingdom work — offering mercy, doing justice, or acting in faithfulness. Ask God to show you ways He wants to use you that you might not have noticed.

LIVE

Sit in the joy and satisfaction of seeking the Lord. If you have not experienced being used by God, imagine what that might feel like.

DAY 168

GOD ENCOUNTERS

On this seventh day, review and reflect on all you have read this week. Take the time to revel in the ways you've encountered God in the past six days.

HOW CAN I GIVE YOU UP?

HOSEA 11:1-5,7-9

1 When Israel was a child, I loved him,
and out of Egypt I called My son.

2 The more they called them,
the more they departed from Me.
They kept sacrificing to the Baals
and burning offerings to idols.

3 It was I who taught Ephraim to walk,
taking them in My arms,
but they never knew that I healed them.

4 I led them with human cords,
with ropes of love.
To them I was like one
who eases the yoke from their jaws;
I bent down to give them food.

5 Israel will not return to the land of Egypt
and Assyria will be his king,
because they refused to repent. . . .

7 My people are bent on turning from Me.
Though they call to Him on high,
He will not exalt them at all.

8 How can I give you up, Ephraim?
How can I surrender you, Israel?
How can I make you like Admah?
How can I treat you like Zeboiim?
I have had a change of heart;
My compassion is stirred!

9 I will not vent the full fury of My anger;
I will not turn back to destroy Ephraim.
For I am God and not man,
the Holy One among you;
I will not come in rage.

READ

Read the passage once to understand the situation. (Include the expanded passage for further information.) Read it again, but this time pause at each phrase or idea and linger there for a moment to really catch what is being said.

THINK

Quiet your mind. Read the passage a third time, aloud. This time notice the word or phrase that most vividly speaks to you of God's unrelenting faithfulness. Pause at this phrase, and hear yourself speak it. Then finish reading the passage.

PRAY

Spend time absorbing the word or phrase into yourself, as though your heart were a sponge slowly soaking up water. Memorize it. Let it intermingle with your concerns, memories, and feelings. Allow your meditation to grow into conversation with God. Notice God pointing out, through this illustration, how His devotedness frees you to experience life differently than you have before.

LIVE

Between now and your next time of prayer, plan at least three occasions throughout your day when you will pause and spend a few minutes mulling over the phrase that showed you the tenacity of God's love. Each time, you'll probably bring different emotions, attitudes, and experiences with you, and that's okay. Let them challenge God's message of commitment to you. Find out how His steadfast love responds to each challenge.

CORPORATE CONFESSION

JOEL 1:8-10

8 Grieve like a young woman dressed in sackcloth,
mourning for the husband of her youth.

9 Grain and drink offerings have been cut off
from the house of the LORD;
the priests, who are ministers of the LORD, mourn.

10 The fields are destroyed;
the land grieves;
indeed, the grain is destroyed;
the new wine is dried up;
and the olive oil fails.

READ

Read the passage and, if possible, the expanded passage.

THINK

In the first chapter of Joel, the prophet speaks of a famine that has significance far beyond mere physical consequences. There are certain passages of Scripture that we love to read, passages of comfort and rest, hope and promise. But there are others — like this one — that confront us with the truth, as hard as it may be to hear.

American Christianity often emphasizes the importance of personal confession of sin. But the concept of corporate sin is rarely discussed. In contrast, confession of corporate sin was a regular occurrence in the ancient Jewish world. National sin grieved the heart of the God-fearing Hebrew, and confessing it was desired and expected.

Take out a piece of paper and write down the corporate sins that our communities, our government, our country, and even our churches need to confess. (Include what wrongdoing has been done and what good-doing has been left undone.)

PRAY

Spend time specifically acknowledging and confessing these corporate sins against God and others. Ask God for forgiveness.

LIVE

Live with the awareness of our collective sins, knowing that God desires repentance for us as a community, a country, and His people. Ask often for corporate forgiveness.

COME BACK TO ME

JOEL 2:12-14

12   Even now —
               this is the LORD's declaration —
     turn to Me with all your heart,
     with fasting, weeping, and mourning.
13   Tear your hearts,
     not just your clothes,
     and return to the LORD your God.
     For He is gracious and compassionate,
     slow to anger, rich in faithful love,
     and He relents from sending disaster.
14   Who knows? He may turn and relent
     and leave a blessing behind Him,
     so you can offer grain and wine
     to the LORD your God.

READ

Read the passage aloud slowly, noting that verse 12 includes words from God Himself.

THINK

Read the passage aloud again, repeating God's words in verse 12 in the tone you think He would have said them.

God says the phrase "return to Me" many times through the prophets. God really does want His people, and He wants them back.

1. What does this passage tell you about what God is like?
2. How surprised are you that God wants His people (including you) back? (Keep in mind that turning back doesn't have to mean you ever dramatically turned away; it might mean you've just been distracted.)

   ☐ Very surprised: You thought God would scold people who wander away or ignore Him.
   ☐ Somewhat surprised: You figured God wouldn't turn away someone who returns, but He would never plead with them.
   ☐ Not surprised: You frequently sense God calling you back and know He's not mad at you.
   ☐ Other:

PRAY

Tell God how you feel about being (or becoming) someone who always returns to Him. Do you always want to? Would you like to always want to? Talk to God about the blessings that come to you when you turn back to Him.

LIVE

Picture this: If God had a body, how would He stand before people and plead for them to come back to Him? What would He do with His hands? His arms? What would His face look like?

A REFUGE AND STRONGHOLD

JOEL 3:14-19

14 Multitudes, multitudes
in the valley of decision!
For the Day of the LORD is near
in the valley of decision.

15 The sun and moon will grow dark,
and the stars will cease their shining.

16 The LORD will roar from Zion
and raise His voice from Jerusalem;
heaven and earth will shake.
But the LORD will be a refuge for His people,
a stronghold for the Israelites.

17 Then you will know
that I am Yahweh your God,
who dwells in Zion, My holy mountain.
Jerusalem will be holy,
and foreigners will never overrun it again.

18 In that day
the mountains will drip with sweet wine,
and the hills will flow with milk.
All the streams of Judah will flow with water,
and a spring will issue from the LORD's house,
watering the Valley of Acacias.

19 Egypt will become desolate,
and Edom a desert wasteland,
because of the violence done to the people of Judah
in whose land they shed innocent blood.

READ

Read the passage, opening yourself up to the situation Joel is prophetically describing here. You might read it a few more times, allowing the words and images to become familiar.

THINK

Ponder the contrast between God as the terrifying roar amid chaos and God as a "stronghold." Which words or images in particular catch your attention? Mull them over. Become aware of specific questions these verses raise for you.

PRAY

Let your questions and meditation lead you into conversation with God. You might think about facets of His character, like His terrifying might or His solid trustworthiness, or you might consider the reality of this future, even though we don't know exactly what it will be like.

If your primary questions about the passage are intellectual, place them before God and ask Him what He has for you. Stay honest with what you do and don't understand, sharing with God how this passage touches your life. Avoid getting lost in academic speculation or trying to force meaning out of the passage. Just ask God how He would like to use this experience of your limitedness today.

LIVE

As you look once more at the two vastly different perspectives on God presented in this passage, which side of God are you most in need of today: His fierce ability to bring justice or His safe protection from harm? Spend time now quietly resting in the presence of this God.

THE GOD OF JUSTICE

AMOS 2:6-8

⁶ The LORD says:

> I will not relent from punishing Israel
> for three crimes, even four,
> because they sell a righteous person for silver
> and a needy person for a pair of sandals.
> ⁷ They trample the heads of the poor
> on the dust of the ground
> and block the path of the needy.
> A man and his father have sexual relations
> with the same girl,
> profaning My holy name.
> ⁸ They stretch out beside every altar
> on garments taken as collateral,
> and in the house of their God,
> they drink wine obtained through fines.

READ

Read the words of God in these verses with the tone of voice you think God might have had when speaking these words.

THINK

The book of Amos communicates clearly and compellingly that God cares deeply about social justice — and He dislikes it when His people turn their heads from doing right. God is truly a God of mercy, yet He is also a God of justice. That means He treats injustice harshly.

What injustices exist around you — among your friends and in your city, state, country, and the entire world? What are we to do about injustice specifically?

Thinking *I'm not a part of an injustice* is easy. But take a hard look around you. In what ways might you be contributing — directly or indirectly — to injustice in the world? In what ways might you get involved — directly or indirectly — to facilitate justice that would reveal the heart of God?

If injustice makes God sick to His stomach, what should the presence of injustice do to you? Does it?

PRAY

Ask God to make injustice in the world as repulsive to you as it is to Him. Ask Him for wisdom to address injustice in a way that honors Him with a godly balance of boldness and tenderness.

LIVE

Read some current news articles. As you absorb the accounts of atrocity, war, and corruption, pray for each situation. Pray that the God of justice will intervene.

SEEKING GOOD

AMOS 5:7,11-15

⁷ Those who turn justice into wormwood
throw righteousness to the ground. . . .

¹¹ Therefore, because you trample on the poor
and exact a grain tax from him,
you will never live in the houses of cut stone
you have built;
you will never drink the wine
from the lush vineyards
you have planted.
¹² For I know your crimes are many
and your sins innumerable.
They oppress the righteous, take a bribe,
and deprive the poor of justice at the gates.
¹³ Therefore, the wise person will keep silent
at such a time,
for the days are evil.

¹⁴ Seek good and not evil
so that you may live,
and the LORD, the God of Hosts,
will be with you,
as you have claimed.
¹⁵ Hate evil and love good;
establish justice in the gate.
Perhaps the LORD, the God of Hosts, will be gracious
to the remnant of Joseph.

READ

Read the passage aloud slowly.

THINK

Read the passage again silently, noticing the pictures in the passage. Which do you find most dreadful?

Pictures of how those who have enough treat those who don't:	
throw righteousness to the ground	trample on the poor
exact a grain tax	oppress the righteous
take bribes	deprive the poor of justice
Pictures of the consequences to those who have enough but don't share:	
luxury homes standing empty	exquisite wine going to waste unused

Read verses 14-15 again aloud. What is God saying to you about seeking good and helping others live?

PRAY

Talk to the Lord about what it would look like for you to seek good.

LIVE

Be alert for situations of injustice in which you can speak up or help someone. If you don't find any, ask someone else to give you ideas.

DAY 175

GOD ENCOUNTERS

On this seventh day, review and reflect on all you have read this week. Take the time to revel in the ways you've encountered God in the past six days.

PLUMB LINE

AMOS 7:1-9

¹ The Lord GOD showed me this: He was forming a swarm of locusts at the time the spring crop first began to sprout — after the cutting of the king's hay. ² When the locusts finished eating the vegetation of the land, I said, "Lord GOD, please forgive! How will Jacob survive since he is so small?"

³ The LORD relented concerning this. "It will not happen," He said.

⁴ The Lord GOD showed me this: The Lord GOD was calling for a judgment by fire. It consumed the great deep and devoured the land. ⁵ Then I said, "Lord GOD, please stop! How will Jacob survive since he is so small?"

⁶ The LORD relented concerning this. "This will not happen either," said the Lord GOD.

⁷ He showed me this: The Lord was standing there by a vertical wall with a plumb line in His hand. ⁸ The LORD asked me, "What do you see, Amos?"

I replied, "A plumb line."

Then the Lord said, "I am setting a plumb line among My people Israel; I will no longer spare them:

⁹   Isaac's high places will be deserted,
       and Israel's sanctuaries will be in ruins;
       I will rise up against the house of Jeroboam
       with a sword."

READ

Read the passage carefully.

THINK

What theme do you see emerging? Write it down in one sentence. Be aware of what thinking might have motivated God to use the plumb line.

LIVE

Take a small, heavy object, like a key, a ring, or a pendant, and hang it from a string. As the object hangs straight toward the ground, the string is your plumb line by which you can measure the uprightness of other items. Take time to ponder this. Play with your plumb line and observe how it works. What do you notice?

PRAY

Setting the text and your plumb line aside, sit with your eyes closed. What are you feeling? What are your concerns and needs? Who are you as the person who is approaching this text today?

Now read the passage again. In what ways do you see the theme you already noted intersecting with your life today? Is there a message God is speaking to you? How does the plumb line hang in the midst of your own life? If you have trouble seeing a connection, read the passage again, pausing in the place that affects you most and leads you into prayer. Write down anything that seems significant.

GOD, THE RADICAL POLITICIAN

OBADIAH 12-14

12 Do not gloat over your brother
in the day of his calamity;
do not rejoice over the people of Judah
in the day of their destruction;
do not boastfully mock
in the day of distress.
13 Do not enter the gate of My people
in the day of their disaster.
Yes, you — do not gloat over their misery
in the day of their disaster
and do not appropriate their possessions
in the day of their disaster.
14 Do not stand at the crossroads
to cut off their fugitives,
and do not hand over their survivors
in the day of distress.

READ

Read the passage aloud slowly. Understand that the prophet Obadiah is speaking to the nation of Edom, who enjoyed watching the nation of Judah experience troubles.

THINK

Put yourself in the place of the nation of Edom. You've had an ancient feud with the Israelites, and they are your bitter enemies. Politics are politics — enemy nations do *not* help each other. Right? Now read the passage again, with its very different viewpoint. Hear God's radical response to Edom's very normal behavior.

God's odd stance has been stated another way in 1 Corinthians 13:6: "Love finds no joy in unrighteousness but rejoices in the truth." What role does the love of God play in political affairs? What role does the love of God play in how nations treat the peoples of the world whom God loves?

PRAY

Ask God to help the nations of the world consider how they treat one another, especially nations who are ancient enemies. Pray for Christians who are active in inserting God's radical love into international politics (for example, Christian Peacemaker Teams).

LIVE

Stand in front of a world map or globe. Put your hand on a nation who has been an enemy of your nation. Pray for the people of that country. Pray for its leaders.

RESISTANT OR OBEDIENT?

JONAH 1:1-3

¹ The word of the LORD came to Jonah son of Amittai: ² "Get up! Go to the great city of Nineveh and preach against it, because their wickedness has confronted Me." ³ However, Jonah got up to flee to Tarshish from the LORD's presence. He went down to Joppa and found a ship going to Tarshish. He paid the fare and went down into it to go with them to Tarshish, from the LORD's presence.

READ

Pray and ask God to give you fresh eyes to see this familiar story in a new way. Then read the passage and chapters 1–2, if possible.

THINK

We might summarize this familiar story by saying that Jonah's resistance to being obedient to God's ways meant His learning a lesson the hard way. But there's more to it than that. In fact, the text tells us that Jonah was fleeing from the Lord's presence. We run away from God too, even if only in subtle ways. When do you run from God?

PRAY

Try praying while holding out your hands, palms up, in front of you. Use this posture as a way to release your desires to God, to receive what He has for you, and to communicate your openness and willingness to obey Him.

Ask the Holy Spirit to search your heart and reveal areas of your life where you resist what God desires. Invite Him to illuminate your unwillingness to obey, and give Him permission to do whatever it takes to show you that He cares deeply for you.

Request forgiveness for those times you have run from God, for your rebellion.

When you are finished, keeping your hands out, listen carefully in the silence.

LIVE

Go and live courageously and obediently in God's purposes for your life.

IN A SULK

JONAH 4:5-11

⁵ Jonah left the city and sat down east of it. He made himself a shelter there and sat in its shade to see what would happen to the city. ⁶ Then the LORD God appointed a plant, and it grew up to provide shade over Jonah's head to ease his discomfort. Jonah was greatly pleased with the plant. ⁷ When dawn came the next day, God appointed a worm that attacked the plant, and it withered.

⁸ As the sun was rising, God appointed a scorching east wind. The sun beat down so much on Jonah's head that he almost fainted, and he wanted to die. He said, "It's better for me to die than to live."

⁹ Then God asked Jonah, "Is it right for you to be angry about the plant?"

"Yes," he replied. "It is right. I'm angry enough to die!"

¹⁰ So the LORD said, "You cared about the plant, which you did not labor over and did not grow. It appeared in a night and perished in a night. ¹¹ Should I not care about the great city of Nineveh, which has more than 120,000 people who cannot distinguish between their right and their left, as well as many animals?"

READ

Allow the words and events of this passage to become familiar to you as you read. Let yourself sink into the scene described.

THINK

As you hear God's conversation with Jonah, think about how you would describe His reaction to Jonah's anger. Now read God's words again, and pay attention to the tone of voice you imagine God using. Is it condemning? Mocking? How might your perception of God shift if the same words were said in a tender but firm voice?

PRAY

What do you feel when you hear Jonah express his anger? Perhaps it makes you nervous or uncomfortable, or maybe there are times when you, too, want to yell at God. Talk to God about what you notice in your response, or write about it in a journal. Give yourself permission to be open and honest.

LIVE

Take some time to consider this statement: "God will love you [even] if you never pray."[11] Do you believe it? Talk to God about your reaction.

Recall your first, instinctive perception of God's response to Jonah. What does this show about what you believe to be God's feelings toward you when you are resentful or disobedient? Ask Him to help you understand over the coming months what His love for you is like and to help you take it in and receive it.

IDOL MAKING

MICAH 1:3-7

³ Look, the LORD is leaving His place
and coming down to trample
the heights of the earth.
⁴ The mountains will melt beneath Him,
and the valleys will split apart,
like wax near a fire,
like water cascading down a mountainside.
⁵ All this will happen because of Jacob's rebellion
and the sins of the house of Israel.
What is the rebellion of Jacob?
Isn't it Samaria?
And what is the high place of Judah?
Isn't it Jerusalem?
⁶ Therefore, I will make Samaria
a heap of ruins in the countryside,
a planting area for a vineyard.
I will roll her stones into the valley
and expose her foundations.
⁷ All her carved images will be smashed to pieces;
all her wages will be burned in the fire,
and I will destroy all her idols.
Since she collected the wages of a prostitute,
they will be used again for a prostitute.

READ

Pause and request that God give you an open heart for what you are about to read. Give Him permission to speak to you specifically about what He wants you to hear. Acknowledge that you desire to hear Him speak to you and will listen attentively.

Now read the passage with listening ears and an open heart.

THINK

Sometimes we let ourselves believe that idols are mere physical objects that people made hundreds, even thousands, of years ago. But theologically speaking, an idol is anything that eclipses our worship of God. And with this definition, *everybody* makes idols today, whether material or immaterial.

What gets between you and a heartfelt, humble, and thankful response to God? To what shrines and idols, gods and goddesses are you tempted to give your allegiance? Make a mental list (or write it on paper, if it helps).

Why do you think you are drawn to believe that certain things will give you more significance, purpose, and meaning than God Himself? Why does God hate those things that take your worship, attention, and devotion? Is God's jealousy selfish? Why or why not?

PRAY

Bring your list of idols before God. Be utterly transparent with Him, acknowledging and confessing the people, places, thoughts, ideas, emotions, and so on that have come between you and God. Invite Him to fight alongside you against these temptations that divert your soul from the truth.

LIVE

When an idol lures you, simply whisper, "God, help me worship You and You alone."

TEACH US ABOUT HIS WAYS

MICAH 4:1-4

¹ In the last days
the mountain of the LORD's house
will be established
at the top of the mountains
and will be raised above the hills.
Peoples will stream to it,

² and many nations will come and say,
"Come, let us go up to the mountain of the LORD,
to the house of the God of Jacob.
He will teach us about His ways
so we may walk in His paths."
For instruction will go out of Zion
and the word of the LORD from Jerusalem.

³ He will settle disputes among many peoples
and provide arbitration for strong nations
that are far away.
They will beat their swords into plows,
and their spears into pruning knives.
Nation will not take up the sword against nation,
and they will never again train for war.

⁴ But each man will sit under his grapevine
and under his fig tree
with no one to frighten him.
For the mouth of the LORD of Hosts
has promised this.

READ

Read the passage aloud slowly.

THINK

Read the passage again, noting what it says about teaching and instruction — how it's found, what it says, and what it results in.

1. What words or ideas touch you in the passage? Perhaps:

   - nations streaming to hear God
   - people wanting to live God's way
   - people giving up weapons to do their work quietly
   - other:

2. Why do you think those words or ideas touch you? How does this connect with what you want in life?

PRAY

Pray for God's true teaching to prevail in troubled places — within troubled people, within troubled relationships, within troubled groups, between troubled nations.

LIVE

Sit quietly before God, mentally rehearsing the sort of person you need to be to bring true teaching that results in such peace.

DAY 182

GOD ENCOUNTERS

On this seventh day, review and reflect on all you have read this week. Take the time to revel in the ways you've encountered God in the past six days.

OUR GOD

MICAH 7:15-20

¹⁵ I will perform miracles for them
as in the days of your exodus
from the land of Egypt.
¹⁶ Nations will see and be ashamed
of all their power.
They will put their hands over their mouths,
and their ears will become deaf.
¹⁷ They will lick the dust like a snake;
they will come trembling out of their hiding places
like reptiles slithering on the ground.
They will tremble in the presence of Yahweh our God;
they will stand in awe of You.

¹⁸ Who is a God like You,
removing iniquity and passing over rebellion
for the remnant of His inheritance?
He does not hold on to His anger forever,
because He delights in faithful love.
¹⁹ He will again have compassion on us;
He will vanquish our iniquities.
You will cast all our sins
into the depths of the sea.
²⁰ You will show loyalty to Jacob
and faithful love to Abraham,
as You swore to our fathers
from days long ago.

PRAY

Before you read, pray about what's on your heart today. Is there something you want to talk to God about? Maybe it's a vague sense of shame or irritation, or maybe something specific is happening. Whatever it is, share your heart with God. Try writing your prayer in a journal. Ask God to speak to you right where you are through today's excerpt.

READ/THINK

As much as you can, set aside what you've been thinking about for a few minutes, trusting that God will hold it for you. Read today's passage, noticing what's happening in Micah's situation and the kinds of problems that God, through him, is addressing in Israel. If you have time, read the expanded passage too, observing in particular what God is like.

Write down what you notice about God and the attributes He displays in this passage.

LIVE

Look at what you wrote about yourself and about God. How do you think God is responding to you and the issues you shared earlier through this passage from Micah? What angers God? What touches His heart? When does He show tenderness, and when does He show firmness?

How do these traits compare to the way you normally perceive God? Where do you think your idea of Him came from? Can you identify elements of your perception that are not of God but are rather reflections of you or other people you know?

Talk to God about what you notice.

PATIENT POWER

NAHUM 1:1-6

¹ The oracle concerning Nineveh. The book of the vision of Nahum the Elkoshite.

² The LORD is a jealous and avenging God;
the LORD takes vengeance
and is fierce in wrath.
The LORD takes vengeance against His foes;
He is furious with His enemies.
³ The LORD is slow to anger but great in power;
the LORD will never leave the guilty unpunished.
His path is in the whirlwind and storm,
and clouds are the dust beneath His feet.
⁴ He rebukes the sea so that it dries up,
and He makes all the rivers run dry.
Bashan and Carmel wither;
even the flower of Lebanon withers.
⁵ The mountains quake before Him,
and the hills melt;
the earth trembles at His presence —
the world and all who live in it.
⁶ Who can withstand His indignation?
Who can endure His burning anger?
His wrath is poured out like fire,
even rocks are shattered before Him.

READ

Read the passage.

THINK

Ponder this passage: "The LORD is slow to anger but great in power."

When you consider the word *power,* what comes to mind? Do you think of *power* as a positive or negative concept? Why?

When you consider God as powerful, is that positive or negative to you? Why? What's the difference between His being powerful and His being slow to anger, or patient? Does the patient factor change your feelings about His power? If so, in what way? What would the world be like if God were powerful and *impatient*?

Why is it important that God is patiently powerful?

PRAY

Spend a few minutes letting the idea of a God who is patient yet powerful rest in your mind. Then ask God what He wants you to know about His power today, right now.

Thank Him for His patience.

Thank Him for His power.

LIVE

Rest today in the midst of your schedule, comforted that the God you serve is both powerful and patient.

WHAT ARE YOU COUNTING ON?

NAHUM 3:14-17

14   Draw water for the siege;
strengthen your fortresses.
Step into the clay and tread the mortar;
take hold of the brick-mold!

15   The fire will devour you there;
the sword will cut you down.
It will devour you like the young locust.
Multiply yourselves like the young locust,
multiply like the swarming locust!

16   You have made your merchants
more numerous than the stars of the sky.
The young locust strips the land
and flies away.

17   Your court officials are like the swarming locust,
and your scribes like clouds of locusts,
which settle on the walls on a cold day;
when the sun rises, they take off,
and no one knows where they are.

READ

Read the passage slowly to yourself. Be aware that this sad passage describes the ancient city of Nineveh, which is doomed. Everything Nineveh counted on has fallen through.

THINK

Read the passage again, noting what Nineveh counted on to keep itself out of trouble.

Why is it so tempting to rely on economic prosperity (merchants and scribes) and the government (court officials)? (We even use phrases such as "having faith in" the stock market or "having faith in" government officials.)

What would your life look like if you relied on God for your future and your safety instead of on the economy or the government?

PRAY

Examine what you have that comes from the economy or the government, such as a job, streetlights, or a public library. Ask God to show you how much you count on these things and what counting on Him in a deeper way would mean.

LIVE

Imagine yourself living in a place where the economy and the government have fallen apart. What might you feel like if you relied totally on God?

SPEAKING OUR MINDS AND HEARTS

HABAKKUK 1:12-17

¹² Are You not from eternity, Yahweh my God?
My Holy One, You will not die.
LORD, You appointed them to execute judgment;
my Rock, You destined them to punish us.

¹³ Your eyes are too pure to look on evil,
and You cannot tolerate wrongdoing.
So why do You tolerate those who are treacherous?
Why are You silent
while one who is wicked swallows up
one who is more righteous than himself?

¹⁴ You have made mankind
like the fish of the sea,
like marine creatures that have no ruler.

¹⁵ The Chaldeans pull them all up with a hook,
catch them in their dragnet,
and gather them in their fishing net;
that is why they are glad and rejoice.

¹⁶ That is why they sacrifice to their dragnet
and burn incense to their fishing net,
for by these things their portion is rich
and their food plentiful.

¹⁷ Will they therefore empty their net
and continually slaughter nations without mercy?

READ

Read Habakkuk 1:12-17.

THINK

Sometimes we have a hard time being completely honest with God. But when we read certain passages of Scripture, such as in the Psalms and here in Habakkuk, we are encouraged to know that not only is God okay with our honesty, but He even invites it. Most prophets speak on behalf of God to us; Habakkuk speaks on behalf of us to God — and he does it with honesty that might make some people blush.

When you read Habakkuk's bold words — "So why do You tolerate those who are treacherous?" — how do you feel?

Does the same level of honesty in Habakkuk's words show up in you when you talk to God? Why or why not? Is that good or bad? What might happen in your life if you could speak to God with such honesty?

PRAY

Consider your life — your friendships, place in life, expectations, dreams, goals, hopes, job, school situation, and so on. About which of these areas do you wish you could speak honestly with God?

Take the risk and tell God exactly what's on your mind. Resist censoring yourself. Speak honestly and openly, assured that God is capable enough to handle your honesty.

LIVE

Know that God invites your honest communication with Him at all times because, above all, He wants your heart.

LIVE BY FAITH

HABAKKUK 2:1-4

1   I will stand at my guard post
and station myself on the lookout tower.
I will watch to see what He will say to me
and what I should reply about my complaint.

2 The LORD answered me:

Write down this vision;
clearly inscribe it on tablets
so one may easily read it.
3   For the vision is yet for the appointed time;
it testifies about the end and will not lie.
Though it delays, wait for it,
since it will certainly come and not be late.
4   Look, his ego is inflated;
he is without integrity.
But the righteous one will live by his faith.

READ

Read the passage aloud slowly, noting that this is a conversation between God and the prophet Habakkuk.

THINK

Habakkuk has just complained to God about the degraded life of Judah and asked God when He will act. In verse 1, Habakkuk insists on an answer, and verses 2-4 are the core of God's answer. Read the passage again with all this in mind.

1. What do you think of Habakkuk's questioning attitude? What does God seem to think of it?
2. In verses 2-4, God speaks to Habakkuk. What does God want Habakkuk to know or do?
3. Which of the words in this passage resonate most with you? Why do you think that is?

PRAY

Respond to God's statement "The righteous one will live by his faith." What does this make you want to say to God? To ask God?

LIVE

Rest in Habakkuk 2:20: "But the LORD is in His holy temple; let everyone on earth be silent in His presence."

REMEMBER MERCY

HABAKKUK 3:1-6

¹ A prayer of Habakkuk the prophet. According to *Shigionoth*.

2 LORD, I have heard the report about You;
LORD, I stand in awe of Your deeds.
Revive Your work in these years;
make it known in these years.
In Your wrath remember mercy!

3 God comes from Teman,
the Holy One from Mount Paran.   *Selah*
His splendor covers the heavens,
and the earth is full of His praise.
4 His brilliance is like light;
rays are flashing from His hand.
This is where His power is hidden.
5 Plague goes before Him,
and pestilence follows in His steps.
6 He stands and shakes the earth;
He looks and startles the nations.
The age-old mountains break apart;
the ancient hills sink down.
His pathways are ancient.

READ

Read Habakkuk's description of God's activities. As you do, let them remind you of actions and characteristics of God that have stood out to you as you've read stories of the Israelites in His Word.

THINK

Think about what it means to ask God to "revive Your work in these years." What was His work like before? How did He deal with Israel? What characterized His relationship with them?

PRAY

Picture Habakkuk inviting you to join him in his prayer that God would act toward you as He did toward Israel. What rises up in you when you consider this? Fear? Frustration? Hope? Explore this with God. What does it show you about your internal picture of Him? Of yourself?

LIVE

Sit silently with God and reexamine what has taken place during your time with Him today. Close with the following prayer: *Merciful God, shine Your light of truth into me in the coming weeks and months, that I might more clearly understand what You're like and how You see me. Let my fears and pride be exposed for what they are, and keep them from distorting my picture of who You are. Give me courage, that I might face my true self, and hope, that I might face You. Help me see in You what Habakkuk saw when he said, "In Your wrath remember mercy!" Amen.*

DAY 189

GOD ENCOUNTERS

On this seventh day, review and reflect on all you have read this week. Take the time to revel in the ways you've encountered God in the past six days.

THE BALANCE BETWEEN BEING JUST AND BEING MERCIFUL

ZEPHANIAH 1:7-11

⁷ Be silent in the presence of the Lord GOD,
for the Day of the LORD is near.
Indeed, the LORD has prepared a sacrifice;
He has consecrated His guests.

⁸ On the day of the LORD's sacrifice
I will punish the officials, the king's sons,
and all who are dressed in foreign clothing.
⁹ On that day I will punish
all who skip over the threshold,
who fill their master's house
with violence and deceit.

¹⁰ On that day —
this is the LORD's declaration —
there will be an outcry from the Fish Gate,
a wailing from the Second District,
and a loud crashing from the hills.
¹¹ Wail, you residents of the Hollow,
for all the merchants will be silenced;
all those loaded with silver will be cut off.

READ

Read these verses in a place that is absolutely quiet.

THINK

Many people see God as a God of comfort, guidance, and love. This image is not wrong, but it is incomplete. God is also a God of justice, one who becomes angry with our complacent and arrogant sin when we dump Him altogether.

How does the fact that God is a God of justice balance in your mind with the fact that God is also a God of mercy (as we know from other places in Scripture)?

Pause and consider areas of complacency and rebellion in your life. Wait and listen for the Holy Spirit to show you. In light of these areas, what do you feel about this God who says He loves you?

PRAY

In the midst of silence, continue searching your heart for recent thoughts and actions that have gone in direct opposition to what God desires for your life. Tell God how you are feeling deep within. He wants to hear from you. Verbalize specifically your rebellion against Him. Ask for His mercy. Ask Him to give you the proper understanding of the balance between His justice and His mercy in the world.

LIVE

When you are tempted to sin today, be aware of how your rebellion angers the heart of God.

GOD SHOWS UP

ZEPHANIAH 2:3,6-10

³ Seek the LORD, all you humble of the earth,
who carry out what He commands.
Seek righteousness, seek humility;
perhaps you will be concealed
on the day of the LORD's anger. . . .

⁶ The seacoast will become pasturelands
with caves for shepherds and folds for sheep.

⁷ The coastland will belong
to the remnant of the house of Judah;
they will find pasture there.
They will lie down in the evening
among the houses of Ashkelon,
for the LORD their God will return to them
and restore their fortunes.

⁸ I have heard the taunting of Moab
and the insults of the Ammonites,
who have taunted My people
and threatened their territory.

⁹ Therefore, as I live —
this is the declaration of the LORD of Hosts,
the God of Israel —
Moab will be like Sodom
and the Ammonites like Gomorrah —
a place overgrown with weeds,
a salt pit, and a perpetual wasteland.
The remnant of My people will plunder them;
the remainder of My nation will dispossess them.

¹⁰ This is what they get for their pride,
because they have taunted and acted arrogantly
against the people of the LORD of Hosts.

READ

Read the passage aloud slowly and silently.

You've probably experienced the wrath of a bully. The nation of Moab had been bullying the nation of Judah. In this passage God says that He plans to sweep in and save Judah. The encouraging words in verses 6-7 are spoken of Judah; verses 8-10 are indictments of Moab to defend Judah.

THINK

Read the passage again, noting the primary sins of Moab. As you read, grieve over their:

- cruelty, insults, and taunts
- put-downs, arrogance, and pride

In what ways do these two sets of sins feed off each other?

When have you experienced such treatment? In what way did God intervene to rescue you? If you don't feel that God did so, take this rescue of Judah and appropriate it for yourself. This isn't fantasy—God did rescue you in some way, even if you didn't realize it.

PRAY

Thank God for rescuing you and providing moments of pastureland in your life. Ask God if He wants to use you to rescue someone. Listen for His guidance in doing so.

LIVE

Sit quietly before God. Feel in your gut the sensation of humiliation at someone else's self-importance. Then feel in your gut the sensations of safety and rescue. Understand that you are reliving Judah's experience.

191

AT HOME IN GOD

ZEPHANIAH 3:9-13

⁹ For I will then restore
   pure speech to the peoples
   so that all of them may call
   on the name of Yahweh
   and serve Him with a single purpose.
¹⁰ From beyond the rivers of Cush
   My supplicants, My dispersed people,
   will bring an offering to Me.
¹¹ On that day you will not be put to shame
   because of everything you have done
   in rebelling against Me.
   For then I will remove
   your proud, arrogant people from among you,
   and you will never again be haughty
   on My holy mountain.
¹² I will leave
   a meek and humble people among you,
   and they will take refuge in the name of Yahweh.
¹³ The remnant of Israel will no longer
   do wrong or tell lies;
   a deceitful tongue will not be found
   in their mouths.
   But they will pasture and lie down,
   with nothing to make them afraid.

READ

Read this passage, carefully listening for what it tells you about sin's impact on our lives.

THINK

How does this passage fill out your perspective on sin — what it's like to live with it, and what it's like to live without it? How does our sin affect us? From Zephaniah's point of view, why does God want us not to sin?

PRAY

Reread Zephaniah's description of a life that is cleared of sin. How does it make you feel? Timid? Hopeful? Sad? Does it feel foreign and unfamiliar? Become aware of God's presence with you now, and expose to Him your response to this vision of life. Explore with Him why the passage makes you feel the way you do.

LIVE

Consider how God is responding to what you just shared with Him. Return to the question, Why does God want us not to sin? Again ponder Zephaniah's answer to this, and let it form your understanding of God's response to you now. What does God desire for you? What kind of life does He want you to have?

TURNAROUND NEEDED

HAGGAI 1:3-6,8-11

[3] The word of the LORD came through Haggai the prophet: [4] "Is it a time for you yourselves to live in your paneled houses, while this house lies in ruins?" [5] Now, the LORD of Hosts says this: "Think carefully about your ways:

[6]   You have planted much
       but harvested little.
       You eat
       but never have enough to be satisfied.
       You drink
       but never have enough to become drunk.
       You put on clothes
       but never have enough to get warm.
       The wage earner puts his wages
       into a bag with a hole in it. . . .

[8] "Go up into the hills, bring down lumber, and build the house. Then I will be pleased with it and be glorified," says the LORD. [9] "You expected much, but then it amounted to little. When you brought the harvest to your house, I ruined it. Why?" This is the declaration of the LORD of Hosts. "Because My house still lies in ruins, while each of you is busy with his own house.

[10]   So on your account,
       the skies have withheld the dew
       and the land its crops.
[11]   I have summoned a drought
       on the fields and the hills,
       on the grain, new wine, olive oil,
       and whatever the ground yields,
       on man and beast,
       and on all that your hands produce."

READ

Read the passage aloud slowly. God isn't demanding that the returned exiles (the Jews) change a thing or two. Their entire lives need a turnaround.

THINK

Read the passage aloud again.

1. How would you describe the turnaround God wants from the returned exiles?
2. How does stinginess affect one's mind so that a life of misery is inevitable?
3. How does this passage speak to you today?

PRAY

Talk to God about any stinginess in your soul. If you find none, look at any misery in your life and ask God to show you if it relates to a stingy, grudging attitude.

LIVE

Sit in the feeling of generosity. Imagine yourself joyously cutting timber, building walls, and honoring God. See yourself living your life this way.

GLORY AND PEACE IN GOD'S HOUSE

HAGGAI 2:1-9

¹ On the twenty-first day of the seventh month, the word of the LORD came through Haggai the prophet: ² "Speak to Zerubbabel son of Shealtiel, governor of Judah, to the high priest Joshua son of Jehozadak, and to the remnant of the people: ³ Who is left among you who saw this house in its former glory? How does it look to you now? Doesn't it seem like nothing to you? ⁴ Even so, be strong, Zerubbabel" — this is the LORD's declaration. "Be strong, Joshua son of Jehozadak, high priest. Be strong, all you people of the land" — this is the LORD's declaration. "Work! For I am with you" — the declaration of the LORD of Hosts. ⁵ "This is the promise I made to you when you came out of Egypt, and My Spirit is present among you; don't be afraid."

⁶ For the LORD of Hosts says this: "Once more, in a little while, I am going to shake the heavens and the earth, the sea and the dry land. ⁷ I will shake all the nations so that the treasures of all the nations will come, and I will fill this house with glory," says the LORD of Hosts. ⁸ "The silver and gold belong to Me" — this is the declaration of the LORD of Hosts. ⁹ "The final glory of this house will be greater than the first," says the LORD of Hosts. "I will provide peace in this place" — this is the declaration of the LORD of Hosts.

READ

Read the passage aloud, injecting the emotion of the characters as much as possible.

THINK

What stands out to you from the words of the LORD of Hosts? Perhaps it's God shaking all the nations so treasures will come, the word *afraid*, or the recurring "Be strong." What does this draw your attention to about yourself, about God, and about the glory and peace God desires His people to have?

PRAY/LIVE

Let your heart get caught up in pondering this insight for a while, as though you are playing with Play-Doh. Reshape two or three experiences (past or current) by the mold of this perspective, and see what they look like. Specifically, what in your life might be helped by this glory and peace?

Now listen for God's input on your current situation(s), remaining in the mold of glory and peace. In what areas might He want you to change your mind-set or take a particular action?

THE PROACTIVE NATURE OF GOD

ZECHARIAH 2:1-5,10-13

¹ I looked up and saw a man with a measuring line in his hand. ² I asked, "Where are you going?"

He answered me, "To measure Jerusalem to determine its width and length."

³ Then the angel who was speaking with me went out, and another angel went out to meet him. ⁴ He said to him, "Run and tell this young man: Jerusalem will be inhabited without walls because of the number of people and livestock in it." ⁵ The declaration of the LORD: "I will be a wall of fire around it, and I will be the glory within it. . . .

¹⁰ "Daughter Zion, shout for joy and be glad, for I am coming to dwell among you" — this is the LORD's declaration. ¹¹ "Many nations will join themselves to the LORD on that day and become My people. I will dwell among you, and you will know that the LORD of Hosts has sent Me to you. ¹² The LORD will take possession of Judah as His portion in the Holy Land, and He will once again choose Jerusalem. ¹³ Let all people be silent before the LORD, for He is coming from His holy dwelling."

READ

Read the passage.

THINK

The prophet Zechariah receives several visions from God and writes about them in detail at the beginning of his book. Take the next several minutes to ponder this vision. In the interaction God says, "Daughter Zion, shout for joy and be glad, for I am coming to dwell among you" (verse 10). Consider God's incredible plan to send His Son, Jesus, to live among us. What comes to mind as you think about God's pursuing His people enough to move literally into their neighborhood?

"Let all people be silent before the LORD, for He is coming from His holy dwelling" (verse 13). What fills your mind as you consider that God is active in human history? How is that reality different from what other people, the media, and our culture say about God's involvement in the world?

What does God's activity say about His character? How do you respond to this type of God?

PRAY

Allow the reality of a loving God pursuing His people, on the move and moving into your neighborhood, guide your prayers right now.

What would your world be like if God moved into the house, apartment, or building next door to you? Allow your communication with God to flow out of your thoughts.

LIVE

As you walk or drive in your neighborhood, consider the implications for your life of having God residing in your — our! — midst. And thank God for the fact that He actively pursues you.

DAY 196

GOD ENCOUNTERS

On this seventh day, review and reflect on all you have read this week. Take the time to revel in the ways you've encountered God in the past six days.

SHOW FAITHFUL LOVE AND COMPASSION

ZECHARIAH 7:4-10

⁴ Then the word of the LORD of Hosts came to me: ⁵ "Ask all the people of the land and the priests: When you fasted and lamented in the fifth and in the seventh months for these 70 years, did you really fast for Me? ⁶ When you eat and drink, don't you eat and drink simply for yourselves? ⁷ Aren't these the words that the LORD proclaimed through the earlier prophets when Jerusalem was inhabited and secure, along with its surrounding cities, and when the southern region and the Judean foothills were inhabited?"

⁸ The word of the LORD came to Zechariah: ⁹ "The LORD of Hosts says this: Make fair decisions. Show faithful love and compassion to one another. ¹⁰ Do not oppress the widow or the fatherless, the foreigner or the poor, and do not plot evil in your hearts against one another."

READ

Read the passage aloud slowly.

THINK

Read the passage aloud again.

1. If God were looking directly at you and saying these verses, what would He mean by the phrase "did you really fast for Me?"
2. Who do you know needing justice, love, and compassion?
3. Which of your religious activities do you think might merely be meeting your own selfish needs? Examine them.

PRAY

Thank God for being interested in people. Admit any ideas you have that God is mostly interested in church programs and what church people are supposed to do.

LIVE

Imagine God being interested in you just because you're you. Now imagine God being interested in someone you don't find interesting. Wonder at that.

ANNULLING THE COVENANT

ZECHARIAH 11:4-11

⁴ Yahweh my God says this: "Shepherd the flock intended for slaughter. ⁵ Those who buy them slaughter them but are not punished. Those who sell them say: Praise the LORD because I have become rich! Even their own shepherds have no compassion for them. ⁶ Indeed, I will no longer have compassion on the inhabitants of the land"—this is the LORD's declaration. "Instead, I will turn everyone over to his neighbor and his king. They will devastate the land, and I will not deliver it from them."

⁷ So I shepherded the flock intended for slaughter, the afflicted of the flock. I took two staffs, calling one Favor and the other Union, and I shepherded the flock. ⁸ In one month I got rid of three shepherds. I became impatient with them, and they also detested me. ⁹ Then I said, "I will no longer shepherd you. Let what is dying die, and let what is going astray go astray; let the rest devour each other's flesh." ¹⁰ Next I took my staff called Favor and cut it in two, annulling the covenant I had made with all the peoples. ¹¹ It was annulled on that day, and so the afflicted of the flock who were watching me knew that it was the word of the LORD.

READ

Read the passage several times slowly, until you begin to grasp the symbolism and what's going on.

THINK

When you consider the consequences God allows to come to Israel for their continual disobedience to Him, what stands out to you? Why do you think God would allow such horrible things to happen to them? What does this have to do with you?

PRAY

Read the passage again, prayerfully. What about God does it highlight? What words or actions especially draw your attention when you consider your life in light of this passage?

LIVE

Consider the following extract from Jan Karon's *These High, Green Hills*:

> "There's something I've been wanting to ask you, Father," said
> Nurse Kennedy, walking with him along the hall.
> "Shoot."
> "Why is it God so often breaks our hearts?"
> "Well, sometimes He does it to increase our faith. That's the
> way He stretches us. But there's another reason, I think, why our
> hearts get broken."
> She looked at him.
> "Usually," he said, "what breaks is what's brittle."[12]

In what area has your heart become brittle toward God? Have you been trying to protect your heart from Him? If so, why? Don't put pressure on yourself to change this: There is probably some reason you have felt the need to protect yourself. But today, with God's help, become aware of it, and explore with Him what might happen if you trust Him with that area of your heart.

A REMINDER OF GOD'S MESSAGE OF LOVE

MALACHI 1:1-5

¹ An oracle: The word of the LORD to Israel through Malachi.

² "I have loved you," says the LORD.

But you ask: "How have You loved us?"

"Wasn't Esau Jacob's brother?" This is the LORD's declaration. "Even so, I loved Jacob, ³ but I hated Esau. I turned his mountains into a wasteland, and gave his inheritance to the desert jackals."

⁴ Though Edom says: "We have been devastated, but we will rebuild the ruins," the LORD of Hosts says this: "They may build, but I will demolish. They will be called a wicked country and the people the LORD has cursed forever. ⁵ Your own eyes will see this, and you yourselves will say, 'The LORD is great, even beyond the borders of Israel.'"

READ

Before reading, close your eyes and pay attention to your breathing. After a few minutes of this silence, whisper, "God, I'm ready to hear from You now. Speak and I will listen."

Then turn to the book of Malachi and read the first five verses.

THINK

God's overriding message to His people, evident throughout all the books of Scripture, is this: "I love you." But our muddled and complex lives blur that message, and we forget the power of it. We need constant reminders of what's important in life, and history is an important reminder of God's incredible love for us. Looking back on the past can help provide the clarity and focus we've lost and give us back a God-minded perspective.

LIVE

Write out the ways God has been faithful to you in the past — big and small — through your relationships, your circumstances, your family, the blessings He has provided, important events, and so on.

Take as much time as you need.

PRAY

Reread verse 5: "Your own eyes will see this, and you yourselves will say, 'The LORD is great, even beyond the borders of Israel.'" Follow these instructions. Pray through your list line by line. Pour out your heart to God in unabashed gratefulness. Thank Him for His faithfulness throughout your life and throughout the lives of many others.

GIVE LIFE AND PEACE

MALACHI 2:5-10

[5] "My covenant with him was one of life and peace, and I gave these to him; it called for reverence, and he revered Me and stood in awe of My name. [6] True instruction was in his mouth, and nothing wrong was found on his lips. He walked with Me in peace and fairness and turned many from sin. [7] For the lips of a priest should guard knowledge, and people should seek instruction from his mouth, because he is the messenger of the LORD of Hosts.

[8] "You, on the other hand, have turned from the way. You have caused many to stumble by your instruction. You have violated the covenant of Levi," says the LORD of Hosts. [9] "So I in turn have made you despised and humiliated before all the people because you are not keeping My ways but are showing partiality in your instruction."

[10] Don't all of us have one Father? Didn't one God create us? Why then do we act treacherously against one another, profaning the covenant of our fathers?

READ

Read the passage aloud slowly.

THINK

Read the passage aloud again, but this time substitute the word *Christian* when the word *priest* appears, because Peter said, as he spoke to Christians, "But you are a chosen race, a royal priesthood, a holy nation, a people for His possession, so that you may proclaim the praises of the One who called you out of darkness into His marvelous light. Once you were not a people, but now you are God's people; you had not received mercy, but now you have received mercy" (1 Peter 2:9-10).

1. In what ways do you enjoy the work of a priest?

   ☐ giving life and peace
   ☐ keeping covenant with God
   ☐ honoring God and standing in reverent awe before God
   ☐ teaching truth and not lies
   ☐ walking with God in peace and fairness
   ☐ turning many from sin
   ☐ other:

2. In what ways do Christians "cause many to stumble" and "make themselves despised and humiliated," not living as God says and not teaching God's truth impartially?

3. In what areas of your life do you need more of God's help to be a priest for Him?

PRAY

Tell God how you feel about being "a royal priesthood." Admit your faults and doubts. Feel the joy of being used by God — even if you don't do it perfectly.

LIVE

Imagine God anointing you anew as a priest to give life to others and peace from God.

FIT FOR GOD

MALACHI 3:1-5

¹ "See, I am going to send My messenger, and he will clear the way before Me. Then the Lord you seek will suddenly come to His temple, the Messenger of the covenant you desire — see, He is coming," says the LORD of Hosts. ² But who can endure the day of His coming? And who will be able to stand when He appears? For He will be like a refiner's fire and like cleansing lye. ³ He will be like a refiner and purifier of silver; He will purify the sons of Levi and refine them like gold and silver. Then they will present offerings to the LORD in righteousness. ⁴ And the offerings of Judah and Jerusalem will please the LORD as in days of old and years gone by.

⁵ "I will come to you in judgment, and I will be ready to witness against sorcerers and adulterers; against those who swear falsely; against those who oppress the widow and the fatherless, and cheat the wage earner; and against those who deny justice to the foreigner. They do not fear Me," says the LORD of Hosts.

THINK

Saint Irenaeus once said, "The glory of God is man fully alive." For a few minutes, isolate the second half of this statement and think about what it means to be "fully alive." Have you ever felt this way? When? What were you doing?

READ

Now read the passage (including the expanded passage for background). Do the words *refiner* and *please* have positive or negative implications to you? How do they intermingle with your idea of being fully alive? Do they act like pins to a balloon? Or do they mesh organically into the bigger picture?

PRAY

With your understanding of being fully alive in one hand and your awareness of God's desire for your purity in the other, explore how much you do or do not see the two connecting. Maybe you can easily see God's presence with you in your picture of yourself fully alive, or maybe that's hard to do; maybe you think living fully must be done behind God's back. Be honest — even if you recognize that your beliefs are not true, tell the truth of what's in your heart.

LIVE

Sit quietly with God, opening yourself to what He might want to say in response to what you've shared with Him today. You might look back at the passage or reconsider Irenaeus's words. Wonder at the freedom intrinsic in someone who is fully alive *and* pure before God.

THE TESTAMENTS, OLD AND NEW

MATTHEW 2:1-6

¹ After Jesus was born in Bethlehem of Judea in the days of King Herod, wise men from the east arrived unexpectedly in Jerusalem, ² saying, "Where is He who has been born King of the Jews? For we saw His star in the east and have come to worship Him."

³ When King Herod heard this, he was deeply disturbed, and all Jerusalem with him. ⁴ So he assembled all the chief priests and scribes of the people and asked them where the Messiah would be born.

⁵ "In Bethlehem of Judea," they told him, "because this is what was written by the prophet:

⁶   And you, Bethlehem, in the land of Judah,
        are by no means least among the leaders of Judah:
        because out of you will come a leader
        who will shepherd My people Israel."

READ

Read the passage, trying to absorb the words from the perspective of a Jew who has never heard of Jesus before.

THINK

In his gospel, Matthew emphasizes the number of Old Testament prophecies fulfilled in the person of Jesus. The Jewish people longed to see the Messiah, the Anointed One, whom they had been expecting for several hundred years. Jesus, Matthew writes, is the one they had been waiting for.

Read the passage again, and note the Old Testament quotation. How do you feel, knowing that God orchestrated these happenings to point to Jesus?

What promises has God made to you, in Scripture or personally, that have yet to come to fruition? Do you wonder if they will ever be fulfilled?

How does Matthew's focus on Old Testament prophecies affect your situation? What implication does it have on your daily life?

PRAY

Take time to thank God for the promises He has kept in your life. Ask God to give you an extra measure of faith to trust Him when you feel He may never keep His other promises to you. Admit the specific areas where you have a hard time trusting that He will be faithful.

LIVE

God keeps His promises. Live in the truth that He is a promise keeper.

DAY 203
_____

GOD ENCOUNTERS

On this seventh day, review and reflect on all you have read this week. Take the time to revel in the ways you've encountered God in the past six days.

LIVE BEFORE GOD

MATTHEW 5:27-29,33-37

27 "You have heard that it was said, Do not commit adultery. 28 But I tell you, everyone who looks at a woman to lust for her has already committed adultery with her in his heart. 29 If your right eye causes you to sin, gouge it out and throw it away. For it is better that you lose one of the parts of your body than for your whole body to be thrown into hell. . . .

33 "Again, you have heard that it was said to our ancestors, You must not break your oath, but you must keep your oaths to the Lord. 34 But I tell you, don't take an oath at all: either by heaven, because it is God's throne; 35 or by the earth, because it is His footstool; or by Jerusalem, because it is the city of the great King. 36 Neither should you swear by your head, because you cannot make a single hair white or black. 37 But let your word 'yes' be 'yes,' and your 'no' be 'no.' Anything more than this is from the evil one."

READ

Read the passage aloud slowly.

THINK

Imagine yourself going to the mailbox today and finding in it a letter addressed to you, containing the words of this passage. Think of yourself opening the letter. Then read the passage aloud again, and as you do, see yourself walking back from the mailbox.

1. What meaning do the words have for you? What is Jesus getting at?
2. How do you pretend this is easier than it really is regarding having a pure thought life? Regarding really meaning what you say?
3. How do these commands speak to the deepest part of you, the part Jesus wants?

PRAY

Ask Jesus to show you situations in which you are likely to say something you don't mean. Ask Him to help you discover what that's about — perhaps impressing people or pretending to be better than you are.

LIVE

Jesus understands how difficult His words are for us. Sense yourself being pulled along with love and grace by Jesus.

PRAY WITH SIMPLICITY

MATTHEW 6:5-13

5 "Whenever you pray, you must not be like the hypocrites, because they love to pray standing in the synagogues and on the street corners to be seen by people. I assure you: They've got their reward! 6 But when you pray, go into your private room, shut your door, and pray to your Father who is in secret. And your Father who sees in secret will reward you. 7 When you pray, don't babble like the idolaters, since they imagine they'll be heard for their many words. 8 Don't be like them, because your Father knows the things you need before you ask Him.

9 "Therefore, you should pray like this:

> Our Father in heaven,
> Your name be honored as holy.
> 10 Your kingdom come.
> Your will be done
> on earth as it is in heaven.
> 11 Give us today our daily bread.
> 12 And forgive us our debts,
> as we also have forgiven our debtors.
> 13 And do not bring us into temptation,
> but deliver us from the evil one.
> [For Yours is the kingdom and the power
> and the glory forever. Amen.]"

READ

Read the passage aloud slowly, noticing what it says about simple prayer versus complex, showy prayer. What is the most important issue for you listed below? Be honest.

Simple Prayer	Complex, Showy Prayer
finding a private place	turning prayer into a public scene
praying to the Father in secret	making a regular show of prayers
using simple, sincere words	using a lot of showy words
watching the focus shift from you to God	using techniques to get what you want from God

THINK

Read the passage again. This time, picture yourself sitting with other people about six feet from Jesus and listening as He says these words. When does Jesus look directly at you as He teaches? What words is He saying because He knows you need them? Why are those words meant for you?

PRAY

Paraphrase the Lord's Prayer (verses 9-13). In other words, add to or change each phrase in a way that makes the prayer specific to you.

LIVE

Sit quietly before God, praying the Lord's Prayer if you wish, or just being silent. Feel the focus shift from you to God. Enjoy that.

AN INVITATION

MATTHEW 9:9-13

⁹ As Jesus went on from there, He saw a man named Matthew sitting at the tax office, and He said to him, "Follow Me!" So he got up and followed Him.

¹⁰ While He was reclining at the table in the house, many tax collectors and sinners came as guests to eat with Jesus and His disciples. ¹¹ When the Pharisees saw this, they asked His disciples, "Why does your Teacher eat with tax collectors and sinners?"

¹² But when He heard this, He said, "Those who are well don't need a doctor, but the sick do. ¹³ Go and learn what this means: I desire mercy and not sacrifice. For I didn't come to call the righteous, but sinners."

READ

Once you are in a quiet place, thank God for the gift of His Word. Then read the passage.

THINK

When have you felt like the outsider? When have people scrutinized and criticized you for the people you associated with? Do you think their judgment was fair? Why or why not?

Ponder these words from Jesus: "I desire mercy and not sacrifice. For I didn't come to call the righteous, but sinners." Where do you think Jesus was going with this statement?

If you were present that day, how might have you responded?

PRAY

Hold your hands open in front of you. Sit in silence for several moments, staring at them. Invite the Holy Spirit to guide your life today. Pray that your hands will be a physical representation of what you desire your heart to be. Acknowledge that you are a physical open invitation to the Holy Spirit for His guidance toward paths of mercy, not religiosity. Ask Him to bring to mind outsiders to whom you can show mercy today.

LIVE

As you are reminded of God's mercy on your life, take the risk of showing mercy to outsiders.

JESUS THE HEALER

MATTHEW 9:18-26

[18] As He was telling them these things, suddenly one of the leaders came and knelt down before Him, saying, "My daughter is near death, but come and lay Your hand on her, and she will live." [19] So Jesus and His disciples got up and followed him.

[20] Just then, a woman who had suffered from bleeding for 12 years approached from behind and touched the tassel on His robe, [21] for she said to herself, "If I can just touch His robe, I'll be made well!"

[22] But Jesus turned and saw her. "Have courage, daughter," He said. "Your faith has made you well." And the woman was made well from that moment.

[23] When Jesus came to the leader's house, He saw the flute players and a crowd lamenting loudly. [24] "Leave," He said, "because the girl isn't dead, but sleeping." And they started laughing at Him. [25] But when the crowd had been put outside, He went in and took her by the hand, and the girl got up. [26] And this news spread throughout that whole area.

READ

Read the passage.

THINK/PRAY

Pick the episode that is more striking to you — either the healing of the hemorrhaging woman or the raising of the official's daughter. (If you choose the first story, read Leviticus 15:25-30 now to better understand her situation.)

Read the passage again, carefully. Immerse yourself in the story as though you are a character in it — an observer or one named in the passage. Use every sense to enter the scene; take part in each moment. Where are you in relation to others? To Jesus? What is it like for you to be there? How are you feeling?

After you exit the scene, talk with Jesus about what you saw and experienced.

LIVE

Think about your experience in the scene, as well as your discussion with Jesus, and jot down anything you want to remember.

Put your pen aside and sit quietly for a few minutes. Listen to the sound of your own breathing and the silence.

End by saying the Lord's Prayer aloud: "Our Father in heaven, Your name be honored as holy. Your kingdom come. Your will be done on earth as it is in heaven. Give us today our daily bread. And forgive us our debts, as we also have forgiven our debtors. And do not bring us into temptation, but deliver us from the evil one. [For Yours is the kingdom and the power and the glory forever. Amen]" (Matthew 6:9-13).

TAKE UP MY YOKE

MATTHEW 11:28-30

[28] "Come to Me, all of you who are weary and burdened, and I will give you rest. [29] All of you, take up My yoke and learn from Me, because I am gentle and humble in heart, and you will find rest for yourselves. [30] For My yoke is easy and My burden is light."

READ

Read the passage slowly.

THINK

Read the passage again, listening for the words or phrases that stand out to you, such as:

- "come to Me"
- "give you rest"
- "learn from Me"
- "I am gentle"
- "you will find rest"
- "My burden is light"

Notice the many different ways Jesus says, "Hang out with Me." Which one do you find most inviting? Why?

What would it feel like to take Jesus' yoke and learn from Him? It's okay to be honest; "find rest for yourselves" may not describe what you think it would really be like. Instead you might think it would be forced and difficult. If so, what would you *desire* for it to be like?

Have you feared that it might require heavy or ill-fitting things? What are they?

PRAY

Jesus speaks very personally and conversationally in this passage, using phrases like "Come to Me." In fact, *I, Me,* or *My* occurs seven times, and *you* occurs five times. So consider that Jesus has been talking to *you.* What is your reply? What do you need to discuss with Jesus today?

LIVE

As you begin to take up Jesus' yoke and walk with Him, turn these words from Jesus over in your mind: *gentle, humble in heart, rest, easy, light.*

SEEING AND HEARING

MATTHEW 13:10-17

¹⁰ Then the disciples came up and asked Him, "Why do You speak to them in parables?"

¹¹ He answered them, "Because the secrets of the kingdom of heaven have been given for you to know, but it has not been given to them. ¹² For whoever has, more will be given to him, and he will have more than enough. But whoever does not have, even what he has will be taken away from him. ¹³ For this reason I speak to them in parables, because looking they do not see, and hearing they do not listen or understand. ¹⁴ Isaiah's prophecy is fulfilled in them, which says:

> You will listen and listen,
> yet never understand;
> and you will look and look,
> yet never perceive.
> ¹⁵   For this people's heart has grown callous;
> their ears are hard of hearing,
> and they have shut their eyes;
> otherwise they might see with their eyes
> and hear with their ears,
> understand with their hearts
> and turn back —
> and I would cure them.

¹⁶ "But your eyes are blessed because they do see, and your ears because they do hear! ¹⁷ For I assure you: Many prophets and righteous people longed to see the things you see yet didn't see them; to hear the things you hear yet didn't hear them."

READ

Read the passage carefully.

THINK

Notice what Jesus says about human hearts. What does He draw attention to about our receptivity to His message? How does He deal with our resistance? What does He want for us?

Now read Jesus' words again, and hear them as if He is saying them to you personally. Meditate on His words until the message becomes familiar. What stands out that relates to your life?

PRAY

Tell Jesus about your meditation — your thoughts and feelings. Listen for His response.

LIVE

Search your memory (or your journal) for any insights God has given you in recent weeks as you have interacted with His Word. What have those truths led you to do? Were there times when God invited you to act on or think about something, but you ignored the request or put it off? Why? Revisit that experience with Jesus. Remember that His greatest desire is not to get you to act a certain way but to engage with you in relationship.

DAY 210

GOD ENCOUNTERS

On this seventh day, review and reflect on all you have read this week. Take the time to revel in the ways you've encountered God in the past six days.

A MATTER OF THE HEART

MATTHEW 15:1-14

¹ Then Pharisees and scribes came from Jerusalem to Jesus and asked, ² "Why do Your disciples break the tradition of the elders? For they don't wash their hands when they eat!"

³ He answered them, "And why do you break God's commandment because of your tradition? ⁴ For God said:

> Honor your father and your mother; and,
> The one who speaks evil of father or mother
> must be put to death.

⁵ But you say, 'Whoever tells his father or mother, "Whatever benefit you might have received from me is a gift committed to the temple" — ⁶ he does not have to honor his father.' In this way, you have revoked God's word because of your tradition. ⁷ Hypocrites! Isaiah prophesied correctly about you when he said:

> ⁸ These people honor Me with their lips,
>   but their heart is far from Me.
> ⁹ They worship Me in vain,
>   teaching as doctrines the commands of men."

¹⁰ Summoning the crowd, He told them, "Listen and understand: ¹¹ It's not what goes into the mouth that defiles a man, but what comes out of the mouth, this defiles a man."

¹² Then the disciples came up and told Him, "Do You know that the Pharisees took offense when they heard this statement?"

¹³ He replied, "Every plant that My heavenly Father didn't plant will be uprooted. ¹⁴ Leave them alone! They are blind guides. And if the blind guide the blind, both will fall into a pit."

READ

Sit at a table with this devotional. Read this passage with your palms open as a way of communicating that you are open to hear from God.

THINK

Jesus seems to spend a lot of time provoking the Pharisees by speaking harshly to them. Of all the religious groups in Israel, Jesus rebukes the Pharisees the most. And yet, these are supposed to be the most devout leaders in the entire nation. Joining Jesus in bashing the Pharisees is tempting. Thinking *I'm glad I'm not like them* is easy. But we often resemble the Pharisees more than we'd like to admit.

Think back and identify a time when your heart responded to Jesus the way the Pharisees responded to Him. What might help you identify the moments when your heart is more Pharisee-like than Jesus-like? Who can you invite to help keep your heart in check?

Ponder the words Matthew quotes from Isaiah (verses 8-9). Under what circumstances does this describe you? What do you think God wants you to do about it?

PRAY

Ask God to give you a Jesus-like heart, one that is humble, transparent, and genuine.

LIVE

Invite others to help you keep your heart in check by giving them permission to ask you tough heart questions.

THE SOFTENED HEART

MATTHEW 19:3-9

³ Some Pharisees approached Him to test Him. They asked, "Is it lawful for a man to divorce his wife on any grounds?"

⁴ "Haven't you read," He replied, "that He who created them in the beginning made them male and female," ⁵ and He also said:

> "For this reason a man will leave
> his father and mother
> and be joined to his wife,
> and the two will become one flesh?

⁶ So they are no longer two, but one flesh. Therefore, what God has joined together, man must not separate."

⁷ "Why then," they asked Him, "did Moses command us to give divorce papers and to send her away?"

⁸ He told them, "Moses permitted you to divorce your wives because of the hardness of your hearts. But it was not like that from the beginning. ⁹ And I tell you, whoever divorces his wife, except for sexual immorality, and marries another, commits adultery."

READ

Read the passage aloud slowly. Consider that this teaching is an example Jesus gave from a longer teaching about forgiveness.

THINK

Matthew recorded this to come just after Jesus telling the parable about the servant who is forgiven a great deal and cannot forgive someone who has harmed him only slightly.

Imagine that you are there as Jesus is teaching. You've heard his parable about the unforgiving servant, and now He speaks of people being hardhearted. As you read the passage again, consider that we divorce ourselves from people in many ways: leaving a church, leaving a project, leaving a friendship. (If you wish, read Matthew 18:23-35 or try to recall the parable of the unforgiving servant. Try to feel for yourself that servant's incredible hardheartedness.)

1. What is hardheartedness really about?
2. How does hardheartedness toward others violate God's will for all of us?
3. Where in your life is hardheartedness a problem?
4. What is God urging you to do to cultivate a softened heart?

PRAY

Ask God to bring to mind those who might want to plead with you, "Be patient with me" (Matthew 18:26,29). Try to picture yourself having mercy on this person. If it seems impossible, ask God to pour out His love into your heart.

LIVE

Sit quietly before God. Become hardhearted — how does this feel in your body? Become softhearted — how does that feel in your body? Stay with the softheartedness for several minutes.

JESUS DROVE THEM OUT

MATTHEW 21:12-17

[12] Jesus went into the temple complex and drove out all those buying and selling in the temple. He overturned the money changers' tables and the chairs of those selling doves. [13] And He said to them, "It is written, My house will be called a house of prayer. But you are making it a den of thieves!"

[14] The blind and the lame came to Him in the temple complex, and He healed them. [15] When the chief priests and the scribes saw the wonders that He did and the children shouting in the temple complex, "*Hosanna* to the Son of David!" they were indignant [16] and said to Him, "Do You hear what these children are saying?"

"Yes," Jesus told them. "Have you never read:

> You have prepared praise
> from the mouths of children and nursing infants?"

[17] Then He left them, went out of the city to Bethany, and spent the night there.

READ

Read the passage aloud.

THINK/PRAY

Imagine you are there when Jesus comes in the temple and cleanses it. To get your imagination going, read the passage a second time, but then set this book aside, close your eyes, and see yourself as a part of the scene.

Who are you? Where are you? Smell the incense and the scent of burning, sacrificed animal flesh. Jump at the loud crash of the tables and the fury in Jesus' voice as the sounds echo in the stunned silence. What are the expressions on the faces around you?

Now let the blind and crippled come into your view. Watch Jesus healing them. Listen to the voices of the children as they play and shout, "Hosanna!" What's your reaction to them? To Jesus' interaction with the disabled? To the indignation of the religious leaders? (Include not only your mental reaction but your physical reaction too, if any.)

Now follow Jesus as He walks out of the city, still fuming. Picture Him initiating a conversation with you about the events of the day. Imagine that He asks you what it was like. Tell Him.

LIVE

In C. S. Lewis's *The Lion, the Witch and the Wardrobe,* the lion, Aslan, "isn't safe. But he's good."[13]

Consider this statement in light of what you've just read about Jesus. How does this view of Jesus — that He sometimes does things that are painful to us — alter your perception of who He is? In what ways does this affect how you relate to Him?

THE LEAST OF THESE

MATTHEW 25:31-40

³¹ "When the Son of Man comes in His glory, and all the angels with Him, then He will sit on the throne of His glory. ³² All the nations will be gathered before Him, and He will separate them one from another, just as a shepherd separates the sheep from the goats. ³³ He will put the sheep on His right and the goats on the left. ³⁴ Then the King will say to those on His right, 'Come, you who are blessed by My Father, inherit the kingdom prepared for you from the foundation of the world.

> ³⁵ For I was hungry
> and you gave Me something to eat;
> I was thirsty
> and you gave Me something to drink;
> I was a stranger and you took Me in;
> ³⁶ I was naked and you clothed Me;
> I was sick and you took care of Me;
> I was in prison and you visited Me.'

³⁷ "Then the righteous will answer Him, 'Lord, when did we see You hungry and feed You, or thirsty and give You something to drink? ³⁸ When did we see You a stranger and take You in, or without clothes and clothe You? ³⁹ When did we see You sick, or in prison, and visit You?'

⁴⁰ "And the King will answer them, 'I assure you: Whatever you did for one of the least of these brothers of Mine, you did for Me.'"

READ

Read the passage aloud slowly. As you read it, understand that Jesus said these words aloud too. They are His words.

THINK

This is a part of an entire sermon (or thematic sermon series) on watchfulness (see Matthew 23–25). The people in this passage were watching for the needy, but they didn't know it was Jesus they were watching. Read the passage again silently and slowly.

1. What words or phrases stand out to you?
2. Who are the overlooked and ignored in your life?
3. Imagine yourself overlooked and ignored. What do you now have in common with Jesus?
4. In what ways is God asking you to give someone food, drink, a room, clothes; to stop and visit someone; to go to a person locked away physically, emotionally, or mentally?

PRAY

Ask Jesus how He exists in the overlooked and ignored. Ponder this mystery. Ask Him to show you your next step in grasping some part of this.

LIVE

As you serve people who are overlooked and ignored, be mindful of the presence of Jesus. See if you can spot Him.

MY GOD, WHY?

MATTHEW 27:45-54

⁴⁵ From noon until three in the afternoon darkness came over the whole land. ⁴⁶ About three in the afternoon Jesus cried out with a loud voice, *"Elí, Elí, lemá sabachtháni?"* that is, "My God, My God, why have You forsaken Me?"

⁴⁷ When some of those standing there heard this, they said, "He's calling for Elijah!"

⁴⁸ Immediately one of them ran and got a sponge, filled it with sour wine, fixed it on a reed, and offered Him a drink. ⁴⁹ But the rest said, "Let's see if Elijah comes to save Him!"

⁵⁰ Jesus shouted again with a loud voice and gave up His spirit. ⁵¹ Suddenly, the curtain of the sanctuary was split in two from top to bottom; the earth quaked and the rocks were split. ⁵² The tombs were also opened and many bodies of the saints who had fallen asleep were raised. ⁵³ And they came out of the tombs after His resurrection, entered the holy city, and appeared to many.

⁵⁴ When the centurion and those with him, who were guarding Jesus, saw the earthquake and the things that had happened, they were terrified and said, "This man really was God's Son!"

READ

If you have time, read Matthew 26:31–27:56. If not, read the shorter passage.

THINK

Church historian Bruce Shelley wrote, "Christianity is the only major religion to have as its central event the humiliation of its God."[14] Consider not only that Jesus' humiliation is immense, but His anguish is deeper than we can imagine. His own people wildly demanded His death. His friends deserted Him. And now even His intimately loving Father has turned away.

Spend time wrestling heart and mind with why the Almighty would choose such a path. Reread Jesus' own words a few times to get closer to His experience.

PRAY

What wells up inside you as you spend time with the paradox of Jesus' death? Wonder? Grief? Distractedness? Tell Jesus about what surfaces. Then gently pull your thoughts back to His sacrifice and death, reading the passage again if you need to. Allow yourself to sink into the event deeply, again being aware of your reaction and talking to Jesus about it.

LIVE

Find a new place to be silent. For example, walk in a quiet place or sit in an empty church sanctuary. Bring your wristwatch or cell phone and set the alarm so you can forget the time until it reminds you. Meditate on Jesus' sacrifice for you, then wait for what He would have you receive from Him.

PARALYZED AND DESPERATE

MARK 2:1-12

¹ When He entered Capernaum again after some days, it was reported that He was at home. ² So many people gathered together that there was no more room, not even in the doorway, and He was speaking the message to them. ³ Then they came to Him bringing a paralytic, carried by four men. ⁴ Since they were not able to bring him to Jesus because of the crowd, they removed the roof above where He was. And when they had broken through, they lowered the mat on which the paralytic was lying.

⁵ Seeing their faith, Jesus told the paralytic, "Son, your sins are forgiven."

⁶ But some of the scribes were sitting there, thinking to themselves: ⁷ "Why does He speak like this? He's blaspheming! Who can forgive sins but God alone?"

⁸ Right away Jesus understood in His spirit that they were thinking like this within themselves and said to them, "Why are you thinking these things in your hearts? ⁹ Which is easier: to say to the paralytic, 'Your sins are forgiven,' or to say, 'Get up, pick up your mat, and walk'? ¹⁰ But so you may know that the Son of Man has authority on earth to forgive sins," He told the paralytic, ¹¹ "I tell you: get up, pick up your mat, and go home."

¹² Immediately he got up, picked up the mat, and went out in front of everyone. As a result, they were all astounded and gave glory to God, saying, "We have never seen anything like this!"

READ

Ask a friend or family member to read the verses aloud to you. Close your eyes and listen intently.

THINK

Imagine yourself in the story, referring to the text again as much as you need to. For a few minutes each, place yourself in the skins of the different individuals. Consider yourself on the roof with the four friends and the paralytic. Become the crippled man on the mat. Think of yourself as one of the four friends. Imagine yourself as someone standing in the crowded room of the house, able to easily see and hear the scribes. And consider yourself the owner of the house.

With which person in the story do you identify the most? Why?

PRAY

Imagine yourself again as the paralytic lying on his stretcher. Jesus looks at you and says, "Son, your sins are forgiven." What is the expression on His face? What is the tone of His voice? What are you feeling when you hear those words?

Talk to Jesus about His actions and your reactions — mental, emotional, physical, spiritual.

LIVE

Consider those people around you who need a life-altering interaction with Jesus. What might you need to do to bring them to the feet of Jesus, even if it means making a big sacrifice for them?

DAY 217

GOD ENCOUNTERS

On this seventh day, review and reflect on all you have read this week. Take the time to revel in the ways you've encountered God in the past six days.

TELLING YOUR WHOLE STORY

MARK 5:25-34

²⁵ A woman suffering from bleeding for 12 years ²⁶ had endured much under many doctors. She had spent everything she had and was not helped at all. On the contrary, she became worse. ²⁷ Having heard about Jesus, she came behind Him in the crowd and touched His robe. ²⁸ For she said, "If I can just touch His robes, I'll be made well!" ²⁹ Instantly her flow of blood ceased, and she sensed in her body that she was cured of her affliction.

³⁰ At once Jesus realized in Himself that power had gone out from Him. He turned around in the crowd and said, "Who touched My robes?"

³¹ His disciples said to Him, "You see the crowd pressing against You, and You say, 'Who touched Me?'"

³² So He was looking around to see who had done this. ³³ Then the woman, knowing what had happened to her, came with fear and trembling, fell down before Him, and told Him the whole truth. ³⁴ "Daughter," He said to her, "your faith has made you well. Go in peace and be free from your affliction."

READ

Read the passage aloud slowly.

THINK

Read the passage again, putting yourself in the place of the woman. (If it helps to imagine yourself instead as a man with an oozing sore, that's fine.)

1. From where did you get the courage to come behind Jesus and touch His clothes?
2. When Jesus looks at you, how do you feel?
3. How does it feel for you to tell Jesus your story — and for Him to listen so well? (Read in the expanded passage how He also listens well when He has a little girl to heal.)
4. How does it feel to be complimented publicly by this holy man?

PRAY

Tell Jesus the "whole truth" about something that's troubling you. Kneel as the woman did. Let the eyes of Jesus rest on you and bless you.

LIVE

Get up from your kneeling position and then sit or stand. Close your eyes and sense that you are living well, living blessed.

FALLING AT HIS FEET

MARK 7:24-30

²⁴ He got up and departed from there to the region of Tyre and Sidon. He entered a house and did not want anyone to know it, but He could not escape notice. ²⁵ Instead, immediately after hearing about Him, a woman whose little daughter had an unclean spirit came and fell at His feet. ²⁶ Now the woman was Greek, a Syrophoenician by birth, and she kept asking Him to drive the demon out of her daughter. ²⁷ He said to her, "Allow the children to be satisfied first, because it isn't right to take the children's bread and throw it to the dogs."

²⁸ But she replied to Him, "Lord, even the dogs under the table eat the children's crumbs."

²⁹ Then He told her, "Because of this reply, you may go. The demon has gone out of your daughter." ³⁰ When she went back to her home, she found her child lying on the bed, and the demon was gone.

READ

Read the expanded passage to get the big picture in which this incident occurs. As you do, identify with Jesus' disciples: Witness His amazing miracles. Feel the exhaustion of not even having time to eat. See the people constantly pressing in on all sides.

Now reread the shorter passage. What is your reaction to the Greek woman's request? How do you feel when Jesus initially turns her down? When He changes His mind?

THINK

Pause to allow the Holy Spirit to help you understand what your initial reactions tell you about your heart.

Then take a moment to look more closely at this woman. What tensions, concerns, and frustrations fill her daily life? What do you see in her face when she's told to "allow the children to be satisfied first"? When she replies? What does she feel when she sees her healed daughter?

Maybe at the end of this meditation you see things in a new light. In what ways does your new perspective mingle with your first reaction?

PRAY/LIVE

Become aware of Jesus in the room with you now, inviting you to talk with Him about what today's passage was like for you. Don't hide feelings and thoughts that have surfaced within you, but openly share with Him any questions, frustrations, or concerns you have. What does Jesus want you to see today? What does He want you to know? Spend several minutes in silence considering what you've experienced.

HEARTSTRINGS

MARK 10:17-22

¹⁷ As He was setting out on a journey, a man ran up, knelt down before Him, and asked Him, "Good Teacher, what must I do to inherit eternal life?"

¹⁸ "Why do you call Me good?" Jesus asked him. "No one is good but One — God. ¹⁹ You know the commandments:

> Do not murder;
> do not commit adultery;
> do not steal;
> do not bear false witness;
> do not defraud;
> honor your father and mother."

²⁰ He said to Him, "Teacher, I have kept all these from my youth."

²¹ Then, looking at him, Jesus loved him and said to him, "You lack one thing: Go, sell all you have and give to the poor, and you will have treasure in heaven. Then come, follow Me." ²² But he was stunned at this demand, and he went away grieving, because he had many possessions.

READ

Pick a pace and read this passage quickly. Read it again at a different pace. Did you notice anything different the second time?

THINK

Write down your thoughts about this story. How are you similar to the rich man? How are you different?

Jesus knows that, though the rich man is morally good, he still has strings attached to his heart that will keep him from being a devoted follower.

Take an internal inventory of your heart. What things are deeply attached to your heart that must be relinquished for you to be a whole-hearted follower of Jesus? They may be possessions, but they may also be thoughts, relationships, activities, and so on.

Later in the chapter, Jesus says this about anyone's chance of getting into God's kingdom: "With men it is impossible, but not with God, because all things are possible with God" (verse 27). Based on these words from Jesus, write in your own words a description of the grace God offers to each one of us.

PRAY

Reflect on God's grace. Thank God for the grace He extends to you. Confess the times when you have abused His grace. Offer God the strings of your heart, those things that keep you from completely following Jesus. Ask God to help you sever those strings and replace them with fray-proof connections to Him.

LIVE

220

Live in freedom and follow Jesus.

THE BIG PICTURE

MARK 12:28-34

²⁸ One of the scribes approached. When he heard them debating and saw that Jesus answered them well, he asked Him, "Which command is the most important of all?"

²⁹ "This is the most important," Jesus answered:

Listen, Israel! The Lord our God, the Lord is One. ³⁰ Love the Lord your God with all your heart, with all your soul, with all your mind, and with all your strength.

³¹ "The second is: Love your neighbor as yourself. There is no other command greater than these."

³² Then the scribe said to Him, "You are right, Teacher! You have correctly said that He is One, and there is no one else except Him. ³³ And to love Him with all your heart, with all your understanding, and with all your strength, and to love your neighbor as yourself, is far more important than all the burnt offerings and sacrifices."

³⁴ When Jesus saw that he answered intelligently, He said to him, "You are not far from the kingdom of God." And no one dared to question Him any longer.

READ

Read the passage aloud slowly.

THINK

Put yourself in the place of the scribe. You have studied theology and can explain its intricate details. You are weary with how most scholars argue over minor issues. You've come to Jesus to ask Him to give you the big picture. Read the passage again, letting Jesus answer you directly.

Be impressed with Jesus' answer: He has combined part of the often-repeated *Shema Israel* (see Deuteronomy 6:4-9) with the last part of a much less quoted command: "Do not take revenge or bear a grudge against members of your community, but love your neighbor as yourself; I am Yahweh" (Leviticus 19:18).

Consider an issue you've been puzzling over, a decision you need to make, or an approach you need to take with a difficult person. How does Jesus' simple but majestic summary help you?

PRAY

Ask God to help you love Him "with all your heart, with all your soul, with all your mind, and with all your strength." Take one at a time, if you wish. Then consider someone you know. Ask God to help you love that person the way you already love yourself. (You feed yourself, you clothe yourself, you give yourself a place to live — that's love.)

LIVE

Picture Jesus saying to you, "Love the Lord God with all your heart, soul, mind, and strength. Love others as you love yourself." Don't take this as a scolding but as the best, wisest thing any person could do.

PETER'S ANGUISH

MARK 14:66-72

⁶⁶ While Peter was in the courtyard below, one of the high priest's servants came. ⁶⁷ When she saw Peter warming himself, she looked at him and said, "You also were with that Nazarene, Jesus."

⁶⁸ But he denied it: "I don't know or understand what you're talking about!" Then he went out to the entryway, and a rooster crowed.

⁶⁹ When the servant saw him again she began to tell those standing nearby, "This man is one of them!"

⁷⁰ But again he denied it. After a little while those standing there said to Peter again, "You certainly are one of them, since you're also a Galilean!"

⁷¹ Then he started to curse and to swear with an oath, "I don't know this man you're talking about!"

⁷² Immediately a rooster crowed a second time, and Peter remembered when Jesus had spoken the word to him, "Before the rooster crows twice, you will deny Me three times." When he thought about it, he began to weep.

READ

As you read the passage, put yourself in Peter's sandals. To get a more vivid picture of what is happening, skim the expanded reading.

THINK

How does Peter feel to be in the courtyard? What has happened since his bold declaration of devotion to Jesus no matter what, earlier in the chapter? What thoughts shoot through Peter's mind that lead him to leave the fireside for the entryway?

Now imagine that the rooster has crowed and reality is caving in on Peter. Sit beside him in his anguish. What is he experiencing? As he remembers Jesus' words, what does Jesus' face look like in his mind's eye? What are the tones of Jesus' voice?

PRAY/LIVE

Let your meditation on Peter's failure lead you to consider your own heart and life. Where have you blown it lately? Talk to Jesus about this. Bravely let yourself feel the depth of what you've done. You might speak a prayer of humility or thanksgiving, or a request for something you need. Notice what you expect Jesus to do or say in response.

Now read the passage again slowly. What is Jesus saying in response to you? Be open to how He may be reacting differently to you or to your failure than you expected. Write down what Jesus' response was and what experiencing that was like.

POINTING THE WAY TO JESUS

LUKE 3:16-20

[16] John answered them all, "I baptize you with water, but One is coming who is more powerful than I. I am not worthy to untie the strap of His sandals. He will baptize you with the Holy Spirit and fire. [17] His winnowing shovel is in His hand to clear His threshing floor and gather the wheat into His barn, but the chaff He will burn up with a fire that never goes out." [18] Then, along with many other exhortations, he proclaimed good news to the people. [19] But Herod the tetrarch, being rebuked by him about Herodias, his brother's wife, and about all the evil things Herod had done, [20] added this to everything else — he locked John up in prison.

READ

Read the passage aloud four times, each time reading it with a different volume.

THINK

These verses tell us about John the Baptist, a torchbearer for the coming of Jesus' ministry, calling people to repent.

Focus first on the words describing the One who is coming. In your life, what would it mean to be the one less powerful who is unworthy, where the main focus is Jesus? What might be some areas of your life where the Holy Spirit will burn the chaff, changing you?

Now think about John's responses in the first few verses of chapter 3, concerning generosity, justice, and honesty.

PRAY

What do you need to repent of in areas where you have failed to be generous, just, and honest in the past week? Invite the Holy Spirit to put everything that is chaff out to be burned up.

Ask God to help you grow in generosity—for example, with your money, time, gifts, passions, energy, and so on.

Ask God to help you grow as an advocate for justice — for example, in your neighborhood, in your city, for the poor, for the unborn, for other people in the world, and so on.

Ask God to reveal areas of dishonesty or deception in your life. Implore Him to give you the grace and courage to live a life of honesty and integrity.

LIVE

Live generously, justly, and honestly today, pointing the way to Jesus.

DAY 224

GOD ENCOUNTERS

On this seventh day, review and reflect on all you have read this week. Take the time to revel in the ways you've encountered God in the past six days.

EVEN SINNERS DO THAT

LUKE 6:27-36

27 "But I say to you who listen: Love your enemies, do what is good to those who hate you, 28 bless those who curse you, pray for those who mistreat you. 29 If anyone hits you on the cheek, offer the other also. And if anyone takes away your coat, don't hold back your shirt either. 30 Give to everyone who asks you, and from one who takes your things, don't ask for them back. 31 Just as you want others to do for you, do the same for them. 32 If you love those who love you, what credit is that to you? Even sinners love those who love them. 33 If you do what is good to those who are good to you, what credit is that to you? Even sinners do that. 34 And if you lend to those from whom you expect to receive, what credit is that to you? Even sinners lend to sinners to be repaid in full. 35 But love your enemies, do what is good, and lend, expecting nothing in return. Then your reward will be great, and you will be sons of the Most High. For He is gracious to the ungrateful and evil. 36 Be merciful, just as your Father also is merciful."

READ

Read the passage aloud slowly.

THINK

Read the passage aloud a second time, but pretend you are Jesus. Get into it and read it like you mean it; say the words and phrases the way you think He would have. Perhaps gently? Perhaps warmly? Perhaps passionately?

Read the passage aloud one more time, but this time put yourself in the place of Jesus' listener; you're sitting in the front row as Jesus speaks and looks directly at you.

1. If Jesus spoke these words to you, what would they mean?
2. Which words would stand out to you?
3. What might Jesus be trying to get across to you?

PRAY

Thank our kind God that He loves His enemies. Thank God that He loves you when you act as if you barely know Him. Take the words that stood out to you (see question 2) and paraphrase those back to God in prayer.

LIVE

Sit quietly and picture the kind of person you would be if you were to:

- do good to those who hate you
- pray for those who mistreat you
- offer the other cheek when someone hits you
- give to everyone who asks you
- do for others what you want from them

DO YOU SEE THIS WOMAN?

LUKE 7:37-47

³⁷ And a woman in the town who was a sinner found out that Jesus was reclining at the table in the Pharisee's house. She brought an alabaster jar of fragrant oil ³⁸ and stood behind Him at His feet, weeping, and began to wash His feet with her tears. She wiped His feet with the hair of her head, kissing them and anointing them with the fragrant oil.

³⁹ When the Pharisee who had invited Him saw this, he said to himself, "This man, if He were a prophet, would know who and what kind of woman this is who is touching Him — she's a sinner!"

⁴⁰ Jesus replied to him, "Simon, I have something to say to you."

"Teacher," he said, "say it."

⁴¹ "A creditor had two debtors. One owed 500 denarii, and the other 50. ⁴² Since they could not pay it back, he graciously forgave them both. So, which of them will love him more?"

⁴³ Simon answered, "I suppose the one he forgave more."

"You have judged correctly," He told him. ⁴⁴ Turning to the woman, He said to Simon, "Do you see this woman? I entered your house; you gave Me no water for My feet, but she, with her tears, has washed My feet and wiped them with her hair. ⁴⁵ You gave Me no kiss, but she hasn't stopped kissing My feet since I came in. ⁴⁶ You didn't anoint My head with olive oil, but she has anointed My feet with fragrant oil. ⁴⁷ Therefore I tell you, her many sins have been forgiven; that's why she loved much. But the one who is forgiven little, loves little."

READ

Read the passage slowly, noticing the major players and actions in the story. Picture the setting's sounds, smells, and sights.

THINK

Now choose one person in the story with whom you identify most — the Pharisee, the sinner, or an onlooker — and read the story again. Imaginatively enter the scene, experiencing everything from that person's perspective. Hear the conversations. Feel the silence in the room as Jesus' feet are tenderly washed. Now listen to Jesus' voice and watch His face as He speaks. What do you feel? What thoughts go through your head?

PRAY

Talk with Jesus about what this experience has stirred up in you.

LIVE

Oswald Chambers said, "If human love does not carry a man beyond himself, it is not love. If love is always discreet, always wise, always sensible and calculating, never carried beyond itself, it is not love at all. It may be affection, it may be warmth of feeling, but it has not the true nature of love in it."[15]

Think about the degree of restraint or abandon you show in your relationship with Jesus (and with others). Consider the conscious or unconscious decisions you are constantly making about the way you'll act in that relationship. When does emotional momentum stir you? What do you do when it does? Under what circumstances do you set limits or hold back? What expectations or fears underlie your decisions? Share these with Jesus. What is something you could do today that would have "the true nature of love in it"?

SITTING AT THE LORD'S FEET

LUKE 10:38-42

[38] While they were traveling, He entered a village, and a woman named Martha welcomed Him into her home. [39] She had a sister named Mary, who also sat at the Lord's feet and was listening to what He said. [40] But Martha was distracted by her many tasks, and she came up and asked, "Lord, don't You care that my sister has left me to serve alone? So tell her to give me a hand."

[41] The Lord answered her, "Martha, Martha, you are worried and upset about many things, [42] but one thing is necessary. Mary has made the right choice, and it will not be taken away from her."

READ

This passage might be very familiar to you. So before reading, pause and ask God to give you fresh eyes and an open heart to absorb it. Then read it carefully.

THINK

Prayerfully let your creativity loose as you engage with this text. First put yourself in the skin of Mary. On that day, what might you be doing? What's going on around you in the house? What are you thinking and feeling when Martha complains about you?

Now put yourself in Martha's shoes. What are you preparing? What are your motivations? What are you feeling? What might you be thinking and feeling after Jesus says those words to you?

LIVE

The text says that Mary "sat at the Lord's feet." Now it's your turn. Take an empty chair and place it in the middle of the room. Sit or kneel in front of it, imagining Jesus seated there. Read the passage again. Stay in this posture, in the silence, and ponder who Jesus is.

PRAY

As you remain before the chair, whisper, "Jesus, who am I more like today: Mary or Martha?" Don't rush this experience. Even if an urge to get up comes, continue to be still and sit in silence. Anticipate that Jesus will communicate with you. Wait for Him and allow Him to speak words of promise, correction, or comfort into your life.

SEEK HIS KINGDOM

LUKE 12:25-34

²⁵ "Can any of you add a cubit to his height by worrying? ²⁶ If then you're not able to do even a little thing, why worry about the rest?

²⁷ "Consider how the wildflowers grow: They don't labor or spin thread. Yet I tell you, not even Solomon in all his splendor was adorned like one of these! ²⁸ If that's how God clothes the grass, which is in the field today and is thrown into the furnace tomorrow, how much more will He do for you — you of little faith? ²⁹ Don't keep striving for what you should eat and what you should drink, and don't be anxious. ³⁰ For the Gentile world eagerly seeks all these things, and your Father knows that you need them.

³¹ "But seek His kingdom, and these things will be provided for you. ³² Don't be afraid, little flock, because your Father delights to give you the kingdom. ³³ Sell your possessions and give to the poor. Make money-bags for yourselves that won't grow old, an inexhaustible treasure in heaven, where no thief comes near and no moth destroys. ³⁴ For where your treasure is, there your heart will be also."

READ

Read the passage aloud slowly. Pretend you and Jesus are sitting in Starbucks, and He's saying these words to you quietly.

THINK

Now pretend that you've come home, and you're going over in your mind what Jesus said to you. Read the passage again.

1. What words or phrases draw you the most?
2. What do you think Jesus is trying to say to you?
3. In order to do what Jesus said, what are you going to have to really trust for?

   ☐ that He will do much more for you
   ☐ that by *giving* instead of *getting,* you'll still have everything you need
   ☐ that God's provision is really enough
   ☐ other:

4. How do you feel about this?

PRAY

Respond to God about truly trusting Him for these practical, important matters. Be honest about what you are and are not ready to do.

LIVE

Sit quietly before God. Receive from Him the idea that He is your treasure: "Where your treasure is, there your heart will be also."

LOST AND FOUND

LUKE 15:1-10

¹ All the tax collectors and sinners were approaching to listen to Him.
² And the Pharisees and scribes were complaining, "This man welcomes sinners and eats with them!"

³ So He told them this parable: ⁴ "What man among you, who has 100 sheep and loses one of them, does not leave the 99 in the open field and go after the lost one until he finds it? ⁵ When he has found it, he joyfully puts it on his shoulders, ⁶ and coming home, he calls his friends and neighbors together, saying to them, 'Rejoice with me, because I have found my lost sheep!' ⁷ I tell you, in the same way, there will be more joy in heaven over one sinner who repents than over 99 righteous people who don't need repentance.

⁸ "Or what woman who has 10 silver coins, if she loses one coin, does not light a lamp, sweep the house, and search carefully until she finds it? ⁹ When she finds it, she calls her women friends and neighbors together, saying, 'Rejoice with me, because I have found the silver coin I lost!' ¹⁰ I tell you, in the same way, there is joy in the presence of God's angels over one sinner who repents."

READ

Open your hands with your palms facing up. Sit for a moment in stillness and ask your heavenly Father to tell you important words that you need to hear today. Communicate that you are open to His guidance. Now read the passage.

THINK

In this passage two things — a sheep and a coin — are lost and then found. And both are celebrated upon their return.

As you think about the two stories of the lost items, which story hits you the most right now? Contemplate why that story jumps out at you today. Read it again, and put yourself in it.

When have you felt lost? Why did you feel that way?

In both stories people — a shepherd, a woman — proactively went after the lost item. How does it feel to know that God Himself is proactively pursuing you for the simple yet profound fact that He loves you deeply?

Notice the element of celebration in these stories. What does this celebration make you feel? What should you begin to celebrate in your life or in the lives of others?

PRAY

Listen for God in these areas: What might He be communicating to you regarding your lostness? Regarding the fact that He desires to find you? Regarding how He celebrates your life?

LIVE

Recognize what God is doing in the world today — in the spectacular and in the mundane — and then celebrate it.

RETURNING TO SAY THANK YOU

LUKE 17:11-19

[11] While traveling to Jerusalem, He passed between Samaria and Galilee. [12] As He entered a village, 10 men with serious skin diseases met Him. They stood at a distance [13] and raised their voices, saying, "Jesus, Master, have mercy on us!"

[14] When He saw them, He told them, "Go and show yourselves to the priests." And while they were going, they were healed.

[15] But one of them, seeing that he was healed, returned and, with a loud voice, gave glory to God. [16] He fell facedown at His feet, thanking Him. And he was a Samaritan.

[17] Then Jesus said, "Were not 10 cleansed? Where are the nine? [18] Didn't any return to give glory to God except this foreigner?" [19] And He told him, "Get up and go on your way. Your faith has made you well."

READ

Read the passage, focusing especially on the questions Jesus asks.

THINK

Not only are lepers deformed by their disease, but Old Testament law also excludes them from community with others. Ten men come to Jesus with this horrific skin disease. These men are physical and relational outsiders. When Jesus heals them, He also helps restore them to their communities.

When have you felt like an outsider and then experienced God's restoring you to community with others or with Himself? Do you tend to be like the nine, who asked for God's help and didn't return, or are you like the one who returned to say thank you? Why?

Think about your last several requests to God in prayer. Have you turned around and come back, shouting your gratitude for how He has answered your requests and blessed you in the process? Why or why not? What needs to happen in your life for you to remember to return when God answers your prayers?

PRAY

Make this prayer time one of intentional thankfulness. Consider your recent requests to God (being specific). Return now and thank Him for answering those requests, big and small.

LIVE

Every time you make a request, turn around and shout your gratitude.

DAY 231

GOD ENCOUNTERS

On this seventh day, review and reflect on all you have read this week. Take the time to revel in the ways you've encountered God in the past six days.

HEALING THE ENEMY

LUKE 22:47-53

⁴⁷ While He was still speaking, suddenly a mob was there, and one of the Twelve named Judas was leading them. He came near Jesus to kiss Him, ⁴⁸ but Jesus said to him, "Judas, are you betraying the Son of Man with a kiss?"

⁴⁹ When those around Him saw what was going to happen, they asked, "Lord, should we strike with the sword?" ⁵⁰ Then one of them struck the high priest's slave and cut off his right ear.

⁵¹ But Jesus responded, "No more of this!" And touching his ear, He healed him. ⁵² Then Jesus said to the chief priests, temple police, and the elders who had come for Him, "Have you come out with swords and clubs as if I were a criminal? ⁵³ Every day while I was with you in the temple complex, you never laid a hand on Me. But this is your hour — and the dominion of darkness."

READ

Read the passage aloud slowly. Keep in mind that this occurs in the Garden of Gethsemane. Jesus has just prayed, "Father, if You are willing, take this cup away from Me — nevertheless, not My will, but Yours, be done" (verse 42). Then Jesus noted that His disciples were sleeping when He'd asked them to watch with Him.

THINK

Read the passage again. This time place yourself in the scene as one of the disciples watching what is going on.

1. How do you feel when Judas arrives with soldiers?
2. How do you feel when one of you strikes the chief priest's slave?
3. How do you feel when Jesus heals this slave — one of His attackers?
4. How do you feel when Jesus points out how silly and dramatic His assailants are? (He has been accessible to them for days and is now *letting them* arrest Him.)

Finally, put yourself in the place of the slave of the chief priest who is healed by Jesus. How do you feel? What do you want to say to Jesus?

PRAY

Consider Jesus' behavior in this scene. What baffles you? What is awakened within you? Fear? A sense of worship? If there is any way this scene might help you trust Jesus more, tell Him.

LIVE

Sit quietly with your hand on one of your ears. See yourself as someone who is about to injure Jesus, but instead He heals you from your own injuries. Sit in that sense of being healed by God. Sit in that sense of finally being able to hear Jesus in your heart with your willing ears.

LOOKING FOR THE LIVING AMONG THE DEAD

LUKE 24:1-12

¹ On the first day of the week, very early in the morning, they came to the tomb, bringing the spices they had prepared. ² They found the stone rolled away from the tomb. ³ They went in but did not find the body of the Lord Jesus. ⁴ While they were perplexed about this, suddenly two men stood by them in dazzling clothes. ⁵ So the women were terrified and bowed down to the ground.

"Why are you looking for the living among the dead?" asked the men. ⁶ "He is not here, but He has been resurrected! Remember how He spoke to you when He was still in Galilee, ⁷ saying, 'The Son of Man must be betrayed into the hands of sinful men, be crucified, and rise on the third day'?" ⁸ And they remembered His words.

⁹ Returning from the tomb, they reported all these things to the Eleven and to all the rest. ¹⁰ Mary Magdalene, Joanna, Mary the mother of James, and the other women with them were telling the apostles these things. ¹¹ But these words seemed like nonsense to them, and they did not believe the women. ¹² Peter, however, got up and ran to the tomb. When he stooped to look in, he saw only the linen cloths. So he went home, amazed at what had happened.

READ

Read the passage carefully, paying attention to the various characters and their responses to the events of the story.

THINK

Which disciple or follower of Jesus do you most identify with in this passage? What is it about that person that reminds you of yourself?

Read the passage again, this time putting yourself in that person's position. What are your thoughts and feelings as you hear that Jesus is alive again? What runs through your mind as you see others' responses? What do you wonder about? Where do you go when you hear the news? What questions do you have?

PRAY

Now picture the risen Jesus approaching you later that day, inviting you to spend time with Him. How do you interact with Him? What do you say? Talk to Him about what all of this has been like for you.

LIVE

Reflect on your prayer time. You might again consider the person in the story you chose and why, or you could think about how your understanding of faithfulness and discipleship was deepened or changed. Write down anything that seems significant.

THE LIGHT OF MEN

JOHN 1:12-18

¹² But to all who did receive Him,
He gave them the right to be children of God,
to those who believe in His name,
¹³ who were born,
not of blood,
or of the will of the flesh,
or of the will of man,
but of God.

¹⁴ The Word became flesh
and took up residence among us.
We observed His glory,
the glory as the One and Only Son from the Father,
full of grace and truth.
¹⁵ (John testified concerning Him and exclaimed,
"This was the One of whom I said,
'The One coming after me has surpassed me,
because He existed before me.'")
¹⁶ Indeed, we have all received grace after grace
from His fullness,
¹⁷ for the law was given through Moses,
grace and truth came through Jesus Christ.
¹⁸ No one has ever seen God.
The One and Only Son —
the One who is at the Father's side —
He has revealed Him.

READ

Read the passage slowly and repeatedly. Don't rush through it. Take your time. Ruminate on the passage. Let it sink into the well of your soul.

THINK

What sticks out to you the most in these verses? Why is the Word coming to earth such a big deal in the great scope of human history?

"The Word became flesh and took up residence among us." What might your life be like if God moved into the house or apartment or locker or dorm room next to yours?

How might the environment of your neighborhood be different if He were your next-door neighbor? How might your own life be different? Be specific.

LIVE

Get a candle (if you don't have one, buy or borrow one). At night, go into a dark room (turn off any lights and shut any curtains). Light the candle and stare at the flame. Consider Jesus, the Word, coming to earth in flesh and blood, becoming the Life-Light for the world.

PRAY

Stand in the dark room, still looking at the small flame. Allow these words to guide your prayers: "Life was in Him, and that life was the light of men. That light shines in the darkness, yet the darkness did not overcome it" (1:4-5).

ANYONE WHO BELIEVES

JOHN 3:9-11,14-15,17-21

[9] "How can these things be?" asked Nicodemus.

[10] "Are you a teacher of Israel and don't know these things?" Jesus replied. [11] "I assure you: We speak what We know and We testify to what We have seen, but you do not accept Our testimony. . . . [14] Just as Moses lifted up the snake in the wilderness, so the Son of Man must be lifted up, [15] so that everyone who believes in Him will have eternal life. . . .

[17] For God did not send His Son into the world that He might condemn the world, but that the world might be saved through Him. [18] Anyone who believes in Him is not condemned, but anyone who does not believe is already condemned, because he has not believed in the name of the One and Only Son of God.

[19] "This, then, is the judgment: The light has come into the world, and people loved darkness rather than the light because their deeds were evil. [20] For everyone who practices wicked things hates the light and avoids it, so that his deeds may not be exposed. [21] But anyone who lives by the truth comes to the light, so that his works may be shown to be accomplished by God."

READ

Before you read the passage, understand that Jesus has just told Nicodemus (a scholar and teacher) that he must be "born of water and the Spirit" (verse 5). But Nicodemus is confused! Now read the passage silently.

THINK

Read the passage again, aloud this time, putting yourself in the place of Nicodemus standing on the rooftop in the moonlight, receiving Jesus' words.

1. Which words or phrases stand out to you? Consider these:

   ☐ "Everyone who believes in Him will have eternal life."
   ☐ "God did not send His Son into the world that He might condemn the world, but that the world might be saved through Him."
   ☐ "Anyone who believes in Him is not condemned."
   ☐ "The light has come into the world."
   ☐ "Anyone who lives by the truth comes to the light, so that his works may be shown to be accomplished by God."

2. Why?

PRAY

Talk to Jesus about any phrases that confused you. Talk to Him about the phrases that captivated you.

LIVE

Sit quietly before God. Put yourself in the place of Nicodemus again — possibly lying in your bed each night, going over these words Jesus said to you. Which words will you drift off with tonight?

DO YOU WANT TO GET WELL?

JOHN 5:1-9

¹ After this, a Jewish festival took place, and Jesus went up to Jerusalem. ² By the Sheep Gate in Jerusalem there is a pool, called Bethesda in Hebrew, which has five colonnades. ³ Within these lay a large number of the sick — blind, lame, and paralyzed [— waiting for the moving of the water, ⁴ because an angel would go down into the pool from time to time and stir up the water. Then the first one who got in after the water was stirred up recovered from whatever ailment he had].

⁵ One man was there who had been sick for 38 years. ⁶ When Jesus saw him lying there and knew he had already been there a long time, He said to him, "Do you want to get well?"

⁷ "Sir," the sick man answered, "I don't have a man to put me into the pool when the water is stirred up, but while I'm coming, someone goes down ahead of me."

⁸ "Get up," Jesus told him, "pick up your mat and walk!" ⁹ Instantly the man got well, picked up his mat, and started to walk.

Now that day was the Sabbath.

READ

Read this passage, being especially aware of how it depicts sickness, lack of wholeness, and the process of healing. These details might remind you of a truth you've considered before, or they might reveal something altogether new.

THINK

Read the verses again. What stands out to you? Why might the Holy Spirit be bringing this to your attention? Perhaps you deeply desire to experience wholeness of mind or spirit because you have been experiencing your woundedness lately. Or perhaps you find yourself questioning whether Jesus really can heal a physical sickness — either your own or someone else's.

PRAY

Ask Jesus what in your life calls for healing. Talk to Him about what you hear.

These possibilities might help get you started: Allowing Jesus to bring healing might require you to let go of something that hurts too much to release, and you don't think you're ready for it right now. Or you desire freedom and wholeness, but you feel stuck, imprisoned, fragmented. Or in this moment you find yourself ready for your healing: Be open to the possibility of Jesus bringing healing when you least expect it, of being instantly healed. On the other hand, perhaps you feel ready and are frustrated that nothing seems to be happening.

LIVE

If your time with Jesus and God's Word today moved you the tiniest bit closer to wholeness, rejoice. If not, simply let things be. Continue talking to Jesus about your situation, being alert to what He has for you.

NO CONDEMNATION

JOHN 8:1-11

¹ But Jesus went to the Mount of Olives.

² At dawn He went to the temple complex again, and all the people were coming to Him. He sat down and began to teach them.

³ Then the scribes and the Pharisees brought a woman caught in adultery, making her stand in the center. ⁴ "Teacher," they said to Him, "this woman was caught in the act of committing adultery. ⁵ In the law Moses commanded us to stone such women. So what do You say?" ⁶ They asked this to trap Him, in order that they might have evidence to accuse Him.

Jesus stooped down and started writing on the ground with His finger. ⁷ When they persisted in questioning Him, He stood up and said to them, "The one without sin among you should be the first to throw a stone at her."

⁸ Then He stooped down again and continued writing on the ground. ⁹ When they heard this, they left one by one, starting with the older men. Only He was left, with the woman in the center. ¹⁰ When Jesus stood up, He said to her, "Woman, where are they? Has no one condemned you?"

¹¹ "No one, Lord," she answered.

"Neither do I condemn you," said Jesus. "Go, and from now on do not sin anymore."

READ

Write out today's passage. Say each word aloud as you go.

THINK

Imagine yourself in the crowd the day these events unfold. Picture the embarrassed and shamed expression on the woman's face. Hear the condescending voices of the religious leaders. Feel the Middle Eastern dirt blowing against you as Jesus bends down and writes something in it.

Now imagine yourself in the same situation as this woman. You're caught in a horrendous sin, exposed. Imagine you and Jesus having the same conversation:

"Has no one condemned you?"

"No one, Lord."

He looks you in the eyes. "Neither do I condemn you. Go, and from now on do not sin anymore."

What are you feeling? Thinking?

PRAY

Confess those acts of spiritual adultery you've engaged in recently. Close your eyes and imagine Jesus standing before you. Hear Him telling you that He doesn't condemn you but that He wants you to stop sinning from now on.

LIVE

Ask the Holy Spirit to give you wisdom and guidance not to condone other people's (or your own) sin and at the same time not to condemn those people (or yourself) either. Ask the Spirit to bring to your mind people you can love while avoiding condemning and condoning.

DAY 238

GOD ENCOUNTERS

On this seventh day, review and reflect on all you have read this week. Take the time to revel in the ways you've encountered God in the past six days.

KNOWING THE GOOD SHEPHERD

JOHN 10:2-5,14-18

2 "The one who enters by the door is the shepherd of the sheep. 3 The door-keeper opens it for him, and the sheep hear his voice. He calls his own sheep by name and leads them out. 4 When he has brought all his own outside, he goes ahead of them. The sheep follow him because they recognize his voice. 5 They will never follow a stranger; instead they will run away from him, because they don't recognize the voice of strangers." . . .

14 "I am the good shepherd. I know My own sheep, and they know Me, 15 as the Father knows Me, and I know the Father. I lay down My life for the sheep. 16 But I have other sheep that are not of this fold; I must bring them also, and they will listen to My voice. Then there will be one flock, one shepherd. 17 This is why the Father loves Me, because I am laying down My life so I may take it up again. 18 No one takes it from Me, but I lay it down on My own. I have the right to lay it down, and I have the right to take it up again. I have received this command from My Father."

READ

Read these words of Jesus aloud slowly. Notice the two sets of closeness expressed: between Jesus and the Father, and between Jesus and the sheep.

THINK

Read these words of Jesus again aloud, as if He were explaining this to you personally. Notice that the word *know* occurs four times. Jesus knows His sheep; they know Jesus. The Father knows Jesus; Jesus knows the Father.

1. What do you make of the centrality of knowing one another?
2. Jesus, the Good Shepherd, does the following for the sheep. Which of these do you most need for Jesus to do for you today?

   ☐ call His own sheep by name
   ☐ lead them out
   ☐ know His own sheep
   ☐ lay down His life for the sheep
   ☐ gather and bring other sheep

3. The sheep recognize Jesus' voice and respond by following Him and knowing Him. How do you need to respond to Jesus today?
4. How are you growing in your capacity to recognize His voice, perhaps through your experiences in this book?

PRAY

Talk to Jesus about what you need from Him. Especially talk about your capacity to recognize His voice. Ask for help with this.

LIVE

Sit quietly before God and practice alert waiting. Receive the assurance that such practice will help you be more alert to Jesus' voice when you hear it.

HOLDING ON TO LIFE

JOHN 12:20-26

[20] Now some Greeks were among those who went up to worship at the festival. [21] So they came to Philip, who was from Bethsaida in Galilee, and requested of him, "Sir, we want to see Jesus."

[22] Philip went and told Andrew; then Andrew and Philip went and told Jesus. [23] Jesus replied to them, "The hour has come for the Son of Man to be glorified.

[24] "I assure you: Unless a grain of wheat falls to the ground and dies, it remains by itself. But if it dies, it produces a large crop. [25] The one who loves his life will lose it, and the one who hates his life in this world will keep it for eternal life. [26] If anyone serves Me, he must follow Me. Where I am, there My servant also will be. If anyone serves Me, the Father will honor him."

READ

If possible, read the expanded passage to see the full picture of what is happening here. Then read this excerpt three times meditatively.

THINK

Write in your own words what you think Jesus means when He talks about a grain of wheat dying and reproducing itself. Think about what you wrote.

Now wait for Jesus to show you an area of your life — a relationship, a decision to be made, and so on — in which you love your life, and are not allowing Him to bring growth or change. In what ways might your stance be destructive or suffocating?

Ponder Romans 12:2: "Do not be conformed to this age, but be transformed by the renewing of your mind." What would this area of your life look like if you were to be transformed, and in so doing, let go?

PRAY

Sit down. Hold your hands in tight fists. Then relax them, open them, and turn your palms upward. Talk with Jesus about what a life of open hands would look like. Ask Him to show you what it means to follow Him.

LIVE

Think again about your tightly held part of life. Try letting go just a little bit, with Jesus' help. Serve Jesus today. Follow Him today.

THE COUNSELOR

JOHN 14:15-17

[15] "If you love Me, you will keep My commands. [16] And I will ask the Father, and He will give you another Counselor to be with you forever. [17] He is the Spirit of truth. The world is unable to receive Him because it doesn't see Him or know Him. But you do know Him, because He remains with you and will be in you."

READ

Because this passage is about the Holy Spirit, ask Him to guide you in a prayerful reading of it. Make your reading a prayer in itself.

THINK

The Holy Spirit is the most neglected personhood of God. We often treat the Spirit like a tagalong part of the Trinity. Yet Jesus promises to leave His disciples (and us as His followers) with this important Counselor. Is it hard for you to imagine that the Holy Spirit is offered to you as a friend? Why or why not?

What does it mean to have the Holy Spirit in you and guiding you throughout your day, as this passage says: "But you do know Him, because He remains with you and will be in you"? Is it comforting? Discomforting? Frustrating? Hard to comprehend? Awe-inspiring? How can you grow today in awareness that the Counselor lives in you?

PRAY

Ask the Holy Spirit, your Counselor, to make you aware of His presence. Pray the words of this Scripture, asking Him to "teach you all things" (verse 26) and remind you of all the things that Jesus told the disciples (and you).

LIVE

As you drive, walk, work, study, and interact with others today, call on your Counselor for His guidance with the thoughts you think, the words you speak, and the decisions you make.

MADE COMPLETELY ONE

JOHN 17:20-23,26

20 I pray not only for these,
but also for those who believe in Me
through their message.
21 May they all be one,
as You, Father, are in Me and I am in You.
May they also be one in Us,
so the world may believe You sent Me.
22 I have given them the glory You have given Me.
May they be one as We are one.
23 I am in them and You are in Me.
May they be made completely one,
so the world may know You have sent Me
and have loved them as You have loved Me. . . .
26 I made Your name known to them
and will make it known,
so the love You have loved Me with
may be in them and I may be in them.

READ

Read the passage aloud slowly, remembering that this is Jesus praying for you ("those who [will] believe in Me").

THINK

Read it again slowly, but this time substitute your name (or your name and "they all") when you read *them* or *they*.

If you need to, read the passage one more time before considering these questions.

1. What are you most excited about Jesus praying for you or saying about you?

   ☐ your message about Jesus
   ☐ to be one with other followers of Jesus
   ☐ to be one with God and Jesus
   ☐ that Jesus has given you glory
   ☐ that Jesus is in you
   ☐ that you'll be made completely one
   ☐ that you'll give the world evidence that God sent Jesus
   ☐ that Jesus made God known to you
   ☐ that God's love for Jesus is in you

2. Why?

PRAY

Thank Jesus for praying for you. Talk to Him about the prayer phrases you found most meaningful. Pray Jesus' prayer for His followers alive today in the world.

LIVE

Walk around today with the sense that Jesus is in you and that this was always His plan — to be in you.

DON'T BE AN UNBELIEVER

JOHN 20:19-29

¹⁹ In the evening of that first day of the week, the disciples were gathered together with the doors locked because of their fear of the Jews. Then Jesus came, stood among them, and said to them, "Peace to you!"

²⁰ Having said this, He showed them His hands and His side. So the disciples rejoiced when they saw the Lord.

²¹ Jesus said to them again, "Peace to you! As the Father has sent Me, I also send you." ²² After saying this, He breathed on them and said, "Receive the Holy Spirit. ²³ If you forgive the sins of any, they are forgiven them; if you retain the sins of any, they are retained."

²⁴ But one of the Twelve, Thomas (called "Twin"), was not with them when Jesus came. ²⁵ So the other disciples kept telling him, "We have seen the Lord!"

But he said to them, "If I don't see the mark of the nails in His hands, put my finger into the mark of the nails, and put my hand into His side, I will never believe!"

²⁶ After eight days His disciples were indoors again, and Thomas was with them. Even though the doors were locked, Jesus came and stood among them. He said, "Peace to you!"

²⁷ Then He said to Thomas, "Put your finger here and observe My hands. Reach out your hand and put it into My side. Don't be an unbeliever, but a believer."

²⁸ Thomas responded to Him, "My Lord and my God!"

²⁹ Jesus said, "Because you have seen Me, you have believed. Those who believe without seeing are blessed."

READ

Read John's description of the first time Jesus appeared to His disciples after His death and resurrection. Pay special attention to Jesus' words to them.

THINK

What does Thomas's response to Jesus' resurrection make you feel? How do you react to Thomas's disbelief? What about Jesus' response to him?

PRAY

Read the passage once more. This time pretend you are one of the disciples. Maybe you will be a believing disciple; maybe you will be Thomas. Pick a role that corresponds with where you actually are in your relationship with Jesus right now. Now play out the story. As you hear Jesus speak to you, respond to Him from your heart. Let Him engage you in conversation.

LIVE

If you're a Thomas, wonder what it would be like to "believe without seeing." If you're like the other disciples, remember to offer grace to others who need to see before believing. Thank God for the faith He has given you — either way.

GOD'S REDEMPTIVE PLAN

ACTS 1:1-11

¹ I wrote the first narrative, Theophilus, about all that Jesus began to do and teach ² until the day He was taken up, after He had given orders through the Holy Spirit to the apostles He had chosen. ³ After He had suffered, He also presented Himself alive to them by many convincing proofs, appearing to them during 40 days and speaking about the kingdom of God.

⁴ While He was together with them, He commanded them not to leave Jerusalem, but to wait for the Father's promise. "This," He said, "is what you heard from Me; ⁵ for John baptized with water, but you will be baptized with the Holy Spirit not many days from now."

⁶ So when they had come together, they asked Him, "Lord, are You restoring the kingdom to Israel at this time?"

⁷ He said to them, "It is not for you to know times or periods that the Father has set by His own authority. ⁸ But you will receive power when the Holy Spirit has come on you, and you will be My witnesses in Jerusalem, in all Judea and Samaria, and to the ends of the earth."

⁹ After He had said this, He was taken up as they were watching, and a cloud took Him out of their sight. ¹⁰ While He was going, they were gazing into heaven, and suddenly two men in white clothes stood by them. ¹¹ They said, "Men of Galilee, why do you stand looking up into heaven? This Jesus, who has been taken from you into heaven, will come in the same way that you have seen Him going into heaven."

READ

Read the passage from the perspective of someone who has never read it before.

THINK

When are you tempted to be a spectator to the movements of God's redemptive plan rather than a participant involved in the action? Why? What are specific ways you can get off the bench and get up to bat for what God is up to in the world? What are some ways you can be a witness to others in your circle of influence?

You know that Jesus will come again in the future. What implications does that reality have on your life?

PRAY

Ask God to give you the courage to take the risk and get into the game, to participate in God's redemptive plan.

LIVE

Ask a close friend or family member to help pray, brainstorm, and discern the ways you can be a participant in God's redemptive plan for your life and the lives of those around you. Ask this person to keep you in check, reminding you that God wants His followers to act on what Jesus said and did.

DAY 245

GOD ENCOUNTERS

On this seventh day, review and reflect on all you have read this week. Take the time to revel in the ways you've encountered God in the past six days.

COMPLETE BOLDNESS

ACTS 4:24-31

²⁴ When they heard this, they all raised their voices to God and said, "Master, You are the One who made the heaven, the earth, and the sea, and everything in them. ²⁵ You said through the Holy Spirit, by the mouth of our father David Your servant:

> Why did the Gentiles rage
> and the peoples plot futile things?
> ²⁶ The kings of the earth took their stand
> and the rulers assembled together
> against the Lord and against His Messiah.

²⁷ "For, in fact, in this city both Herod and Pontius Pilate, with the Gentiles and the people of Israel, assembled together against Your holy Servant Jesus, whom You anointed, ²⁸ to do whatever Your hand and Your plan had predestined to take place. ²⁹ And now, Lord, consider their threats, and grant that Your slaves may speak Your message with complete boldness, ³⁰ while You stretch out Your hand for healing, signs, and wonders to be performed through the name of Your holy Servant Jesus." ³¹ When they had prayed, the place where they were assembled was shaken, and they were all filled with the Holy Spirit and began to speak God's message with boldness.

READ

Read the passage aloud slowly, keeping in mind that Peter and John were just released from police custody for preaching about Jesus. Most of this passage is their prayer.

THINK

Read the passage aloud again. What touches you most? How do you explain the "complete boldness" of these men who have just suffered for Jesus?

Read the passage one more time, noting when a member of the Trinity is mentioned: God, Jesus (and His designation, Messiah), the Holy Spirit. Clearly, Peter and John, as well as these followers of Jesus, were living in the reality of the Trinity — active and living among them! What might it look like to live your life today immersed in the reality and power of the Trinity?

PRAY

Paraphrase the prayer of Peter, John, and Jesus' followers (verses 24-30) as it fits your life today, including what God has done in the past (verses 24-28), what is happening today (verse 29), and how you wish for God to work today (verse 30).

LIVE

Remind yourself throughout the day that a follower of Jesus is immersed in the Trinitarian reality — really!

JESUS, THE LORD

ACTS 7:51–8:1

[51] "You stiff-necked people with uncircumcised hearts and ears! You are always resisting the Holy Spirit; as your ancestors did, so do you. [52] Which of the prophets did your fathers not persecute? They even killed those who announced beforehand the coming of the Righteous One, whose betrayers and murderers you have now become. [53] You received the law under the direction of angels and yet have not kept it."

[54] When they heard these things, they were enraged in their hearts and gnashed their teeth at him. [55] But Stephen, filled by the Holy Spirit, gazed into heaven. He saw God's glory, with Jesus standing at the right hand of God, and he said, [56] "Look! I see the heavens opened and the Son of Man standing at the right hand of God!"

[57] Then they screamed at the top of their voices, covered their ears, and together rushed against him. [58] They threw him out of the city and began to stone him. And the witnesses laid their robes at the feet of a young man named Saul. [59] They were stoning Stephen as he called out: "Lord Jesus, receive my spirit!" [60] Then he knelt down and cried out with a loud voice, "Lord, do not charge them with this sin!" And saying this, he fell asleep.

[1] Saul agreed with putting him to death.

On that day a severe persecution broke out against the church in Jerusalem, and all except the apostles were scattered throughout the land of Judea and Samaria.

READ

Read the passage aloud once. Then read it again silently and slowly, paying careful attention to your response.

THINK

Stephen calls Jesus "Lord," and his actions agree. Have you ever read or heard stories of other martyrs like Stephen, people who died for Jesus' sake? What do these stories make you feel?

PRAY

Become aware of Jesus inviting you to share with Him your thoughts and feelings. Perhaps stories of martyrdom make you angry, grieved, or afraid. Maybe you find yourself pulling away from such stories. You might have questions. Maybe you want only to sit silently with Jesus. As you open your heart's reaction to Him, let that become your prayer.

LIVE

Read the passage again, this time prayerfully. Look for clues to help you discern Jesus' response to Stephen's martyrdom, as well as Jesus' response to you. Write down anything you want to remember or think about later.

THE MIRACULOUS RELEASE

ACTS 12:7-15

[7] Suddenly an angel of the Lord appeared, and a light shone in the cell. Striking Peter on the side, he woke him up and said, "Quick, get up!" Then the chains fell off his wrists. [8] "Get dressed," the angel told him, "and put on your sandals." And he did so. "Wrap your cloak around you," he told him, "and follow me." [9] So he went out and followed, and he did not know that what took place through the angel was real, but thought he was seeing a vision. [10] After they passed the first and second guard posts, they came to the iron gate that leads into the city, which opened to them by itself. They went outside and passed one street, and immediately the angel left him.

[11] Then Peter came to himself and said, "Now I know for certain that the Lord has sent His angel and rescued me from Herod's grasp and from all that the Jewish people expected." [12] When he realized this, he went to the house of Mary, the mother of John Mark, where many had assembled and were praying. [13] He knocked at the door in the gateway, and a servant named Rhoda came to answer. [14] She recognized Peter's voice, and because of her joy, she did not open the gate but ran in and announced that Peter was standing at the gateway.

[15] "You're crazy!" they told her. But she kept insisting that it was true. Then they said, "It's his angel!"

READ

Imagine you are in a roomful of your friends, and they have asked you to read them a story. With this scenario in mind, read the passage.

THINK

Good stories grab hold of us and won't let go. This story is no exception. Scripture sometimes "messes" with us in appropriate ways. How does this passage mess with you and your understanding of God?

The people praying for Peter's release from prison didn't believe it when he was standing at the door. They thought Rhoda was crazy or it must be someone else or an angel of Peter (but not Peter himself). Is it hard to believe that the Holy Spirit is powerful enough to perform such sensational acts? Why or why not? If this were to happen today, would you be skeptical or cynical? Why or why not?

How often do you pray for God to work and, when He does, react with shock or disbelief? What does this reveal about the faith behind your prayers?

PRAY

What can you pray that God will do — something you *wholeheartedly believe* He will answer? Pray for that with bold confidence and hope, knowing that God is powerful and is listening to your prayer.

LIVE

Be keenly aware today of how the Holy Spirit is working — in the sensational, in the mundane, or in both.

BELIEVE ON THE LORD JESUS

ACTS 16:25-34

25 About midnight Paul and Silas were praying and singing hymns to God, and the prisoners were listening to them. 26 Suddenly there was such a violent earthquake that the foundations of the jail were shaken, and immediately all the doors were opened, and everyone's chains came loose. 27 When the jailer woke up and saw the doors of the prison open, he drew his sword and was going to kill himself, since he thought the prisoners had escaped.

28 But Paul called out in a loud voice, "Don't harm yourself, because all of us are here!"

29 Then the jailer called for lights, rushed in, and fell down trembling before Paul and Silas. 30 Then he escorted them out and said, "Sirs, what must I do to be saved?"

31 So they said, "Believe on the Lord Jesus, and you will be saved — you and your household." 32 Then they spoke the message of the Lord to him along with everyone in his house. 33 He took them the same hour of the night and washed their wounds. Right away he and all his family were baptized. 34 He brought them into his house, set a meal before them, and rejoiced because he had believed God with his entire household.

READ

Read the passage aloud slowly, keeping in mind that just before this, Paul and Silas (after doing good) are stripped by a crowd, beaten black and blue by officials, and put in jail.

THINK

Read the passage again, being mindful that the Greek word for "salvation" has to do with deliverance for the future but also living a new kind of life in the here and now.

1. Why do you think the jailer is so dramatically affected by Paul's and Silas's behavior?
2. Why would the jailer have an idea of what it meant to "believe on the Lord Jesus"?
3. Picture these scenes:

   - the jailer making his prisoners feel at home with his family
   - the jailer dressing the wounds his coworkers had inflicted
   - Paul and Silas baptizing the family
   - the group eating a festive meal together, not knowing what would happen to Paul and Silas the next day

PRAY

Talk to God about what touches you most in this passage. What does that tell you about what you need from God? Ask God for that.

LIVE

Ponder the next twenty-four hours. In what area might you rejoice even though circumstances might not be happy? Who might you love who isn't expecting it? Watch for unexpected events and celebrate them.

PAINFUL CONSEQUENCES

ACTS 19:11-17

¹¹ God was performing extraordinary miracles by Paul's hands, ¹² so that even facecloths or work aprons that had touched his skin were brought to the sick, and the diseases left them, and the evil spirits came out of them.

¹³ Then some of the itinerant Jewish exorcists attempted to pronounce the name of the Lord Jesus over those who had evil spirits, saying, "I command you by the Jesus that Paul preaches!" ¹⁴ Seven sons of Sceva, a Jewish chief priest, were doing this. ¹⁵ The evil spirit answered them, "I know Jesus, and I recognize Paul — but who are you?" ¹⁶ Then the man who had the evil spirit leaped on them, overpowered them all, and prevailed against them, so that they ran out of that house naked and wounded. ¹⁷ This became known to everyone who lived in Ephesus, both Jews and Greeks. Then fear fell on all of them, and the name of the Lord Jesus was magnified.

READ

Read the passage.

THINK

Often God allows us to experience unpleasant consequences of choices we make, sometimes so we realize how our choices affect our relationships with Him and other people. For example, He might allow ugly parts of our character to be exposed, with embarrassing and painful results. Why do you think God uses consequences to draw people's attention to the thorny parts of their hearts? What do you think God wanted the sons of Sceva to learn about themselves through this experience?

PRAY

Recall a difficult experience that helped you see more of your weaknesses or faults. Ponder the state of your relationship with God before the experience. How did it change? Think about your relationships with others, both before and after the experience. What changed? In other words, in what ways did your newfound awareness impact how you relate to others?

LIVE

Mull over these words, written by Teresa of Avila in her *Interior Castle*: "We are fonder of consolations than we are of the cross. Test us, Lord — for You know the truth — so that we may know ourselves."[16] Can you identify with her confession? Can you identify with her request to be more fully exposed to God and to see herself more clearly? Sit and talk with Jesus about your reaction to testing from God, contrasting it with your reaction to feel-good experiences.

FAITH JOURNEY

ACTS 22:1-10

[1] "Brothers and fathers, listen now to my defense before you." [2] When they heard that he was addressing them in the Hebrew language, they became even quieter. [3] He continued, "I am a Jewish man, born in Tarsus of Cilicia but brought up in this city at the feet of Gamaliel and educated according to the strict view of our patriarchal law. Being zealous for God, just as all of you are today, [4] I persecuted this Way to the death, binding and putting both men and women in jail, [5] as both the high priest and the whole council of elders can testify about me. After I received letters from them to the brothers, I traveled to Damascus to bring those who were prisoners there to be punished in Jerusalem.

[6] "As I was traveling and near Damascus, about noon an intense light from heaven suddenly flashed around me. [7] I fell to the ground and heard a voice saying to me, 'Saul, Saul, why are you persecuting Me?'

[8] "I answered, 'Who are You, Lord?'

"He said to me, 'I am Jesus the Nazarene, the One you are persecuting!' [9] Now those who were with me saw the light, but they did not hear the voice of the One who was speaking to me.

[10] "Then I said, 'What should I do, Lord?'

"And the Lord told me, 'Get up and go into Damascus, and there you will be told about everything that is assigned for you to do.'"

READ

Read the passage from the perspective of Paul's mother. What might she be thinking as she hears these words?

THINK

Paul's faith began in an amazing way on the road to Damascus (see the beginning of Acts 9 for more details). He was bold to share his story and ultimately The Story, the one of God and man. This passage gives us a thorough yet succinct explanation of the person Paul was before he met Christ, how he met Christ, and the person he became after he met Christ.

Reflect on your story—how you came to faith and how your faith journey is continuing today. Who were you before Christ? What was meeting Christ like? In what ways is your life different now as a result of meeting Him? Are other people different today because of your interaction with Jesus?

LIVE

Think about how you might describe your life-altering encounter with the living God and your faith journey. Now write or type your story of faith in just two or three paragraphs. Finally, ask someone you know to help you hone it to include the most appropriate details.

PRAY

Pray that God will provide you an opportunity to present your story and The Story (of God and man) with another person in the next week. When you sense the open door plainly before you, take the risk and share the stories.

DAY 252

GOD ENCOUNTERS

On this seventh day, review and reflect on all you have read this week. Take the time to revel in the ways you've encountered God in the past six days.

WHY ARE YOU PERSECUTING ME?

ACTS 26:12-18

¹² "I was traveling to Damascus under these circumstances with authority and a commission from the chief priests. ¹³ King Agrippa, while on the road at midday, I saw a light from heaven brighter than the sun, shining around me and those traveling with me. ¹⁴ We all fell to the ground, and I heard a voice speaking to me in the Hebrew language, 'Saul, Saul, why are you persecuting Me? It is hard for you to kick against the goads.'

¹⁵ "Then I said, 'Who are You, Lord?'

"And the Lord replied: 'I am Jesus, the One you are persecuting. ¹⁶ But get up and stand on your feet. For I have appeared to you for this purpose, to appoint you as a servant and a witness of what you have seen and of what I will reveal to you. ¹⁷ I will rescue you from the people and from the Gentiles. I now send you to them ¹⁸ to open their eyes so they may turn from darkness to light and from the power of Satan to God, that by faith in Me they may receive forgiveness of sins and a share among those who are sanctified.'"

READ

Read the passage aloud slowly. This is Paul speaking before King Agrippa, telling about his conversion.

THINK

Read the passage aloud again, this time noting all the personal pronouns in this very personal conversation: *I, me, you.*

Read it a third time, noting how the conversation focuses on the past and the future.

1. Why do you think Jesus doesn't just say, "I'm the Son of God. Your doctrine is wrong. Change it"?
2. How do you respond to Jesus' giving Saul a job to do even though he's been murdering Christians? What does this tell you about Jesus?
3. Consider what Paul might have prayed next; there he is, blind, with his underlings leading him to safety.

PRAY

Have a conversation with Jesus similar to Paul's.

First, Jesus asks you, "Why are you . . . ?" How do you respond?

Next, Jesus tells you exactly who He is — a glimpse of Him you have missed: "I am Jesus, the One you are . . ."

Finally, Jesus says, "Stand on your feet . . . I have appeared to you for this purpose." What is the purpose? How do you respond?

Live today asking Jesus this question: *Is there anything about You I'm missing out on? That I don't understand or accept? Show me.*

PRIDE COMES BEFORE A FALL

ROMANS 2:17-24

[17] Now if you call yourself a Jew, and rest in the law, boast in God, [18] know His will, and approve the things that are superior, being instructed from the law, [19] and if you are convinced that you are a guide for the blind, a light to those in darkness, [20] an instructor of the ignorant, a teacher of the immature, having the full expression of knowledge and truth in the law— [21] you then, who teach another, don't you teach yourself? You who preach, "You must not steal"—do you steal? [22] You who say, "You must not commit adultery"—do you commit adultery? You who detest idols, do you rob their temples? [23] You who boast in the law, do you dishonor God by breaking the law? [24] For, as it is written: The name of God is blasphemed among the Gentiles because of you.

READ

Whisper to yourself the words of this passage.

THINK

Paul, writing mostly to Gentiles (non-Jews) in the church in Rome, finds himself addressing Jews in this passage, and warns those who have become arrogant because of their ancestral heritage. He warns that their arrogance, laziness, and apathy do not sit well with God. It leads to all sorts of thoughts and behaviors that dishonor God, including saying one thing and actually doing another.

You may or may not have Jewish roots, but this passage is relevant to all of us. What areas of your own heart might be arrogant or apathetic because of your upbringing, your heritage, or what you have done (and not done) in the past?

What might your friends who are far from God think or feel about this? What can be done about it?

When was the last time you said or taught one thing yet acted quite differently? What emotions might God feel when He sees us thinking or acting contrary to His character?

PRAY

Sit for a few minutes in silence, asking God to help you know the feeling of true humility. Then call on Him to forgive you where your life has not lived up to what you claim to believe. (Be specific.)

LIVE

Courageously invite others around you to help you remain humble. Give them permission to do what it takes to help your life match your words.

HOPING AGAINST HOPE

ROMANS 4:16-21

[16] This is why the promise is by faith, so that it may be according to grace, to guarantee it to all the descendants — not only to those who are of the law but also to those who are of Abraham's faith. He is the father of us all [17] in God's sight. As it is written: I have made you the father of many nations. He believed in God, who gives life to the dead and calls things into existence that do not exist. [18] He believed, hoping against hope, so that he became the father of many nations according to what had been spoken: So will your descendants be. [19] He considered his own body to be already dead (since he was about 100 years old) and also considered the deadness of Sarah's womb, without weakening in the faith. [20] He did not waver in unbelief at God's promise but was strengthened in his faith and gave glory to God, [21] because he was fully convinced that what He had promised He was also able to perform.

READ

Read the passage aloud slowly.

THINK

Read the passage again, but silently.

1. What did God do for Abraham?
2. If you were Abraham, which of the following efforts would be most difficult for you?

   ☐ daring to call things into existence that do not exist
   ☐ believing in spite of hopeless circumstances
   ☐ living on the basis of what God had spoken
   ☐ not focusing on hopeless circumstances
   ☐ not wavering in unbelief
   ☐ being strengthened in faith and giving glory to God
   ☐ being fully convinced that what God promised He is able to perform
   ☐ other:

Read the passage again. What words or phrases stand out to you?

PRAY

Thank God for Abraham, "father of us all." Ask God to help you trust Him and His way.

LIVE

Sit quietly before God. Get used to the idea that you really can embrace Him and what He does. Imagine one way your life might be different if you do this.

ENSLAVED TO RIGHTEOUSNESS

ROMANS 6:15-21

¹⁵ What then? Should we sin because we are not under law but under grace? Absolutely not! ¹⁶ Don't you know that if you offer yourselves to someone as obedient slaves, you are slaves of that one you obey — either of sin leading to death or of obedience leading to righteousness? ¹⁷ But thank God that, although you used to be slaves of sin, you obeyed from the heart that pattern of teaching you were transferred to, ¹⁸ and having been liberated from sin, you became enslaved to righteousness. ¹⁹ I am using a human analogy because of the weakness of your flesh. For just as you offered the parts of yourselves as slaves to moral impurity, and to greater and greater lawlessness, so now offer them as slaves to righteousness, which results in sanctification. ²⁰ For when you were slaves of sin, you were free from allegiance to righteousness. ²¹ So what fruit was produced then from the things you are now ashamed of? For the end of those things is death.

THINK

Search yourself for an area where you don't walk in freedom but continue to struggle with sin. When do you easily give in to temptation? Why? Are there times when you don't feel the pull so strongly? Why? What comfort, relief, or pleasure does the sin give you (no matter how short-lived or shallow)? What pain or discomfort does it bring? What do you fear you would lose if you gave up the sin?

READ

Read the passage with your specific sin in mind. Sift these verses through your life experience. How do they hold up? Do you find Paul's description of sin — "because we are not under law but under grace" — to be accurate? What about his perspective on "having been liberated from sin" — living in obedience to His commands? Take time to identify what you do and don't agree with.

PRAY

Talk to God about the things you've uncovered. If you have unanswered questions or problems you can't reconcile, share them. If you're frustrated, express it to Him. Maybe you will challenge Him to show you freedom, as you agree to take on the challenge of giving His ways a shot.

LIVE

"Having been liberated from sin, you became enslaved to righteousness." Rest in this freedom today.

NOTHING CAN SEPARATE US FROM GOD'S LOVE

ROMANS 8:31-39

31 What then are we to say about these things?
If God is for us, who is against us?

32 He did not even spare His own Son
but offered Him up for us all;
how will He not also with Him grant us everything?

33 Who can bring an accusation against God's elect?
God is the One who justifies.

34 Who is the one who condemns?
Christ Jesus is the One who died,
but even more, has been raised;
He also is at the right hand of God
and intercedes for us.

35 Who can separate us from the love of Christ?
Can affliction or anguish or persecution
or famine or nakedness or danger or sword?

36 As it is written:
Because of You we are being put to death all day long;
we are counted as sheep to be slaughtered.

37 No, in all these things we are more than victorious
through Him who loved us.

38 For I am persuaded that not even death or life,
angels or rulers,
things present or things to come, hostile powers,

39 height or depth, or any other created thing
will have the power to separate us
from the love of God that is in Christ Jesus our Lord!

READ

Read the passage four times very slowly.

THINK

Logically understanding that God loves us is fairly easy. But grasping this truth to its fullest extent in our hearts and souls — in every corner of our everyday existence — requires more. We think we know God loves us, but we don't often ponder this profound truth, this important element of our identity as God's children.

Read the passage again. This time underline the phrases that speak directly to you and encourage your heart. With each underline, say aloud, "Thank You, God, for how much You love me."

"Who can separate us from the love of Christ?" When you read Paul's words, what flows through your mind and heart?

PRAY

Sit in silence with one thought in mind: *I am loved by God.* If your mind begins to wander, simply whisper, "Thank You for loving me, Jesus." Claim the promises of this passage as your own.

LIVE

Live confidently knowing that nothing "will have the power to separate us from the love of God." He loves you that much!

THE MESSAGE OF FAITH

ROMANS 10:8-13

[8] On the contrary, what does it say? The message is near you, in your mouth and in your heart. This is the message of faith that we proclaim: [9] If you confess with your mouth, "Jesus is Lord," and believe in your heart that God raised Him from the dead, you will be saved. [10] One believes with the heart, resulting in righteousness, and one confesses with the mouth, resulting in salvation. [11] Now the Scripture says, Everyone who believes on Him will not be put to shame, [12] for there is no distinction between Jew and Greek, since the same Lord of all is rich to all who call on Him. [13] For everyone who calls on the name of the Lord will be saved.

READ

Read the passage aloud slowly.

THINK

Read the passage again silently.

1. Look at the rich phrases and see which one speaks to you most:

   ☐ "The message is near you, in your mouth and in your heart."
   ☐ "the message of faith that we proclaim"
   ☐ "believe in your heart that God raised Him from the dead, you will be saved"
   ☐ "confesses with the mouth"
   ☐ "the same Lord of all is rich to all who call on Him"
   ☐ "Everyone who believes on Him will not be put to shame."
   ☐ "Everyone who calls on the name of the Lord will be saved."

2. Why does this phrase touch you?
3. In what way would you like this phrase to become a stronger reality in your life?

PRAY

Thank God for His nearness, His willingness to be embraced, His willingness to hear us, resulting in salvation. Talk to God about your next step in believing on Him.

LIVE

Sit quietly before God, imagining what it feels like to live trusting Him and believing in your heart — a life without shame.

DAY 259

GOD ENCOUNTERS

On this seventh day, review and reflect on all you have read this week. Take the time to revel in the ways you've encountered God in the past six days.

A LIVING SACRIFICE

ROMANS 12:1-3

[1] Therefore, brothers, by the mercies of God, I urge you to present your bodies as a living sacrifice, holy and pleasing to God; this is your spiritual worship. [2] Do not be conformed to this age, but be transformed by the renewing of your mind, so that you may discern what is the good, pleasing, and perfect will of God.

[3] For by the grace given to me, I tell everyone among you not to think of himself more highly than he should think. Instead, think sensibly, as God has distributed a measure of faith to each one.

READ

Read the passage twice, aloud.

THINK

Choose a theme that speaks to you—perhaps the idea of being transformed by the renewing of your mind or perhaps discerning the perfect will of God. What does this passage say about that issue?

PRAY

Pick one phrase from the passage that pinpoints the theme that impacts you. Repeat that phrase to yourself slowly several times. Each time you say it, notice your internal response. What thoughts, memories, or feelings does it stir up?

Now bring these thoughts back to the passage, line by line, in a conversation with God: He speaks to you through the words in the passage, then you respond to what He said. (For example, if you feel you are being "conformed to this age," you bring that feeling to each line of the passage and see how God replies.) When you're finished, repeat the phrase to yourself one last time, checking your heart's reaction. Is it different? Don't worry if this process leaves unanswered questions. Just be open to what God is showing you through your meditation.

LIVE

Consider what it means to "present your bodies as a living sacrifice." What would placing this activity before God as your spiritual worship look like? How would it change some of your day-to-day activities?

GOVERNMENT AND GOD

ROMANS 13:1-7

[1] Everyone must submit to the governing authorities, for there is no authority except from God, and those that exist are instituted by God. [2] So then, the one who resists the authority is opposing God's command, and those who oppose it will bring judgment on themselves. [3] For rulers are not a terror to good conduct, but to bad. Do you want to be unafraid of the authority? Do what is good, and you will have its approval. [4] For government is God's servant for your good. But if you do wrong, be afraid, because it does not carry the sword for no reason. For government is God's servant, an avenger that brings wrath on the one who does wrong. [5] Therefore, you must submit, not only because of wrath, but also because of your conscience. [6] And for this reason you pay taxes, since the authorities are God's public servants, continually attending to these tasks. [7] Pay your obligations to everyone: taxes to those you owe taxes, tolls to those you owe tolls, respect to those you owe respect, and honor to those you owe honor.

THINK

There are all sorts of opinions out there regarding how our government should be run. And people have a hard time talking about church and government in the same paragraphs. *Separation of church and state,* we think.

But when was the last time you thanked God for people in office or prayed for their leadership? Have you ever thought about the truth that God is powerful and in control of the world in such a way that He is not surprised by who is in office, regardless of that person's political views?

In this passage, Paul commands, "Pay your obligations to everyone: taxes to those you owe taxes, tolls to those you owe tolls, respect to those you owe respect, and honor to those you owe honor." What is your obligation as a citizen to this country and to the kingdom of God? In what specific ways can you respect your leaders?

READ

Read the passage.

PRAY

Find a list of names of your local officials (mayor, city council members, county officials), as well as your state and federal officials (governor, congressmen and women, senators, Supreme Court justices, vice president, and president). Pray for each one of them by name. Pray that God would use them to lead wisely and justly.

LIVE

Consider writing a short note or letter of encouragement to one or two of the government officials you prayed for, telling them you are thankful for what they do.

DEBATABLE MATTERS

ROMANS 14:6-10,13

⁶ Whoever observes the day, observes it for the honor of the Lord. Whoever eats, eats for the Lord, since he gives thanks to God; and whoever does not eat, it is for the Lord that he does not eat it, yet he thanks God. ⁷ For none of us lives to himself, and no one dies to himself. ⁸ If we live, we live for the Lord; and if we die, we die for the Lord. Therefore, whether we live or die, we belong to the Lord. ⁹ Christ died and came to life for this: that He might rule over both the dead and the living. ¹⁰ But you, why do you criticize your brother? Or you, why do you look down on your brother? For we will all stand before the tribunal of God. . . .

¹³ Therefore, let us no longer criticize one another. Instead decide never to put a stumbling block or pitfall in your brother's way.

READ

Read the passage aloud slowly, keeping in mind that Paul has been addressing a controversy about what foods are right to eat.

THINK

Read the passage aloud again, imagining that Paul, your brother in Christ, is sitting next to you in a window seat, saying these things to you.

1. Why do people insist on their own way about debatable matters?
2. When you're critical, what words and tone do you usually use? When you're being condescending, what facial expression and arm gestures do you use?
3. What does this passage say about why moral superiority is so silly?

Read the passage aloud again. Which phrase speaks most deeply to you?

PRAY

Take the phrase that spoke to you and talk to God about it. Ask Him to let that truth sink into your deepest self. Ask Him to guide you in that truth.

LIVE

When Mother Teresa was asked how someone might pray for her, she asked that person to pray that she would not get in the way of what God wanted to do. Move through life with that consciousness, acting with God's love but not getting in the way of what God wants to do.

STRENGTH IS FOR SERVICE

ROMANS 15:1-6

[1] Now we who are strong have an obligation to bear the weaknesses of those without strength, and not to please ourselves. [2] Each one of us must please his neighbor for his good, to build him up. [3] For even the Messiah did not please Himself. On the contrary, as it is written, The insults of those who insult You have fallen on Me. [4] For whatever was written in the past was written for our instruction, so that we may have hope through endurance and through the encouragement from the Scriptures. [5] Now may the God who gives endurance and encouragement allow you to live in harmony with one another, according to the command of Christ Jesus, [6] so that you may glorify the God and Father of our Lord Jesus Christ with a united mind and voice.

THINK

Paul specifies that we are to help others in areas where we are strong. What are some areas in which you have received training, direction, or guidance? What are some of your natural gifts and strengths?

READ

Read the passage with a heart of gratitude for those who, past and present, have stepped in to bear your weakness, even if you don't remember specific details.

PRAY

Ponder what this passage says about Jesus and how He dealt with people's troubles. Now think about His call to follow Him (see Matthew 16:24). When you think about being like Jesus in this way, what questions, thoughts, and feelings come up? Share these with Him.

LIVE

Contemplate the role that service to others plays in your daily life. There are a variety of forms this might take, for example, lending a listening ear or emotional support, doing manual labor or other chores for someone, or giving money, food, shelter, or clothing to a person in need. Has your service to others become another form of overwork? Or is it truly integrated into your life in a comfortable and valuable way? Have you been selfish in the use of your time? Should you be giving more of yourself to others than you currently do?[17]

CONSIDER YOUR CALLING

1 CORINTHIANS 1:26-31

[26] Brothers, consider your calling: Not many are wise from a human perspective, not many powerful, not many of noble birth. [27] Instead, God has chosen what is foolish in the world to shame the wise, and God has chosen what is weak in the world to shame the strong. [28] God has chosen what is insignificant and despised in the world — what is viewed as nothing — to bring to nothing what is viewed as something, [29] so that no one can boast in His presence. [30] But it is from Him that you are in Christ Jesus, who became God-given wisdom for us — our righteousness, sanctification, and redemption, [31] in order that, as it is written: The one who boasts must boast in the Lord.

READ

Ruminate over these verses. Take your time and read them slowly.

THINK

What sticks out to you in this passage concerning God and your relationship with Him?

When have you tried to "boast in His presence," either overtly or subtly?

Consider the entire story of Scripture, starting with Genesis. Think about the types of people God fights for and the types He uses to impact human history: Abraham, Moses, Gideon, Saul (later Paul), Peter, and so on. Many of them started out inadequate or less-than-qualified for the job. How does this make you feel about God's desire to use you in His grand plan for the world?

PRAY

Write down your thoughts and prayers in these two areas:

1. "Brothers, consider your calling." Think about what your life was like — specifically and generally — before meeting Christ. (If you don't remember because you let Christ in when you were really young, think about the person you were even five years ago.)
2. Reflect on the person you are today — the ways you are different due to God's involvement in your life.

Thank God for what He's done.

LIVE

Live confidently today, knowing that God wants to use you — yes, even you — for His ultimate purpose and plan. Live openly before Him, realizing that you are an instrument in a world desperately in need of hope.

YOU ARE A SANCTUARY

1 CORINTHIANS 3:11-17

[11] For no one can lay any other foundation than what has been laid down. That foundation is Jesus Christ. [12] If anyone builds on that foundation with gold, silver, costly stones, wood, hay, or straw, [13] each one's work will become obvious, for the day will disclose it, because it will be revealed by fire; the fire will test the quality of each one's work. [14] If anyone's work that he has built survives, he will receive a reward. [15] If anyone's work is burned up, it will be lost, but he will be saved; yet it will be like an escape through fire.

[16] Don't you yourselves know that you are God's sanctuary and that the Spirit of God lives in you? [17] If anyone destroys God's sanctuary, God will destroy him; for God's sanctuary is holy, and that is what you are.

READ

Read the passage aloud slowly.

THINK

Read it aloud again, imagining Paul speaking to you as a good father would speak to you (see 1 Corinthians 4:14-17).

In the metaphor where each of us is a building, Jesus is the foundation. What might someone use for their foundation that would "be revealed by fire"? (In general, this would be anything other than Jesus, but be specific for yourself and others like you.)

The sort of building that you are is a temple, or sanctuary. A temple is where people go to pray. Not only is God Himself present in the temple (you), but both the Holy Spirit and Jesus also live inside you and intercede for you (see Romans 8:26-27,34). What might you do to keep your temple a sacred space?

Read the passage again silently. What does it make you want to be or do or entrust to God?

PRAY

Talk to God about your being a temple for Him — even celebrate it! Then ask what you need to know and do to make the Trinity feel at home inside you.

LIVE

Move through life today, musing to yourself about truly being a temple in which the Trinity dwells. Do something to celebrate that.

DAY 266

GOD ENCOUNTERS

On this seventh day, review and reflect on all you have read this week. Take the time to revel in the ways you've encountered God in the past six days.

A LITTLE YEAST

1 CORINTHIANS 5:1-6

[1] It is widely reported that there is sexual immorality among you, and the kind of sexual immorality that is not even tolerated among the Gentiles — a man is living with his father's wife. [2] And you are inflated with pride, instead of filled with grief so that he who has committed this act might be removed from your congregation. [3] For though I am absent in body but present in spirit, I have already decided about the one who has done this thing as though I were present. [4] When you are assembled in the name of our Lord Jesus with my spirit and with the power of our Lord Jesus, [5] turn that one over to Satan for the destruction of the flesh, so that his spirit may be saved in the Day of the Lord.

[6] Your boasting is not good. Don't you know that a little yeast permeates the whole batch of dough?

READ

Read the passage.

THINK

Have you ever observed the process of baking bread? By the work of a pinch of yeast, a small ball of dough doubles in size. Consider how this process is similar to what happens with sin and tolerance among Christians. In what way does "boasting" make the problem worse?

PRAY

Think of a particular experience you've had with sin lately — either your own or that of someone you're close to. How did you respond? Did the sin break your heart? Did you confront it? Did you avoid or ignore it?

Picture Jesus sitting with you. Talk to Him about what happened. Explore your heart with Him and ask Him to uncover why you responded the way you did.

LIVE

Consider this statement by Julian of Norwich: "[God] comes down to the lowest part of our need. For he never despises that which he himself has made."[18] Do you believe it's true about you? About others you know? Write down what this touches in you and anything you sense God is inviting you to do in response.

RISKING SOMEONE'S ETERNAL RUIN

1 CORINTHIANS 8:7-9

[7] However, not everyone has this knowledge. In fact, some have been so used to idolatry up until now that when they eat food offered to an idol, their conscience, being weak, is defiled. [8] Food will not make us acceptable to God. We are not inferior if we don't eat, and we are not better if we do eat. [9] But be careful that this right of yours in no way becomes a stumbling block to the weak.

READ

This passage was part of an actual letter. Pretend you have just pulled this letter from your mailbox. Read the words as though they are handwritten by a friend.

THINK

Paul gives instruction here to the church in Corinth regarding meat sacrificed to idols. Translated to our current culture, this instruction would be similar to Christians who believe that people should never drink alcohol versus Christians who believe that people have the freedom to drink alcohol, depending on their maturity in their Christian walk.

Think of a situation when you could have been more sensitive to other believers who may have a different understanding than you. How can you grow to be more sensitive to others without becoming soft on the truth? What sacrifices in your own life need to be made to ensure you aren't tripping up other believers?

Where is the limit on our freedom in Christ?

PRAY

Ask God to search your heart in the area of sensitive interaction with other believers. Consider not only *what* you say or do but also *how* you say or do it. Ask the Holy Spirit to give you wisdom and compassion for healthy, God-honoring relationships with other believers.

Finally, ask God to show you if there is anyone you need to request forgiveness from due to an interaction that involved differing views on these types of issues.

LIVE

If applicable, boldly but humbly seek out those individuals and ask their forgiveness for your lack of sensitivity. Consider also talking with friends or family members in the near future about what freedom in Christ expressed appropriately might look like.

DRINKING FROM THE SPIRITUAL ROCK

1 CORINTHIANS 10:1-10

[1] Now I want you to know, brothers, that our fathers were all under the cloud, all passed through the sea, [2] and all were baptized into Moses in the cloud and in the sea. [3] They all ate the same spiritual food, [4] and all drank the same spiritual drink. For they drank from a spiritual rock that followed them, and that rock was Christ. [5] But God was not pleased with most of them, for they were struck down in the wilderness.

[6] Now these things became examples for us, so that we will not desire evil things as they did. [7] Don't become idolaters as some of them were; as it is written, The people sat down to eat and drink, and got up to play. [8] Let us not commit sexual immorality as some of them did, and in a single day 23,000 people fell dead. [9] Let us not test Christ as some of them did and were destroyed by snakes. [10] Nor should we complain as some of them did, and were killed by the destroyer.

READ

Read the passage aloud slowly, realizing that Paul is referring to how the Israelites exited Egypt, crossed the Red Sea, and journeyed to the Promised Land.

THINK

Read the passage again.

1. What miracles did the Israelites experience? (Note: Some people read verse 4 to mean that the same rock followed them or appeared at each of their resting places — and "that rock was Christ." So Christ journeyed with them.)
2. "But God was not pleased with most of them, for they were struck down." Try to understand and explain how they could have developed such a bad attitude.
3. Which of these ways that the Israelites wanted their own way captivates you most?

   ☐ becoming idolaters
   ☐ committing sexual immorality
   ☐ testing Christ
   ☐ complaining

PRAY

Read the passage one more time. Thank God that He draws you to experience His wonder and grace every day. Ask Him to keep you away from temptation and to teach you how to deal with it.

LIVE

Be alert and expectant today, noticing God's wonder and grace, and thanking Him for it. See yourself as learning from the Israelites' mistakes.

MY BODY, WHICH IS FOR YOU

1 CORINTHIANS 11:23-29

²³ For I received from the Lord what I also passed on to you: On the night when He was betrayed, the Lord Jesus took bread, ²⁴ gave thanks, broke it, and said, "This is My body, which is for you. Do this in remembrance of Me."

²⁵ In the same way, after supper He also took the cup and said, "This cup is the new covenant established by My blood. Do this, as often as you drink it, in remembrance of Me." ²⁶ For as often as you eat this bread and drink the cup, you proclaim the Lord's death until He comes.

²⁷ Therefore, whoever eats the bread or drinks the cup of the Lord in an unworthy way will be guilty of sin against the body and blood of the Lord. ²⁸ So a man should examine himself; in this way he should eat the bread and drink from the cup. ²⁹ For whoever eats and drinks without recognizing the body, eats and drinks judgment on himself.

THINK

Briefly think back on the last time you took Communion. What was it like for you? Did it feel routine or special? In what ways? Who was there with you? Did the presence of that person(s) change the experience for you in any way? How did you prepare yourself?

READ

Read the passage, being especially aware of how you usually approach Communion.

PRAY

Be aware of the Holy Spirit's presence with you now. Meditate on what stands out to you in Paul's description of the communion experience. What is your reaction to his words? Do you resonate with his serious tone? Do you feel challenged by anything in particular? Invite the Holy Spirit to examine your heart and to filter out any junk He finds there — and make you clean.

LIVE

Take time to examine your heart now, as at Communion. What do you need to clear up with God? With another person? Meditate on this Anglican prayer from *The Book of Common Prayer*: "We do not presume to come to this thy Table, O merciful Lord, trusting in our own righteousness, but in thy manifold and great mercies. We are not worthy so much as to gather up the crumbs under thy Table. But thou art the same Lord whose property is always to have mercy. Grant us therefore, gracious Lord, so to eat the flesh of thy dear Son Jesus Christ, and to drink his blood, that we may evermore dwell in him, and he in us. *Amen*."[19]

Find out the next time your church plans to offer Communion, and set aside time on your calendar to revisit this prayer of examination before you participate.

NOTHING WITHOUT LOVE

1 CORINTHIANS 13:3-7

³ And if I donate all my goods to feed the poor,
and if I give my body in order to boast
but do not have love, I gain nothing.

⁴ Love is patient, love is kind.
Love does not envy,
is not boastful, is not conceited,

⁵ does not act improperly,
is not selfish, is not provoked,
and does not keep a record of wrongs.

⁶ Love finds no joy in unrighteousness
but rejoices in the truth.

⁷ It bears all things, believes all things,
hopes all things, endures all things.

READ

Ask God to give you fresh insight into these familiar words, allowing you to learn things that you haven't before. Now read the passage.

THINK

Whether we know Scripture well or not, most of us have heard this passage read during a wedding ceremony. Its words are encouraging and uplifting, and we might hope the couple won't forget them (and us either). But as you know, reading the words is much easier than living by them.

Ponder this sentence: "If I give my body in order to boast but do not have love, I gain nothing." What specifically does this mean in your own life?

Consider the list that defines love. Read line by line, asking yourself these two questions: In what ways am I living this out well? In what ways do I need to improve?

PRAY

Pick the one that needs more improvement, and communicate it to God. Ask Him to remodel your life in such a way that you quickly see changes in this area. Ask for the ability to recognize when you're not exemplifying the godly love described in this passage.

LIVE

Someplace where you will see it often today — in your cell phone, on your hand, or at the top of a notebook — write the one way you want to improve. When you see it, ask yourself how you might express that attribute to those around you.

BE STEADFAST

1 CORINTHIANS 15:51-58

[51] Listen! I am telling you a mystery:

> We will not all fall asleep,
> but we will all be changed,
> [52] in a moment, in the blink of an eye,
> at the last trumpet.
> For the trumpet will sound,
> and the dead will be raised incorruptible,
> and we will be changed.
> [53] For this corruptible must be clothed
> with incorruptibility,
> and this mortal must be clothed
> with immortality.
> [54] When this corruptible is clothed
> with incorruptibility,
> and this mortal is clothed
> with immortality,
> then the saying that is written will take place:
> Death has been swallowed up in victory.
> [55] Death, where is your victory?
> Death, where is your sting?
> [56] Now the sting of death is sin,
> and the power of sin is the law.
> [57] But thanks be to God, who gives us the victory
> through our Lord Jesus Christ!

[58] Therefore, my dear brothers, be steadfast, immovable, always excelling in the Lord's work, knowing that your labor in the Lord is not in vain.

READ

Read this passage a few times, slowly and meditatively.

THINK

What phrase or idea in this passage stands out to you? Perhaps you are drawn toward the "last trumpet" or being free from the fear of death, or maybe you are more drawn to the concept of excelling in the Lord's work. Allow this idea to unfold in your mind. What does it mean for your life today?

PRAY

Talk to the Master about how this makes you feel. If you have questions for Him, don't hold on to them: Let Jesus hear them and then let them go. Trust that your questions will be answered at the right time.

Once you have shared your concerns with Jesus, sit with Him in silence, being open to whatever He might say in response.

LIVE

Consider Paul's instruction to the Christians in Corinth to "be steadfast, immovable, always excelling in the Lord's work." Ponder: What is the "work" you have been made for? Consider your interests, abilities, skills, passions. When do you feel most alive? (The work you've been made for may or may not correspond to your current vocation.)

What holds you back from pursuing this work with your whole heart — however that might look at this stage in your life? Consider the legitimate reasons, as well as the reasons that might be illegitimate but are still preventing you from moving ahead. Talk to God about this. Ask Him to show you what He would have you do, even if that's the simple step of waiting on Him to slowly reveal your work over time.

DAY 273

GOD ENCOUNTERS

On this seventh day, review and reflect on all you have read this week. Take the time to revel in the ways you've encountered God in the past six days.

YES!

2 CORINTHIANS 1:17-22

[17] So when I planned this, was I irresponsible? Or what I plan, do I plan in a purely human way so that I say "Yes, yes" and "No, no" simultaneously? [18] As God is faithful, our message to you is not "Yes and no." [19] For the Son of God, Jesus Christ, who was preached among you by us — by me and Silvanus and Timothy — did not become "Yes and no"; on the contrary, a final "Yes" has come in Him. [20] For every one of God's promises is "Yes" in Him. Therefore, the "Amen" is also spoken through Him by us for God's glory. [21] Now it is God who strengthens us, with you, in Christ and has anointed us. [22] He has also sealed us and given us the Spirit as a down payment in our hearts.

READ

Read the passage slowly, at least three times.

THINK

In these verses, Paul writes to the church in the city of Corinth about the promises of God through the fulfillment of Jesus. Read the passage again and circle the word *yes* each time it appears in the text.

So often we hear the word *no,* but this passage says, "Every one of God's promises is 'Yes' in Him." What does it mean to hear *yes* from God?

What would your life look like (specifically) if you accepted that "the 'Amen' is also spoken through Him by us for God's glory"?

PRAY

Allow God to affirm you as you simply sit with Him.

Invite Him to bring His promises of "yes" to your mind and heart. What specific promises has He given to you? Embrace those promises and ask Him to place these stamps of "yes" on your heart so you can carry them with you.

LIVE

Write down one or two specific "yeses" God has given you. Carry that note around with you. Consider sharing these promises with a friend, roommate, family member, classmate, or coworker today.

UNVEILED FACES

2 CORINTHIANS 3:12-18

[12] Therefore, having such a hope, we use great boldness. [13] We are not like Moses, who used to put a veil over his face so that the Israelites could not stare at the the end of what was fading away, [14] but their minds were closed. For to this day, at the reading of the old covenant, the same veil remains; it is not lifted, because it is set aside only in Christ. [15] Even to this day, whenever Moses is read, a veil lies over their hearts, [16] but whenever a person turns to the Lord, the veil is removed. [17] Now the Lord is the Spirit, and where the Spirit of the Lord is, there is freedom. [18] We all, with unveiled faces, are looking as in a mirror at the glory of the Lord and are being transformed into the same image from glory to glory; this is from the Lord who is the Spirit.

READ

Read the passage aloud slowly.

THINK

Again, slowly read verses 12-15 with a mood of despair. Then read verses 16-18 with a mood of joy, mystery, and surprise.

1. What words or phrases stand out to you? Why?
2. If you didn't choose words or phrases from verses 16-18, do that now. Read them again and note the frequency of these words: *face, glory, freedom, transformed.*

PRAY

Paraphrase verses 16-18 back to God with something like: "Whenever I turn my face to You, O God, You remove the veil and there we are, face-to-face! I will suddenly recognize You as a living, personal presence, not a remote, unknown figure. And when You are personally present, a living Spirit, that old, constricting legalism is recognized as obsolete. I'm free of it! All of us are! Nothing between me and You, my face shining with the glory of Your face. And so I am transformed. My life gradually becomes brighter and more beautiful as You enter my life and I become like You."

LIVE

Sit quietly before God, basking in one of these phrases:

- "the Lord is the Spirit"
- "unveiled faces"
- "being transformed into the same image from glory to glory"

TREASURE IN CLAY JARS

2 CORINTHIANS 4:5-13

⁵ For we are not proclaiming ourselves but Jesus Christ as Lord, and ourselves as your slaves because of Jesus. ⁶ For God who said, "Let light shine out of darkness," has shone in our hearts to give the light of the knowledge of God's glory in the face of Jesus Christ.

⁷ Now we have this treasure in clay jars, so that this extraordinary power may be from God and not from us. ⁸ We are pressured in every way but not crushed; we are perplexed but not in despair; ⁹ we are persecuted but not abandoned; we are struck down but not destroyed. ¹⁰ We always carry the death of Jesus in our body, so that the life of Jesus may also be revealed in our body. ¹¹ For we who live are always given over to death because of Jesus, so that Jesus' life may also be revealed in our mortal flesh. ¹² So death works in us, but life in you. ¹³ And since we have the same spirit of faith in keeping with what is written, I believed, therefore I spoke, we also believe, and therefore speak.

READ

Read the passage aloud once. Read it a second time, and if a word catches your attention, stop and toss it around in your mind. Listen briefly for what your heart is saying in reply. Then keep reading.

THINK

In the silence that follows your reading, meditate on what you heard. How do you relate to the pressured, perplexed, and persecuted lifestyle Paul and other Christians in the first century led? If you can't relate, what other people around you might be run-down and struggling?

PRAY

Tell God what you've been thinking about. What is your response to the trouble and pain in or around you? If it's your own pain, share with God what you wish you could do in response. If it's the pain of another, notice your impulse to help, fix, or ignore. Be open to God's response to you. Let your sharing lead you into a silent prayer of thankfulness, humility, or request.

LIVE

In her book *Going on Retreat,* Margaret Silf describes what she calls a "retreat on the streets": Small groups of people meet to pray, then they go off into the city with only a few dollars to spend on food that day, taking opportunities to talk with the homeless, unemployed, disturbed, or addicted. At the end of the day, the group gathers to share thoughts and feelings, and to pray.[20]

While this kind of retreat may not be appropriate for you at this time, think about how you could intentionally seek to engage with the needs and feelings of disadvantaged people around you. What would your life look like if you let the light within you shine amid the darkness?

276

A NEW CREATION

2 CORINTHIANS 5:14-21

[14] For Christ's love compels us, since we have reached this conclusion: If One died for all, then all died. [15] And He died for all so that those who live should no longer live for themselves, but for the One who died for them and was raised.

[16] From now on, then, we do not know anyone in a purely human way. Even if we have known Christ in a purely human way, yet now we no longer know Him in this way. [17] Therefore, if anyone is in Christ, he is a new creation; old things have passed away, and look, new things have come. [18] Everything is from God, who reconciled us to Himself through Christ and gave us the ministry of reconciliation: [19] That is, in Christ, God was reconciling the world to Himself, not counting their trespasses against them, and He has committed the message of reconciliation to us. [20] Therefore, we are ambassadors for Christ, certain that God is appealing through us. We plead on Christ's behalf, "Be reconciled to God." [21] He made the One who did not know sin to be sin for us, so that we might become the righteousness of God in Him.

READ

Read the passage.

THINK

What implications does this passage have for your life right now?

Meditate on these words: "If anyone is in Christ, he is a new creation; old things have passed away, and look, new things have come." (You might consider their radical inclusiveness.)

"Be reconciled to God." How can you become reconciled to God? What would that entail? Do you feel deserving of reconciliation? Why or why not?

PRAY

Thank God that He gives you a fresh start with your life and a fresh start every single morning. Let your thankfulness spill over; tell God that you are grateful to have new life in Him.

Ask God to help you become a better friend to Him and to help you understand what a friend He is to you!

LIVE

"We are ambassadors for Christ." Who can you tell today about what God is doing in the world?

HEART OPENED WIDE

2 CORINTHIANS 6:1-13

[1] Working together with Him, we also appeal to you, "Don't receive God's grace in vain." [2] For He says:

> I heard you in an acceptable time,
> and I helped you in the day of salvation.

Look, now is the acceptable time; now is the day of salvation.
[3] We give no opportunity for stumbling to anyone, so that the ministry will not be blamed. [4] But as God's ministers, we commend ourselves in everything:

> by great endurance, by afflictions,
> by hardship, by difficulties,
> [5] by beatings, by imprisonments,
> by riots, by labors,
> by sleepless nights, by times of hunger,
> [6] by purity, by knowledge,
> by patience, by kindness,
> by the Holy Spirit, by sincere love,
> [7] by the message of truth,
> by the power of God;
> through weapons of righteousness
> on the right hand and the left,
> [8] through glory and dishonor,
> through slander and good report;
> as deceivers yet true;
> [9] as unknown yet recognized;
> as dying and look — we live;
> as being disciplined yet not killed;
> [10] as grieving yet always rejoicing;
> as poor yet enriching many;
> as having nothing yet possessing everything.

[11] We have spoken openly to you, Corinthians; our heart has been opened wide. [12] You are not limited by us, but you are limited by your own affections. [13] I speak as to my children. As a proper response, you should also be open to us.

READ

Read the passage aloud slowly.

THINK

Read the passage again, noting any words that stand out to you.

1. What does this passage have to say to someone who thinks life is boring?
2. What does it say to someone who thinks living for God is boring?
3. With what sort of heart did Paul and his friends do their work for God?

Read the passage one more time — very slowly.

4. What words or phrases are most meaningful to you?
5. How do they connect with your life right now?

PRAY

Talk to God about the opportunity to live with a heart opened wide. Ask Him to show you how to work hard with a life of power and rejoicing.

LIVE

Sit in the word *live*. Picture yourself fully alive, partnering with God in what He is doing (or wants to do) in you, and in the people and circumstances around you.

GRIEF THAT LEADS TO REPENTANCE

2 CORINTHIANS 7:8-13

[8] For even if I grieved you with my letter, I do not regret it — even though I did regret it since I saw that the letter grieved you, yet only for a little while. [9] Now I rejoice, not because you were grieved, but because your grief led to repentance. For you were grieved as God willed, so that you didn't experience any loss from us. [10] For godly grief produces a repentance not to be regretted and leading to salvation, but worldly grief produces death. [11] For consider how much diligence this very thing — this grieving as God wills — has produced in you: what a desire to clear yourselves, what indignation, what fear, what deep longing, what zeal, what justice! In every way you showed yourselves to be pure in this matter. [12] So even though I wrote to you, it was not because of the one who did wrong, or because of the one who was wronged, but in order that your diligence for us might be made plain to you in the sight of God. [13] For this reason we have been comforted.

In addition to our comfort, we rejoiced even more over the joy Titus had, because his spirit was refreshed by all of you.

LIVE

Because we are spirits in bodies, tangible objects or physical activities can help us enter into prayer. If it's daytime, close the curtains or go into a room without windows. Light a candle and spend a few minutes watching the flame before you read and pray today. Let your awareness of the flame quiet your tendency to be aware only of yourself.

READ

Read the passage twice. According to Paul, what are God's reasons for using grief to bring us to repentance? How does Paul describe a life of repentance that is brought back closer to God?

THINK

Now set the text aside and take a few moments to sit with your eyes closed and recall recent experiences you've had with sin. Did you repent? If so, how did God lead you to that? Did you resist? What turned you around? If you didn't repent, do you notice ways that God was reaching out to you that you refused? What were the thoughts that held you back?

PRAY

Go back to the passage again. Prayerfully reread Paul's perspective on repentance. How does his outlook interact with your current situation? Is there a message you sense God is speaking to you?

DAY 280

GOD ENCOUNTERS

On this seventh day, review and reflect on all you have read this week. Take the time to revel in the ways you've encountered God in the past six days.

GENEROUS OFFERINGS

2 CORINTHIANS 9:8-15

[8] And God is able to make every grace overflow to you, so that in every way, always having everything you need, you may excel in every good work. [9] As it is written:

> He scattered;
> He gave to the poor;
> His righteousness endures forever.

[10] Now the One who provides seed for the sower and bread for food will provide and multiply your seed and increase the harvest of your righteousness. [11] You will be enriched in every way for all generosity, which produces thanksgiving to God through us. [12] For the ministry of this service is not only supplying the needs of the saints, but is also overflowing in many acts of thanksgiving to God. [13] They will glorify God for your obedience to the confession of the gospel of Christ, and for your generosity in sharing with them and with others through the proof provided by this service. [14] And they will have deep affection for you in their prayers on your behalf because of the surpassing grace of God in you. [15] Thanks be to God for His indescribable gift.

READ

Read the passage, imagining that Paul is speaking these words specifically to you.

THINK

Paul talks here about generosity as an important element of God's character. Taking care of the poor is close to the heart of God. Jesus spoke — and lived — generously, just like His Father.

Do you think followers of God are known as being generous people? Why or why not?

In what ways can you grow in your generosity with your time? Your love? Your money? Your abilities? Your possessions? Your life?

PRAY

Walk around inside and outside your home. Look at your possessions: clothes, electronic equipment, books, furniture, paintings on the walls, maybe even the car in your driveway, and so on. What does all this stuff make you think? (Even if most of it belongs to others, like your parents, what's running through your head and heart?) Use Paul's words as the foundation for your communication with God, praying as you walk around.

Talk with God about your desire to be more generous with the objects you possess. Ask Him to bring to mind the people you could be more generous with today and in what way. Ask God to make you more like Him — a person of generosity.

LIVE

Go and live with generosity at the forefront of your mind.

GOD'S HIDDEN SERVANTS

2 CORINTHIANS 11:21,23-30

[21] I say this to our shame: We have been weak.

But in whatever anyone dares to boast—I am talking foolishly—I also dare: . . .

> [23] Are they servants of Christ?
> I'm talking like a madman—I'm a better one:
> with far more labors,
> many more imprisonments,
> far worse beatings, near death many times.
> [24] Five times I received 39 lashes from Jews.
> [25] Three times I was beaten with rods by the Romans.
> Once I was stoned by my enemies.
> Three times I was shipwrecked.
> I have spent a night and a day
> in the open sea.
> [26] On frequent journeys, I faced
> dangers from rivers,
> dangers from robbers,
> dangers from my own people,
> dangers from the Gentiles,
> dangers in the city,
> dangers in the open country,
> dangers on the sea,
> and dangers among false brothers;
> [27] labor and hardship,
> many sleepless nights, hunger and thirst,
> often without food, cold, and lacking clothing.

[28] Not to mention other things, there is the daily pressure on me: my care for all the churches. [29] Who is weak, and I am not weak? Who is made to stumble, and I do not burn with indignation? [30] If boasting is necessary, I will boast about my weaknesses.

READ

Read the passage aloud slowly, keeping in mind that the Corinthians were partial to slick preachers.

THINK

Which sort of teachers (of the Bible, of spiritual things) do you gravitate toward: the animated, joking, smooth servants of God or the hidden, suffering, unrecognized servants of God?

Paul was the second type. In those days, they didn't know him as we do — the great apostle Paul who wrote nearly half the New Testament. He may not have been all that popular a fellow.

Read the passage again silently. If you were to admire the apostle Paul, what in this passage describes what you would admire him for?

Keep in mind that Paul was also a person of joy. His joy was not in being well-known and appreciated. Instead he was one who encouraged his reader to "rejoice in the Lord always" (Philippians 4:4). When do you need Paul's sort of joy in your life?

PRAY

Ask God to give you discernment (not judgment) about His servants and which ones are best to follow. Ask God to give you great satisfaction in serving Him regardless of how successful that service may look.

LIVE

Watch today for an opportunity to feel the desperation for another who is at the end of his or her rope, or to have an angry fire in your gut when someone is duped into sin. Make an effort to weep for those who weep and rejoice with those who rejoice.

RELATIONSHIPS ARE MESSY

2 CORINTHIANS 12:16-21

[16] Now granted, I have not burdened you; yet sly as I am, I took you in by deceit! [17] Did I take advantage of you by anyone I sent you? [18] I urged Titus to come, and I sent the brother with him. Did Titus take advantage of you? Didn't we walk in the same spirit and in the same footsteps?

[19] You have thought all along that we were defending ourselves to you. No, in the sight of God we are speaking in Christ, and everything, dear friends, is for building you up. [20] For I fear that perhaps when I come I will not find you to be what I want, and I may not be found by you to be what you want; there may be quarreling, jealousy, outbursts of anger, selfish ambitions, slander, gossip, arrogance, and disorder. [21] I fear that when I come my God will again humiliate me in your presence, and I will grieve for many who sinned before and have not repented of the moral impurity, sexual immorality, and promiscuity they practiced.

READ

Read the passage aloud slowly.

THINK

Enter the scenes that Paul is describing. Envision the individual members of the Corinthian church he's writing to. Replay Paul's history with them — how he first came to the cosmopolitan city preaching the message of Christ for the first time. Many believed and repented, and many formed new churches. Since then, those churches have helped support him financially, and he's acted as a spiritual mentor and father to them. Imagine what goes on in his mind as he anticipates visiting them again; think about what his last visit was like.

PRAY

Now read the passage again aloud. Notice the messiness of human relationships — misunderstandings, conflicts, and tensions. In the silence that follows your reading, consider your own relationships. Pick one in which you've felt the most recent tension or problems. Open up to God, asking Him to show you what He wants you to know about it.

LIVE

Write down in a journal what God uncovered for you about your problematic relationship. Ask Him to make clear anything He is asking you to notice or do about it, then sit quietly and attentively as you wait for His response. Don't assume that you should necessarily do anything; instead, be open to how God leads you.

IN NEED OF CORRECTION

GALATIANS 1:6-12

⁶ I am amazed that you are so quickly turning away from Him who called you by the grace of Christ and are turning to a different gospel — ⁷ not that there is another gospel, but there are some who are troubling you and want to change the good news about the Messiah. ⁸ But even if we or an angel from heaven should preach to you a gospel other than what we have preached to you, a curse be on him! ⁹ As we have said before, I now say again: If anyone preaches to you a gospel contrary to what you received, a curse be on him!

¹⁰ For am I now trying to win the favor of people, or God? Or am I striving to please people? If I were still trying to please people, I would not be a slave of Christ.

¹¹ Now I want you to know, brothers, that the gospel preached by me is not based on human thought. ¹² For I did not receive it from a human source and I was not taught it, but it came by a revelation from Jesus Christ.

READ

Read the passage aloud. Reflect by writing your thoughts down in a journal or typing them into your computer.

THINK

This feels like a scathing lecture from Paul — and it certainly is. He is disgusted because the church in Galatia has turned from the true message of the gospel to other teachers who want to change the good news.

Consider carefully: What are the essentials of the gospel — the good news of Jesus Christ? What does it most certainly include? What does it most certainly not include?

Have you ever been tempted to turn from the message of the gospel or to add to, delete, or alter portions of it to make it conveniently fit your life? Have you ever heard others add to, delete, or alter the message of the gospel? What might be done about that? What are the consequences of doing such a thing?

What might Paul say to you if he were here today?

PRAY

Prayerfully reflect on the importance of the gospel message. Ask God to give you a mind that discerns and carefully weighs the truth of the gospel and that knows how the gospel should be applied to your life.

LIVE

Spend a few minutes searching for and reading at least three key passages in your Bible that speak specifically to the meaning of the gospel.

FAITH NOT WORKS

GALATIANS 2:16,19-21

[16] [We] know that no one is justified by the works of the law but by faith in Jesus Christ. And we have believed in Christ Jesus so that we might be justified by faith in Christ and not by the works of the law, because by the works of the law no human being will be justified. . . . [19] For through the law I have died to the law, so that I might live for God. I have been crucified with Christ [20] and I no longer live, but Christ lives in me. The life I now live in the body, I live by faith in the Son of God, who loved me and gave Himself for me. [21] I do not set aside the grace of God, for if righteousness comes through the law, then Christ died for nothing.

READ

Read the passage aloud slowly.

THINK

Read it again silently.

1. What did Paul find that was better than works of the law?
2. Which of the following astonishing statements by Paul do you find most intriguing?

   ☐ "By the works of the law no human being will be justified."
   ☐ "We might be justified by faith in Christ and not by the works of the law."
   ☐ "Christ lives in me."
   ☐ "The life I now live in the body, I live by faith in the Son of God."

Read the passage one more time — very slowly — letting it sink into the innermost parts of you.

PRAY

Talk to God about Paul's amazing statements. Which of them do you want help in making true of yourself? To what degree do you really believe that Christ lives in you? If you need help believing this, tell God.

LIVE

Take something with you through your day to remind yourself that the life you now live is not yours, but is Christ's life in you. The item could be a cross, a piece of paper with this statement written on it, a stone on which you have written *LIFE,* or whatever will help remind you.

GROWTH: A RESULT OF HOW HARD YOU TRY?

GALATIANS 3:2-6

² I only want to learn this from you: Did you receive the Spirit by the works of the law or by hearing with faith? ³ Are you so foolish? After beginning with the Spirit, are you now going to be made complete by the flesh? ⁴ Did you suffer so much for nothing—if in fact it was for nothing? ⁵ So then, does God supply you with the Spirit and work miracles among you by the works of the law or by hearing with faith?

⁶ Just as Abraham believed God, and it was credited to him for righteousness.

READ

As you read this passage, try not to identify yourself too firmly with the author's anger, but stay open to any similarities you recognize between yourself and his listeners.

THINK/PRAY

Ponder one question that particularly challenges you. For example, "Does God give me the Holy Spirit because I try so hard to be good? Or because I trust Him to do it?" Or ask yourself what "foolish" efforts you're making toward a transformational work that He's begun in you. Share your heart's response openly with the Father. Bring Him your questions and concerns, and ask for His help in opening up to His model of growth.

LIVE

Take several minutes to try stepping outside your usual foolishness. Taste what it could be like to see growth as a process of letting God complete what was begun by Him. Rest in the presence of His Holy Spirit, supplied for you. Don't worry about how you'll grow spiritually; don't try to make a plan for how you'll change yourself. Use this time to practice simply being, finding out what it is to be yourself in the presence of Love.

DAY 287

GOD ENCOUNTERS

On this seventh day, review and reflect on all you have read this week. Take the time to revel in the ways you've encountered God in the past six days.

AN HEIR THROUGH GOD

GALATIANS 4:1-7

¹ Now I say that as long as the heir is a child, he differs in no way from a slave, though he is the owner of everything. ² Instead, he is under guardians and stewards until the time set by his father. ³ In the same way we also, when we were children, were in slavery under the elemental forces of the world. ⁴ When the time came to completion, God sent His Son, born of a woman, born under the law, ⁵ to redeem those under the law, so that we might receive adoption as sons. ⁶ And because you are sons, God has sent the Spirit of His Son into our hearts, crying, "*Abba*, Father!" ⁷ So you are no longer a slave but a son, and if a son, then an heir through God.

READ

Read the passage at least five times. Take your time. Slow down and reflect on what you read.

THINK

Paul is a master craftsman of metaphors. And so we find him here in the middle of another word picture, contrasting the difference between the rights and privileges of a slave and those of an heir. We were once slaves, but as believers we are now called sons and daughters — heirs — and God desires for us to live in freedom, not slavery: "so that we might receive adoption as sons."

What does it mean for you to receive adoption in Christ? What does it mean to have freedom in your relationship with Him? How do you temper that freedom so as not to abuse God's grace?

In what ways does being an heir rather than a slave change your interaction with your Father? Be specific.

PRAY

Imagine yourself in the lap of your Father, crying, "Abba, Father!" With the mind-set of a child, pray like a child. Begin your prayer with "Papa." Pray freely and without fear, knowing that this childlike and intimate language is not only permissible but desirable. Tell Him your fears. Tell Him your joys. Tell Him your dreams.

LIVE

Pray frequently, creatively, and confidently, knowing that you have great freedom to approach your heavenly Papa, who is always accessible to you.

FRUITFUL LOVE

GALATIANS 5:16-17,19-23

¹⁶ I say then, walk by the Spirit and you will not carry out the desire of the flesh. ¹⁷ For the flesh desires what is against the Spirit, and the Spirit desires what is against the flesh; these are opposed to each other, so that you don't do what you want. . . .

¹⁹ Now the works of the flesh are obvious: sexual immorality, moral impurity, promiscuity, ²⁰ idolatry, sorcery, hatreds, strife, jealousy, outbursts of anger, selfish ambitions, dissensions, factions, ²¹ envy, drunkenness, carousing, and anything similar. I tell you about these things in advance — as I told you before — that those who practice such things will not inherit the kingdom of God.

²² But the fruit of the Spirit is love, joy, peace, patience, kindness, goodness, faith, ²³ gentleness, self-control. Against such things there is no law.

READ

Read the passage aloud slowly. Read verses 16-17 and 19-21 again slowly. What words or phrases stand out to you? Why do you think they stand out? Read verses 22-23 again slowly. What words or phrases stand out to you? Why do you think they stand out?

THINK

These two ways of life — self-focus and God-focus — negate each other. To live the first way shuts out the second. To live the second way shuts out the first. The first is empowered by the idea that we must get what we want when we want it. The second is empowered by a faithful, fruitful love for God.

PRAY

Talk to God about the ideas that stood out to you in verses 22-23. Tell God why these are attractive to you. Tell God how they reflect His deep character.

LIVE

Hold one of the following words in front of you today: *joy, peace, patience, goodness, gentleness, self-control.* Let that word permeate what you do.

THE WORLD IS CRUCIFIED TO ME

GALATIANS 6:11-16

¹¹ Look at what large letters I use as I write to you in my own handwriting. ¹² Those who want to make a good impression in the flesh are the ones who would compel you to be circumcised — but only to avoid being persecuted for the cross of Christ. ¹³ For even the circumcised don't keep the law themselves; however, they want you to be circumcised in order to boast about your flesh. ¹⁴ But as for me, I will never boast about anything except the cross of our Lord Jesus Christ. The world has been crucified to me through the cross, and I to the world. ¹⁵ For both circumcision and uncircumcision mean nothing; what matters instead is a new creation. ¹⁶ May peace come to all those who follow this standard, and mercy to the Israel of God!

READ

Carefully read the passage.

THINK

This passage is rebuking first-century Christians for believing that ceremonial Jewish acts like circumcision could alleviate all guilt before God. Consider how you relate to this message. Who are you interested in impressing? How much energy do you expend figuring out ways to be more accepted by others? Is your security rooted in others, or is it rooted in your total acceptance by God?

Do you ever imagine God taking sides — either with you against the world or with everyone else against you? How would your life look if you lived to please only Him?

PRAY

Let your thoughts lead you into conversation with God. Interact with Him on what you're thinking about, remembering that He loves and accepts you. You might write things down as they come to mind, but don't let your writing shrink your awareness so you forget God's presence. Confide in Him why you do what you do, even if you know your reasons are selfish or foolish.

LIVE

Return to the question of how your life would look if you lived only to please Him — to "never boast about anything except the cross of our Lord Jesus Christ." What one thing, even if tiny and internal, could you do to start living this way? Maybe you begin by asking God to give you a view of what it is like to be "crucified . . . to the world."

WHO WE ARE

EPHESIANS 1:11-19

¹¹ We have also received an inheritance in Him, predestined according to the purpose of the One who works out everything in agreement with the decision of His will, ¹² so that we who had already put our hope in the Messiah might bring praise to His glory.

¹³ When you heard the message of truth, the gospel of your salvation, and when you believed in Him, you were also sealed with the promised Holy Spirit. ¹⁴ He is the down payment of our inheritance, for the redemption of the possession, to the praise of His glory.

¹⁵ This is why, since I heard about your faith in the Lord Jesus and your love for all the saints, ¹⁶ I never stop giving thanks for you as I remember you in my prayers. ¹⁷ I pray that the God of our Lord Jesus Christ, the glorious Father, would give you a spirit of wisdom and revelation in the knowledge of Him. ¹⁸ I pray that the perception of your mind may be enlightened so you may know what is the hope of His calling, what are the glorious riches of His inheritance among the saints, ¹⁹ and what is the immeasurable greatness of His power to us who believe, according to the working of His vast strength.

THINK

Consider your identity. Who are you — *really*? In what do you find your true identity and sense of worth? In other words, what makes you, you? Are the sources of your self-worth healthy or unhealthy? Jot down a few notes about how you see your identity.

READ

Read the passage silently, but mouth the words of the verses as you read. What does this passage say about your identity? What is Christ's role in shaping your identity? Refer to your notes. How does this picture of your identity compare to those initial thoughts?

PRAY

Paul includes several elements in his prayers for the church at Ephesus. It is full of thanksgiving, petitions for revelation of the Father, an enlightened mind, knowledge of Christ, and strength.

Make Paul's prayer in verses 15-19 your own. For example, *I ask You — the God of my Lord Jesus Christ, the glorious Father — to give me wisdom and knowledge to know You personally.* And so on.

Next, ask God to bring to mind an individual who needs prayer. Come before God and pray these verses for that person's current situation and overall life. Pray for his or her identity. Make your prayer specific by replacing the applicable words in today's passage with the individual's name.

Are there others for whom you could pray this prayer? Spend time interceding for them as well.

LIVE

If the Spirit nudges you to do so, tell the person that you prayed specifically for him or her. Read that person the prayer from Scripture.

ALIVE WITH THE MESSIAH

EPHESIANS 2:1-6

[1] And you were dead in your trespasses and sins [2] in which you previously walked according to the ways of this world, according to the ruler who exercises authority over the lower heavens, the spirit now working in the disobedient. [3] We too all previously lived among them in our fleshly desires, carrying out the inclinations of our flesh and thoughts, and we were by nature children under wrath as the others were also. [4] But God, who is rich in mercy, because of His great love that He had for us, [5] made us alive with the Messiah even though we were dead in trespasses. You are saved by grace! [6] Together with Christ Jesus He also raised us up and seated us in the heavens.

READ

Read the passage aloud slowly.

THINK

Read the passage again, noting how we "walked according to the ways of this world," as described in the first part of the paragraph and all that God has done in the second part.

1. How do you relate to the way you "previously walked," described in verses 1-3?
2. How difficult or easy is it for you to believe that the old life is not in sync with the life Christ has for us?
3. Repeat in your own words what God has done in verses 4-6. What does this tell you about what God is really like?
4. How difficult or easy is it for you to believe that God is like that?

PRAY

Ask God to help you more easily believe in the goodness of life with Him (verses 1-3) and in the goodness of God's own self (verses 4-6). Respond to God about what it's like to be surrounded by such goodness.

LIVE

Be aware of having an interactive life with this God who is unendingly compassionate and who makes us really alive all day long.

DEPTH OF GOD'S LOVE

EPHESIANS 3:10-20

[10] This is so God's multi-faceted wisdom may now be made known through the church to the rulers and authorities in the heavens. [11] This is according to His eternal purpose accomplished in the Messiah, Jesus our Lord. [12] In Him we have boldness and confident access through faith in Him. [13] So then I ask you not to be discouraged over my afflictions on your behalf, for they are your glory.

[14] For this reason I kneel before the Father [15] from whom every family in heaven and on earth is named. [16] I pray that He may grant you, according to the riches of His glory, to be strengthened with power in the inner man through His Spirit, [17] and that the Messiah may dwell in your hearts through faith. I pray that you, being rooted and firmly established in love, [18] may be able to comprehend with all the saints what is the length and width, height and depth of God's love, [19] and to know the Messiah's love that surpasses knowledge, so you may be filled with all the fullness of God.

[20] Now to Him who is able to do above and beyond all that we ask or think according to the power that works in us.

READ

As you read this passage, look for a word or theme that refreshes you. Maybe this will be Paul's specific description of God's strength and power, or the picture of having "boldness and confident access through faith in Him."

THINK/PRAY

Think about the portion of the passage you chose. Why do you think it touches you today? Are you feeling tired? Trapped? Discouraged?

Now sit in silence, picturing yourself opening the door to Christ and letting Him come inside to be with you in your troubles. Talk to Him about what is bringing you down.

Look back at the passage, and read — a few times, slowly — the part that spoke to you. What message does Christ want you to hear today? Savor this message and let it speak to your need.

LIVE

Pick a word from the passage that symbolizes what uplifted you. Write it down or doodle a picture that represents its meaning to you. Now put it where you will often see it and reflect on it. Maybe you'll use a sticky note and put it on your steering wheel, your bathroom mirror, or your microwave door. When you see it throughout the day, pause to recall Christ's word to you.

DAY 294

GOD ENCOUNTERS

On this seventh day, review and reflect on all you have read this week. Take the time to revel in the ways you've encountered God in the past six days.

UNITY OF THE SPIRIT

EPHESIANS 4:1-6

[1] Therefore I, the prisoner for the Lord, urge you to walk worthy of the calling you have received, [2] with all humility and gentleness, with patience, accepting one another in love, [3] diligently keeping the unity of the Spirit with the peace that binds us. [4] There is one body and one Spirit — just as you were called to one hope at your calling — [5] one Lord, one faith, one baptism, [6] one God and Father of all, who is above all and through all and in all.

READ

Read this passage with another believer, if possible.

THINK

Think about walking "worthy of the calling you have received." Ponder Paul's words: "Diligently keeping the unity of the Spirit with the peace that binds us." What does "unity of the Spirit" look like? Do you know other followers of Christ who are walking with you in unity?

"There is one body and one Spirit — just as you were called to one hope at your calling." Does this describe your relationships? Your church community? The body of Christ around the world? What can be done to strengthen this oneness with other believers?

With another believer (or several), brainstorm ways — little and big — to help create greater oneness in Christ.

PRAY

When you walk beside roads today, use that as a trigger to pray for unity among other believers — in your personal circles, in your town, and around the world.

LIVE

Do what you can to live in unity with others.

BEING FILLED BY THE SPIRIT

EPHESIANS 5:15-20

[15] Pay careful attention, then, to how you walk—not as unwise people but as wise — [16] making the most of the time, because the days are evil. [17] So don't be foolish, but understand what the Lord's will is. [18] And don't get drunk with wine, which leads to reckless actions, but be filled by the Spirit:

[19] speaking to one another
in psalms, hymns, and spiritual songs,
singing and making music
from your heart to the Lord,
[20] giving thanks always for everything
to God the Father
in the name of our Lord Jesus Christ.

READ

Read the passage aloud slowly.

THINK

Read the passage again, picturing yourself in the crowd of people listening to this letter read aloud (as was done in those days). The writer, Paul, spent two years with your group and knows you well.

1. What does being foolish mean to you?
2. How would you go about being "filled by the Spirit"? What would that look like for you?

Read the passage again and notice what words or phrases stand out to you. Why do you think they speak to you that way?

PRAY

Speak back to God the words that spoke to you. Tell God what they mean to you and what you would like to do about them. Talk to God about how well He knows you, that He would speak to you so personally.

LIVE

Each time you drink a liquid today, pause and picture yourself being filled with the Spirit of God. Enjoy that.

RELATIONSHIPS FOR LIVING WELL

EPHESIANS 6:1-9

[1] Children, obey your parents as you would the Lord, because this is right. [2] Honor your father and mother, which is the first commandment with a promise, [3] so that it may go well with you and that you may have a long life in the land. [4] Fathers, don't stir up anger in your children, but bring them up in the training and instruction of the Lord.

[5] Slaves, obey your human masters with fear and trembling, in the sincerity of your heart, as to Christ. [6] Don't work only while being watched, in order to please men, but as slaves of Christ, do God's will from your heart. [7] Serve with a good attitude, as to the Lord and not to men, [8] knowing that whatever good each one does, slave or free, he will receive this back from the Lord. [9] And masters, treat your slaves the same way, without threatening them, because you know that both their Master and yours is in heaven, and there is no favoritism with Him.

READ

Read the passage, letting it call to mind the relevant relationships in your life.

THINK

Mull over what this passage is saying about whole and healthy relationships — children to parents, fathers to children, and employees to employers [slaves to masters]. What is your reaction to the description given of each relationship? Perhaps you feel longing or maybe sadness or annoyance? Explore your reaction.

PRAY

Pick one relationship this passage brought to mind and take a few minutes to observe what kind of child, parent, employee, or student you are. How does your fulfillment of this role compare to the standard Paul sets? Ponder the models in your life for that role. How were you parented? How do your role models relate to their employers? Talk to Jesus about this, and share with Him any disappointment, gratitude, or frustration you feel about your own role and your role models.

LIVE

What is Jesus' invitation to you in the relationship you selected? Perhaps it is just to continue growing in your awareness of what kind of person you are in relationships. Or perhaps you sense Jesus leading you toward a specific action. Make a note of what you hear so you can refer to it.

THE POSTURE OF GRATEFULNESS

PHILIPPIANS 1:3-6

³ I give thanks to my God for every remembrance of you, ⁴ always praying with joy for all of you in my every prayer, ⁵ because of your partnership in the gospel from the first day until now. ⁶ I am sure of this, that He who started a good work in you will carry it on to completion until the day of Christ Jesus.

READ

Read the passage. After doing so, write out the entire passage. Then read it again.

THINK

The subject of thankfulness in prayer will come up many times in this devotional, but there's no way to offer too much gratitude when we communicate with God. Of course it seems to be in our nature to approach God only when times are tough, when we feel like venting, or when we have a need. God listens to all our prayers, but it's hard to pray heartfelt, God-honoring prayers with an ungrateful and complaining spirit. We should *always* be grateful for *something* in prayer.

Paul models a thankful heart for us here as he reflects on the church in Philippi. On a scale of one to ten — one being "frequently ungrateful" and ten being "always thankful" — what number would you give your prayers? What number would your friends give your prayers? What would it take for your prayers to move toward ten?

LIVE/PRAY

Find a small photo of an old friend or family member. Place it in a location where you will see it often. Every time you look at the photo, pause and thank God for who that person is, what that person means to you, and who God is forming that person to become. Be reminded that God, who started this great work in him or her, will "carry it on to completion" one day.

HE HUMBLED HIMSELF

PHILIPPIANS 2:2-11

2 Fulfill my joy by thinking the same way, having the same love, sharing the same feelings, focusing on one goal. 3 Do nothing out of rivalry or conceit, but in humility consider others as more important than yourselves. 4 Everyone should look out not only for his own interests, but also for the interests of others.

5   Make your own attitude that of Christ Jesus,

6   who, existing in the form of God,
        did not consider equality with God
        as something to be used for His own advantage.
7   Instead He emptied Himself
        by assuming the form of a slave,
        taking on the likeness of men.
        And when He had come as a man
        in His external form,
8   He humbled Himself by becoming obedient
        to the point of death —
        even to death on a cross.
9   For this reason God highly exalted Him
        and gave Him the name
        that is above every name,
10   so that at the name of Jesus
        every knee will bow —
        of those who are in heaven and on earth
        and under the earth —
11   and every tongue should confess
        that Jesus Christ is Lord,
        to the glory of God the Father.

READ

Read the passage aloud slowly, noticing the following words: *advantage, humbled, emptied, obedient, exalted.*

THINK

1. Read verses 5-8 again and consider what amazes you about Jesus, perhaps that He:

   - "did not consider equality with God"
   - "emptied Himself"
   - "assum[ed] the form of a slave"
   - "humbled Himself by becoming obedient to the point of death"

2. Read verses 9-11 again and consider what amazes you about God, perhaps that He:

   - "highly exalted Him [Jesus]"
   - is honored by how people bow to worship Jesus Christ

3. Now read verses 2-4 again and consider what God is calling you to be or do.

4. In what way does your admiration for Jesus' and God's radical behavior (verses 5-11) inspire you to the behavior described in verses 2-4?

PRAY

Tell Jesus what you admire about His willingness to come to earth and His way of being while here. Tell God what you admire about His humility. Ask them to help you do whatever came to you in question 3.

LIVE

Look for opportunities today to help someone get ahead. If and when you do, sense Jesus' companionship in your efforts.

THINK THIS WAY

PHILIPPIANS 3:15-21

[15] Therefore, all who are mature should think this way. And if you think differently about anything, God will reveal this also to you. [16] In any case, we should live up to whatever truth we have attained. [17] Join in imitating me, brothers, and observe those who live according to the example you have in us. [18] For I have often told you, and now say again with tears, that many live as enemies of the cross of Christ. [19] Their end is destruction; their god is their stomach; their glory is in their shame. They are focused on earthly things, [20] but our citizenship is in heaven, from which we also eagerly wait for a Savior, the Lord Jesus Christ. [21] He will transform the body of our humble condition into the likeness of His glorious body, by the power that enables Him to subject everything to Himself.

READ

Read the passage two times slowly.

THINK

Read again what Paul says about how those who are mature should think. Write down honestly what you feel and think about it, without judging your own reaction.

Now read again what Paul says about those who "think differently about anything." What thoughts, memories, or feelings do you have as you read this? Jot them down.

Finally, read again, paying special attention to what Christians have to look forward to. What does this make you feel? Note the promise that evokes the greatest response in you.

LIVE

Think about a circumstance in your life that frustrates you with its monotony or pointlessness. Once again become aware of the goal in this passage: a simple and trusting openness to God and total commitment to what He has for you.

Now consider the following statement by Oswald Chambers: "The spiritual saint never believes circumstances to be haphazard, or thinks of his life as secular and sacred; he sees everything he is dumped down in as the means of securing the knowledge of Jesus Christ."[21] Do you believe that the God who intends to make you "into the likeness of His glorious body" is the same God who has allowed your circumstance? Why or why not?

PRAY

Ask Jesus to help you become totally committed to wanting to "live up to whatever truth we have attained." Ask Him to help you recognize and avoid being "focused on earthly things." Thank Him that your "citizenship is in heaven."

DAY 301

GOD ENCOUNTERS

On this seventh day, review and reflect on all you have read this week. Take the time to revel in the ways you've encountered God in the past six days.

SHAPING WORRIES INTO PRAYERS

PHILIPPIANS 4:6-9

⁶ Don't worry about anything, but in everything, through prayer and petition with thanksgiving, let your requests be made known to God. ⁷ And the peace of God, which surpasses every thought, will guard your hearts and minds in Christ Jesus.

⁸ Finally brothers, whatever is true, whatever is honorable, whatever is just, whatever is pure, whatever is lovely, whatever is commendable — if there is any moral excellence and if there is any praise — dwell on these things. ⁹ Do what you have learned and received and heard and seen in me, and the God of peace will be with you.

READ

Read the passage, including the expanded passage, if possible.

THINK

How do you handle something that worries you? Do you ignore the problem so you can put off thinking about it for as long as possible? Do you feel depressed and pessimistic about it, pretty sure of negative results, no matter what? Do you spend a lot of energy identifying a solution and working toward it? Whatever your answer, pinpoint your primary way of reacting. See if you know why you handle worry the way you do.

Now consider one worry you have today and how you've been dealing (or not dealing) with it.

PRAY

Sit in silence for a few minutes with your eyes closed. Breathe deeply and let your mind quiet down. Become aware of God's presence.

Express to God your concern. Even though He knows the situation, tell Him all about it, every detail. In what way has your anxiety affected other areas of your life, such as relationships, work, or school? What's the worst-case scenario you're afraid might happen? Whether rational or irrational, share with God what you fear.

LIVE

Recall the Person you've experienced God to be in the past weeks and months. Reflect on previous notes you've made about experiencing God through His Word and prayer. From that, focus on three of His attributes. How do these elements of His character relate to your situation? What do they indicate about His presence with you right now? Picture this God in your mind. Remember today that this is the God who has heard your concern, the God of peace who will be with you.

HE IS THE HEAD

COLOSSIANS 1:15-23

¹⁵ He is the image of the invisible God,
the firstborn over all creation.
¹⁶ For everything was created by Him,
in heaven and on earth,
the visible and the invisible,
whether thrones or dominions
or rulers or authorities —
all things have been created through Him and for Him.
¹⁷ He is before all things,
and by Him all things hold together.
¹⁸ He is also the head of the body, the church;
He is the beginning,
the firstborn from the dead,
so that He might come to have
first place in everything.
¹⁹ For God was pleased to have
all His fullness dwell in Him,
²⁰ and through Him to reconcile
everything to Himself
by making peace
through the blood of His cross —
whether things on earth or things in heaven.

²¹ Once you were alienated and hostile in your minds because of your evil actions. ²² But now He has reconciled you by His physical body through His death, to present you holy, faultless, and blameless before Him — ²³ if indeed you remain grounded and steadfast in the faith and are not shifted away from the hope of the gospel that you heard. This gospel has been proclaimed in all creation under heaven, and I, Paul, have become a servant of it.

READ

Wherever you are, stand up and read the passage aloud. Stand prayerfully in a posture that communicates to God respect and receptivity to His Word.

THINK

This passage speaks of the supremacy and power of God manifested through Jesus Christ. What specific attribute or characteristic of Jesus sticks out to you most in this passage? Why do you think it does?

"He is the image of the invisible God, the firstborn over all creation." What are specific, practical ways in which you can see the invisible God in Jesus?

What does the following mean? "He is the beginning, the firstborn from the dead, so that He might come to have first place in everything." What implications does this have in your life today? Wonder about the supremacy of Christ.

PRAY

Reflect on the attribute of Christ that struck you (for example, maybe it was that "He is before all things"). In what ways would the world be different if Christ did not possess that attribute? In what ways would your life be different? How and why?

LIVE

Live your day knowing that you serve — and are loved by — the God who holds the entire world together!

PERFECT BOND OF UNITY

COLOSSIANS 3:3-5,12-17

³ For you have died, and your life is hidden with the Messiah in God. ⁴ When the Messiah, who is your life, is revealed, then you also will be revealed with Him in glory.

⁵ Therefore, put to death what belongs to your worldly nature: sexual immorality, impurity, lust, evil desire, and greed, which is idolatry. . . .

¹² Therefore, God's chosen ones, holy and loved, put on heartfelt compassion, kindness, humility, gentleness, and patience, ¹³ accepting one another and forgiving one another if anyone has a complaint against another. Just as the Lord has forgiven you, so you must also forgive. ¹⁴ Above all, put on love — the perfect bond of unity. ¹⁵ And let the peace of the Messiah, to which you were also called in one body, control your hearts. Be thankful. ¹⁶ Let the message about the Messiah dwell richly among you, teaching and admonishing one another in all wisdom, and singing psalms, hymns, and spiritual songs, with gratitude in your hearts to God. ¹⁷ And whatever you do, in word or in deed, do everything in the name of the Lord Jesus, giving thanks to God the Father through Him.

READ

Read the passage aloud slowly.

THINK

Read the passage again and consider these segments included in the process of stepping into the new life.

1. A new life is possible (verses 3-4).
2. We get rid of the old life (verse 5).
3. We put on the new life (verses 12-14).
4. We consider background thoughts and behaviors needed to put on the new life (verses 15-17).

Which segment of this process speaks to you most right now? Reread the verses that correspond to that segment. Now, what word or phrase in that segment speaks to you? Why do you think that is? How does that idea relate to the other segments? How does it relate to love, the "perfect bond of unity"?

PRAY

Pray back to God the segment that speaks to you, personalizing it. For example, based on verse 15, *Please let the peace of Christ control my heart — show me that true peace of Christ!*

LIVE

Sit quietly in the idea that your old life really is dead. All the good, loving attitudes and behaviors of Jesus are open to you. Allow yourself to be invited to step into that today.

VIRTUE CHECKLIST

COLOSSIANS 4:2-6

[2] Devote yourselves to prayer; stay alert in it with thanksgiving. [3] At the same time, pray also for us that God may open a door to us for the message, to speak the mystery of the Messiah, for which I am in prison, [4] so that I may reveal it as I am required to speak. [5] Act wisely toward outsiders, making the most of the time. [6] Your speech should always be gracious, seasoned with salt, so that you may know how you should answer each person.

READ

Read this passage several times, each time narrowing your focus to the part that challenges you the most.

THINK

What did you focus on? Was it a virtuous action that is not part of your lifestyle? Or perhaps it was something you already do, but you noticed something different about the way or reason why Paul says to do it. What is your emotional response when you think of changing this area of your life? Do you feel eager? Overwhelmed? Threatened or protective? Unsure?

PRAY

Talk with Jesus about the item on Paul's list of virtues that challenged you most and about how you responded to it. Sit in silence to wait for what Jesus might have to say to you.

LIVE

As you read the following statement made by Saint Bernard of Clairvaux, also consider what Paul tells Christians to do in today's passage: "If then you are wise, you will show yourself rather as a reservoir than as a canal. For a canal spreads abroad water as it receives it, but a reservoir waits until it is filled before overflowing, and thus communicates, without loss to itself, its superabundant water. In the Church at the present day, we have many canals, few reservoirs."[22]

Are you more like a canal, a reservoir, or something else altogether? Would others who know you agree? Talk with Jesus about this and be open to what He is showing you about yourself. In what way is He inviting you to live differently?

SEEK TO PLEASE GOD

1 THESSALONIANS 2:3-8

³ For our exhortation didn't come from error or impurity or an intent to deceive. ⁴ Instead, just as we have been approved by God to be entrusted with the gospel, so we speak, not to please men, but rather God, who examines our hearts. ⁵ For we never used flattering speech, as you know, or had greedy motives — God is our witness — ⁶ and we didn't seek glory from people, either from you or from others. ⁷ Although we could have been a burden as Christ's apostles, instead we were gentle among you, as a nursing mother nurtures her own children. ⁸ We cared so much for you that we were pleased to share with you not only the gospel of God but also our own lives, because you had become dear to us.

READ

Read the passage, noting the word *approved*.

THINK

It's tempting to promote ourselves, to see ourselves more highly than we ought. If we examine ourselves honestly, we will have to admit that we are often trying to win the approval of the crowd.

Think back over the past week. What decisions did you make solely to look good in the eyes of others? What would it take for you to go through today without making decisions based on trying to make yourself look good? What would it take for you to live today for only God's approval?

PRAY

Confess those recent circumstances when you were tempted to seek approval from other people. Ask God to help you be free of living to please people. Ask Him to help you focus your desire for acceptance and approval entirely on Him.

LIVE

Before every decision, before every comment, ask yourself, *What is my motive? Is it to get approval from the crowd or to get approval from God?* Let these questions make you aware today of how — and why — you make decisions.

GOOD NEWS ABOUT YOUR FAITH AND LOVE

1 THESSALONIANS 3:6-13

⁶ But now Timothy has come to us from you and brought us good news about your faith and love and reported that you always have good memories of us, wanting to see us, as we also want to see you. ⁷ Therefore, brothers, in all our distress and persecution, we were encouraged about you through your faith. ⁸ For now we live, if you stand firm in the Lord. ⁹ How can we thank God for you in return for all the joy we experience before our God because of you, ¹⁰ as we pray very earnestly night and day to see you face to face and to complete what is lacking in your faith?

¹¹ Now may our God and Father Himself, and our Lord Jesus, direct our way to you. ¹² And may the Lord cause you to increase and overflow with love for one another and for everyone, just as we also do for you. ¹³ May He make your hearts blameless in holiness before our God and Father at the coming of our Lord Jesus with all His saints. Amen.

READ

Read the passage aloud slowly.

THINK

Ask God to bring to mind those you know who live their lives before God routinely showing "faith and love" (a really alive faith) and giving others joy. You may not know these people well or see them often (they may be missionaries from your church, friends of friends, or speakers you've listened to), but the way they live reassures you that this kind of life is possible. Read the passage again in light of these people.

PRAY

First, thank God for these people, that:

- their faith and love make you feel better
- they think well of you and you want to see them
- their faith is so alive it keeps you more alive
- you experience joy because of them

Second, pray for these people who, although they may seem so mature, still need your prayers. Pray that:

- if their faith falters, someone (maybe you) can help them
- God the Father and the Lord Jesus will direct their way
- Jesus will cause them "to increase and overflow with love for one another and for everyone"
- they may be "blameless in holiness before our God"

LIVE

Rejoice restfully that people who love God and live the Word really do exist in this world.

DAY 308

GOD ENCOUNTERS

On this seventh day, review and reflect on all you have read this week. Take the time to revel in the ways you've encountered God in the past six days.

THE HOPE OF SALVATION

1 THESSALONIANS 5:1-10

[1] About the times and the seasons: Brothers, you do not need anything to be written to you. [2] For you yourselves know very well that the Day of the Lord will come just like a thief in the night. [3] When they say, "Peace and security," then sudden destruction comes on them, like labor pains come on a pregnant woman, and they will not escape. [4] But you, brothers, are not in the dark, for this day to overtake you like a thief. [5] For you are all sons of light and sons of the day. We do not belong to the night or the darkness. [6] So then, we must not sleep, like the rest, but we must stay awake and be serious. [7] For those who sleep, sleep at night, and those who get drunk are drunk at night. [8] But since we belong to the day, we must be serious and put the armor of faith and love on our chests, and put on a helmet of the hope of salvation. [9] For God did not appoint us to wrath, but to obtain salvation through our Lord Jesus Christ, [10] who died for us, so that whether we are awake or asleep, we will live together with Him.

READ

Read the passage twice.

THINK

When you think about the end of the world and Jesus' return to earth, what do you feel? Nervous? Excited? Halfhearted interest? In everyday life, how often do you think, feel, act, or plan as though you really believe that Jesus will come back someday soon?

PRAY

Prayerfully think about Paul's statement: "You . . . are not in the dark." What does it stir up in you? Do you feel confident or uncertain about where you stand with Jesus? Talk to Him about your reaction to this phrase.

LIVE

Ruth Haley Barton voices the questions "Is God really good? If I trust myself to him, isn't there a good chance that I will wind up where I least want to be or that God will withhold what I want the most? Isn't God a little bit like Lucy in the Peanuts comic strip, who pulls the football away just as Charlie Brown gives himself completely to the kick, causing him to fall flat on his face?"[23]

Take a moment to absorb these questions and reconsider Paul's statement that "God did not appoint us to wrath, but to obtain salvation." How do your deep-down-inside expectations of God correspond with Paul's perspective? With the perspective Barton describes? Share with God your honest beliefs about Him and your expectations of how He'll treat you.

Suspend for a few minutes whatever disbelief you have, and imagine you truly believe God is trustworthy. How might you live differently?

WE GIVE THANKS

2 THESSALONIANS 1:3-4

³ We must always thank God for you, brothers. This is right, since your faith is flourishing and the love each one of you has for one another is increasing. ⁴ Therefore, we ourselves boast about you among God's churches — about your endurance and faith in all the persecutions and afflictions you endure.

READ

Read this passage very slowly and cautiously. Imagine yourself as a surgeon carefully cutting and dissecting it. Give focused attention to each word.

THINK/PRAY

What or whom are you grateful for today? Why? Pause and give thanks to God for these now.

Who is growing in their faith, maturing into God's likeness, and loving others well? Thank God for them now, including names and details.

Who needs to grow more in their faith, needs to mature further into God's likeness, and could love others more appropriately and generously? Thank God for them and pray for them now, including names and details.

Which followers of Christ have fallen on hard times but are determined and are persevering? Thank God for them and pray for them now, including names and details. Pray also for the persecuted church — those Christ-followers around the globe who are being arrested and tortured and murdered simply because of what they believe. Thank God for their incredible passion and commitment to Jesus. Finally, ask God to give you the same courage, commitment, and love for Christ.

LIVE

Carry all these individuals in your thoughts today. Ask God to bring them to mind during the coming week. As you remember them, thanking God for them, pray for them.

LIFE IN THE SPIRIT

2 THESSALONIANS 2:13-17

[13] But we must always thank God for you, brothers loved by the Lord, because from the beginning God has chosen you for salvation through sanctification by the Spirit and through belief in the truth. [14] He called you to this through our gospel, so that you might obtain the glory of our Lord Jesus Christ. [15] Therefore, brothers, stand firm and hold to the traditions you were taught, either by our message or by our letter.

[16] May our Lord Jesus Christ Himself and God our Father, who has loved us and given us eternal encouragement and good hope by grace, [17] encourage your hearts and strengthen you in every good work and word.

READ

Read the passage aloud slowly. Then recall the small, inconsequential things that have occupied your thoughts in the last few moments, hours, or days.

THINK

Read the passage again, noting how Paul viewed an average life as so spectacular because he was immersed in the Trinitarian reality (God, Jesus, and Holy Spirit in verses 13-14).

1. Which of these truths about God's unseen reality most captivate you?

   □ You are "loved by the Lord."
   □ You have a "belief in the truth."
   □ You're invited to sanctification by the Spirit.
   □ You "obtain the glory of our Lord Jesus Christ."
   □ God calls you through the gospel.
   □ God gives you "eternal encouragement and good hope."
   □ God can "encourage your heart."
   □ God can "strengthen you in every good work."
   □ God can "strengthen you in . . . word."

2. Think about today's events — even mundane ones. Which of the truths mentioned in question 1 do you need to link with each event?

PRAY

Pray about each event, that you will live in this unseen reality, that you'll see how these truths are present. For example, pray about a conversation or a homework assignment or a work project, that you'll participate in it knowing you are loved and receiving God's gifts of unending help and confidence.

LIVE

Pick one of these truths about life in the Spirit and sense its reality. If you have trouble doing this, ask God to help you.

IF YOU DON'T WORK, YOU DON'T EAT

2 THESSALONIANS 3:6-15

⁶ Now we command you, brothers, in the name of our Lord Jesus Christ, to keep away from every brother who walks irresponsibly and not according to the tradition received from us. ⁷ For you yourselves know how you must imitate us: We were not irresponsible among you; ⁸ we did not eat anyone's food free of charge; instead, we labored and struggled, working night and day, so that we would not be a burden to any of you. ⁹ It is not that we don't have the right to support, but we did it to make ourselves an example to you so that you would imitate us. ¹⁰ In fact, when we were with you, this is what we commanded you: "If anyone isn't willing to work, he should not eat." ¹¹ For we hear that there are some among you who walk irresponsibly, not working at all, but interfering with the work of others. ¹² Now we command and exhort such people by the Lord Jesus Christ that quietly working, they may eat their own food. ¹³ Brothers, do not grow weary in doing good.

¹⁴ And if anyone does not obey our instruction in this letter, take note of that person; don't associate with him, so that he may be ashamed. ¹⁵ Yet don't treat him as an enemy, but warn him as a brother.

READ

Read the passage carefully.

THINK

Why do you think Paul is making such a big deal out of Christians who are irresponsible? Why is he encouraging those in Thessalonica to make a big deal out of it? In what ways do you think laziness and irresponsibility impact relationships?

PRAY

Read the passage again, this time listening for a word or phrase that stands out to you, such as "doing good," "interfering," or "don't treat him as an enemy, but warn him as a brother." Chew on this for a few minutes. Share with God what pops up in you as you consider it.

Now read again the part of the passage that contains the word or phrase. Why do you think this word is standing out to you today? Does it trigger a fear? Does it challenge you? What part of your life does it touch?

LIVE

Read the whole passage one last time. This time, listen for the action or attitude God is inviting you to take on this week. Maybe He's asking you to lovingly sit down with a friend and speak plainly about her irresponsibility. Maybe He wants you to start looking for a job or to stop borrowing or using stuff that isn't yours. Make a note of how you can take steps in the direction God is indicating. If you are especially aware of God's presence with you when you take these steps, what might the impact be?

LOVE FROM A PURE HEART

1 TIMOTHY 1:3-7

³ As I urged you when I went to Macedonia, remain in Ephesus so that you may instruct certain people not to teach different doctrine ⁴ or to pay attention to myths and endless genealogies. These promote empty speculations rather than God's plan, which operates by faith. ⁵ Now the goal of our instruction is love that comes from a pure heart, a good conscience, and a sincere faith. ⁶ Some have deviated from these and turned aside to fruitless discussion. ⁷ They want to be teachers of the law, although they don't understand what they are saying or what they are insisting on.

THINK

Paul as mentor has sent carefully written instructions to his disciple Timothy. This is the first volume of his guidance for Timothy, urging him as a young leader to mature in Christ. Among the complexities of life, Paul boils the message down to one simple concept: love. Not just love, but "love that comes from a pure heart, a good conscience, and a sincere faith."

READ

With this background in mind, meditate on the passage.

PRAY

While remaining open to God, consider what love looks like when it's "from a pure heart, a good conscience, and a sincere faith." Then ask God the following questions, pausing between each one to listen to the Holy Spirit's response:

God, what about my love is not from a pure heart? Ask God to help remove the selfishness in your life.

Father, what about my love is not from a good conscience? Ask for courage to be authentic with God, others, and yourself.

Lord, what about my life and love is not from a sincere faith? Ask God to give you the willingness and to help you be more open to His purposes, even if doing so feels uncertain and scary.

LIVE

Go live and love selflessly, authentically, and openly.

QUIET LIFE IN ALL GODLINESS

1 TIMOTHY 2:1-2,8-9

¹ First of all, then, I urge that petitions, prayers, intercessions, and thanksgivings be made for everyone, ² for kings and all those who are in authority, so that we may lead a tranquil and quiet life in all godliness and dignity. . . .

⁸ Therefore, I want the men in every place to pray, lifting up holy hands without anger or argument. ⁹ Also, the women are to dress themselves in modest clothing, with decency and good sense, not with elaborate hairstyles, gold, pearls, or expensive apparel.

READ

Read the passage aloud slowly.

THINK

Read the passage again, noting what is said about prayer:

- how to pray: "in every place" and "lifting up holy hands"
- government-related prayer: petitions, intercessions, and thanksgivings
- tone of prayer: "without anger or argument"
- pray for: "everyone" and "those who are in authority"
- outcome of prayer: live tranquil and quiet lives

Read the passage one more time. What do you think God is telling you about how you need to pray?

PRAY

Lift holy hands as you ask God to lead you in praying that governments will be guided by Him, "so that we may lead a tranquil and quiet life."

LIVE

Sit quietly with your hands raised, outstretched, eager for God's Word to permeate the nations of our planet.

DAY 315

GOD ENCOUNTERS

On this seventh day, review and reflect on all you have read this week. Take the time to revel in the ways you've encountered God in the past six days.

PRECONDITIONS OF LEADERSHIP

1 TIMOTHY 3:1-13

¹ This saying is trustworthy: "If anyone aspires to be an overseer, he desires a noble work." ² An overseer, therefore, must be above reproach, the husband of one wife, self-controlled, sensible, respectable, hospitable, an able teacher, ³ not addicted to wine, not a bully but gentle, not quarrelsome, not greedy — ⁴ one who manages his own household competently, having his children under control with all dignity. ⁵ (If anyone does not know how to manage his own household, how will he take care of God's church?) ⁶ He must not be a new convert, or he might become conceited and fall into the condemnation of the Devil. ⁷ Furthermore, he must have a good reputation among outsiders, so that he does not fall into disgrace and the Devil's trap.

⁸ Deacons, likewise, should be worthy of respect, not hypocritical, not drinking a lot of wine, not greedy for money, ⁹ holding the mystery of the faith with a clear conscience. ¹⁰ And they must also be tested first; if they prove blameless, then they can serve as deacons. ¹¹ Wives, too, must be worthy of respect, not slanderers, self-controlled, faithful in everything. ¹² Deacons must be husbands of one wife, managing their children and their own households competently. ¹³ For those who have served well as deacons acquire a good standing for themselves, and great boldness in the faith that is in Christ Jesus.

READ

Read this passage a few times slowly and carefully.

THINK

As you absorb the moral expectations presented in this passage, what is your reaction? Perhaps you desire to change, or perhaps you feel irritated. Maybe you feel shame or guilt. Maybe relief. Does reading this make you want to be a leader? If not, why not? Share your reaction with God.

PRAY

Take several minutes to read the text again slowly, letting each instruction direct you toward a new area of your heart to examine with the Holy Spirit. (Don't feel that you must work your way through the entire passage: The goal is to uncover content for prayer, not get through the entire list.) In which areas does your life look different from the model Paul is describing? For example, you've been more pushy than gentle with someone, or you have a problem with self-control. Tell God about what you find.

LIVE

Ask God to show you what it would look like to embrace transformation in an area you've examined today, realizing that starting with baby steps might be just right for you. Take courage that "our personalities are transformed — not lost — in the furnace of God's love."[24] God's transformation will not obliterate your personality; instead, the process will make you more into the one-of-a-kind you who God made you to be.

TEACH THESE THINGS

1 TIMOTHY 4:10-16

[10] In fact, we labor and strive for this, because we have put our hope in the living God, who is the Savior of everyone, especially of those who believe.

[11] Command and teach these things. [12] Let no one despise your youth; instead, you should be an example to the believers in speech, in conduct, in love, in faith, in purity. [13] Until I come, give your attention to public reading, exhortation, and teaching. [14] Do not neglect the gift that is in you; it was given to you through prophecy, with the laying on of hands by the council of elders. [15] Practice these things; be committed to them, so that your progress may be evident to all. [16] Pay close attention to your life and your teaching; persevere in these things, for by doing this you will save both yourself and your hearers.

READ

Read the passage, focusing on the words *teach* and *practice*.

THINK

In these verses, Paul, as almost a father figure, passes on wise words to young Timothy — and to us — about modeling our faith.

How can we be a part of that, no matter how old we are?

On a scale of one to ten — one being spiritual flabbiness and ten being spiritually fit — how would you rate your spiritual fitness? Why did you give yourself that rating?

How well is your life teaching in these five areas: "in speech, in conduct, in love, in faith, in purity"? Very well? In which areas? Not so well? In which areas? How can you make your life a better teacher in all of these?

PRAY

See if you can open your life to God like you would open a book. Consider the areas (such as school, family, work, and other activities), and write them down if that helps. Acknowledge to God your openness and then invite Him to do His work in your life — encouraging you, challenging you, and shaping your words, your demeanor, your love, your faith, and your integrity.

LIVE

Write these five words on an index card: *speech, conduct, love, faith, purity*. Ask God to help you teach with your life in these specific areas throughout your day.

DEVOTED TO GOOD WORKS

1 TIMOTHY 5:1-4,7-10

¹ Do not rebuke an older man, but exhort him as a father, younger men as brothers, ² older women as mothers, and with all propriety, the younger women as sisters.

³ Support widows who are genuinely widows. ⁴ But if any widow has children or grandchildren, they must learn to practice godliness toward their own family first and to repay their parents, for this pleases God. . . . ⁷ Command this also, so they won't be blamed. ⁸ But if anyone does not provide for his own, that is his own household, he has denied the faith and is worse than an unbeliever.

⁹ No widow should be placed on the official support list unless she is at least 60 years old, has been the wife of one husband, ¹⁰ and is well known for good works — that is, if she has brought up children, shown hospitality, washed the saints' feet, helped the afflicted, and devoted herself to every good work.

READ

Read the passage aloud slowly.

THINK

Before reading the passage again, consider the following cultural ideas. Which ones have you unconsciously accepted?

- ☐ Older people and younger people don't mix much.
- ☐ Older people are retired, so they don't do good works. (You don't know many people who help out with works such as showing hospitality and helping the afflicted.)
- ☐ Older people are tired and don't want to do much at church anymore.
- ☐ Older people aren't generally the people you go to for advice.
- ☐ Older people have Social Security benefits and don't need anyone's help.
- ☐ Older people are people you feel sorry for, not reverently honor.

Read the passage again. Envision the sort of older person Paul was talking about. What older person do you know who is like the one Paul describes? In what small ways might you show respect to this person? Try to wrap your mind around the idea that you can *look forward* to being such an older person.

PRAY

Thank God for older people in your life who resemble Paul's description. Pray for those who need more of what Paul describes. Pray for yourself that you'll be this sort of older person.

LIVE

Sit quietly. Pretend your joints don't work as well as they used to. Ponder what it would be like to still be eager to get up every day to be with Jesus and partner with Him in what He's doing in the world.

GODLINESS WITH CONTENTMENT

1 TIMOTHY 6:6-12

⁶ But godliness with contentment is a great gain.

⁷   For we brought nothing into the world,
    and we can take nothing out.
⁸   But if we have food and clothing,
    we will be content with these.

⁹ But those who want to be rich fall into temptation, a trap, and many foolish and harmful desires, which plunge people into ruin and destruction. ¹⁰ For the love of money is a root of all kinds of evil, and by craving it, some have wandered away from the faith and pierced themselves with many pains.

¹¹   But you, man of God, run from these things,
    and pursue righteousness, godliness, faith,
    love, endurance, and gentleness.
¹²   Fight the good fight for the faith;
    take hold of eternal life
    that you were called to
    and have made a good confession about
    in the presence of many witnesses.

READ

Read the passage twice.

THINK

Mull over Paul's advice to Timothy. Do you agree with his statements and assumptions about material wealth? About the value of godliness over riches? Why or why not? Explore your thoughts and share them with God.

PRAY

Consider your belongings, including favorite things and stuff you don't usually think about. In what ways might some of these items get in the way of your faith and godliness? In what way does your attachment to these possessions alter your view of who you are? (Don't be too quick to answer here.)

LIVE

Read the passage again, considering more carefully Paul's description of pursuing righteousness. Do you notice an especially strong desire for any of these qualities? Listen for what God may be saying to you through the text and through your desire. Is He inviting you to do anything — even something small — in response to this time today?

PURSUE RIGHTEOUSNESS

2 TIMOTHY 2:22-26

²² Flee from youthful passions, and pursue righteousness, faith, love, and peace, along with those who call on the Lord from a pure heart. ²³ But reject foolish and ignorant disputes, knowing that they breed quarrels. ²⁴ The Lord's slave must not quarrel, but must be gentle to everyone, able to teach, and patient, ²⁵ instructing his opponents with gentleness. Perhaps God will grant them repentance leading them to the knowledge of the truth. ²⁶ Then they may come to their senses and escape the Devil's trap, having been captured by him to do his will.

READ

Slowly read these verses. Let their message saturate your heart and mind.

THINK

In Paul's second leadership letter to Timothy, he writes words of encouragement and challenge that we, too, need to take to heart in the coming week. Paul is talking about some aspects of a mature faith.

Imagine he is sitting beside you, speaking these words to you directly. How do you feel when you hear them? What part of the passage resonates most with you? Why? Maybe "youthful passions" seems a little patronizing. Perhaps "righteousness, faith, love, and peace" seem impossible or defeating. Maybe with some people you've lost hope that "God will grant them repentance."

PRAY

Sit in a comfortable position, being silent and as still as you can. Ask God *why* He has given you this particular piece of instruction through Paul (the one that resonated most with you). Listen for the gentle whisper of God's voice in the midst of the silence. Maybe He will show you a spot of childishness or one of righteousness. Maybe He will offer you hope.

LIVE

As you continue to sit in silence, explore what God might want you to do with this piece of instruction. How are you to live it out today? This week? This month?

INSPIRED BY GOD AND PROFITABLE

2 TIMOTHY 3:1-5,15-17

¹ But know this: Difficult times will come in the last days. ² For people will be lovers of self, lovers of money, boastful, proud, blasphemers, disobedient to parents, ungrateful, unholy, ³ unloving, irreconcilable, slanderers, without self-control, brutal, without love for what is good, ⁴ traitors, reckless, conceited, lovers of pleasure rather than lovers of God, ⁵ holding to the form of godliness but denying its power. Avoid these people! . . .

¹⁵ And you know that from childhood you have known the sacred Scriptures, which are able to give you wisdom for salvation through faith in Christ Jesus. ¹⁶ All Scripture is inspired by God and is profitable for teaching, for rebuking, for correcting, for training in righteousness, ¹⁷ so that the man of God may be complete, equipped for every good work.

READ

Read the passage aloud slowly.

THINK

Before dismissing the first paragraph as a description of people other than yourself, consider that Western culture, in general (and our individual selves, in particular), tends to be lovers of self, lovers of money, proud, and unholy.

Read the passage again. This time notice the enormous change from the first paragraph to the second.

1. How does the way Scripture moves us (verse 16) help us to be different from the general culture?
2. Scripture is inspired by God — words given by our relational God, not a bunch of rules. Picture God speaking to you, teaching, correcting, and training you in righteousness.

Can you picture God doing these things in ways exactly right for you? In gentle yet firm ways? To rescue you before you blow it?

PRAY

Ask God to help you be open to His showing you truth, exposing your rebellion, correcting your mistakes, and training you in righteousness. Ask Him to show you specific details, if any, that you need to know at this moment.

LIVE

Imagine what living an interactive life with God would be like, one in which all day long you experience Him gently showing you truth, exposing your rebellion, correcting your mistakes, and training you to live His way. Why would this be the best way to live?

DAY 322

GOD ENCOUNTERS

On this seventh day, review and reflect on all you have read this week. Take the time to revel in the ways you've encountered God in the past six days.

THE RIGHTEOUS JUDGE

2 TIMOTHY 4:1-8

[1] I solemnly charge you before God and Christ Jesus, who is going to judge the living and the dead, and because of His appearing and His kingdom: [2] Proclaim the message; persist in it whether convenient or not; rebuke, correct, and encourage with great patience and teaching. [3] For the time will come when they will not tolerate sound doctrine, but according to their own desires, will multiply teachers for themselves because they have an itch to hear something new. [4] They will turn away from hearing the truth and will turn aside to myths. [5] But as for you, be serious about everything, endure hardship, do the work of an evangelist, fulfill your ministry.

[6] For I am already being poured out as a drink offering, and the time for my departure is close. [7] I have fought the good fight, I have finished the race, I have kept the faith. [8] There is reserved for me in the future the crown of righteousness, which the Lord, the righteous Judge, will give me on that day, and not only to me, but to all those who have loved His appearing.

READ

Read Paul's instructions to his apprentice Timothy, trying to identify the primary theme.

THINK

What common thread runs through all of Paul's statements and instructions here? Perhaps it's the tone of what he's saying (such as urgent or tender), or maybe it's that every statement somehow relates to a particular object or event (such as Christ's judgment of everyone, or people-pleasing versus God-pleasing). Write down the theme you see.

PRAY

Read the passage again with the theme in mind. Notice how each part of the passage unpacks the meaning even more. What especially stands out to you? Perhaps it's the reason that repentance and evangelism are so important or the anticipation of standing before God as He looks at your life. Think about what you discover, and be transparent with God about it.

LIVE

Now read the passage once more, this time listening for what you sense God, through the text, is saying to you personally. Maybe He's drawing your attention to your need to please people, or maybe you're relieved to understand more clearly that repentance isn't about being perfect but about living in accordance with reality. What will you do with what God is showing you? Sit in silence for a few minutes. Jot down your new intention.

APOSTLE OF CHRIST

TITUS 1:1-4

[1] Paul, a slave of God and an apostle of Jesus Christ, to build up the faith of God's elect and their knowledge of the truth that leads to godliness, [2] in the hope of eternal life that God, who cannot lie, promised before time began. [3] In His own time He has revealed His message in the proclamation that I was entrusted with by the command of God our Savior:

[4] To Titus, my true son in our common faith.

Grace and peace from God the Father and Christ Jesus our Savior.

READ

Read the opening words of greeting from Paul to Titus in these verses.

THINK

Paul describes himself as "an apostle of Jesus Christ, to build up the faith of God's elect." Are you God's slave and Christ's apostle? Do those terms accurately describe your life? Why or why not? How can your life be lived in such a way that you are building up the "knowledge of the truth that leads to godliness" to those around you? How can your life be promoting the faith among others by word and action? Take time to consider these questions, being specific.

Paul gives the purpose of his life to Titus: to "build up the faith of God's elect and their knowledge of the truth that leads to godliness, in the hope of eternal life that God, who cannot lie, promised before time began." In what way does God give us hope of eternal life?

PRAY

Ask Christ to help you be His representative. Invite Him to reveal to you how you might best respond to His Word.

LIVE

Respond to what you hear from God, remembering that you go forth into this day as a representative of Christ.

A GOD-FILLED LIFE

TITUS 2:11-14

[11] For the grace of God has appeared with salvation for all people, [12] instructing us to deny godlessness and worldly lusts and to live in a sensible, righteous, and godly way in the present age, [13] while we wait for the blessed hope and appearing of the glory of our great God and Savior, Jesus Christ. [14] He gave Himself for us to redeem us from all lawlessness and to cleanse for Himself a people for His own possession, eager to do good works.

READ

Read the passage aloud slowly.

THINK

Read the passage aloud again, this time picturing the words being spoken by someone you look up to and admire. Which of these rich words or phrases stand out to you? Why do you need these words and ideas at this moment in your life?

Read it one more time, picturing yourself saying the words to someone you wish to encourage.

PRAY

Ask God to guide you in one or all of these movements of growth:

☐ turning your back on "godlessness and worldly lusts"
☐ taking on a "sensible, righteous, and godly way"
☐ believing that this is "the present age"
☐ being "eager to do good works"
☐ other:

LIVE

Consider God, who is goodness. Inhale that goodness. See how much God wishes to bring you along. Try on the belief that this new life starts right now.

WASHED INSIDE AND OUT

TITUS 3:1-11

¹ Remind them to be submissive to rulers and authorities, to obey, to be ready for every good work, ² to slander no one, to avoid fighting, and to be kind, always showing gentleness to all people. ³ For we too were once foolish, disobedient, deceived, enslaved by various passions and pleasures, living in malice and envy, hateful, detesting one another.

⁴ But when the goodness of God and His love
for mankind appeared,
⁵ He saved us —
not by works of righteousness that we had done,
but according to His mercy,
through the washing of regeneration
and renewal by the Holy Spirit.
⁶ He poured out this Spirit on us abundantly
through Jesus Christ our Savior,
⁷ so that having been justified by His grace,
we may become heirs with the hope of eternal life.

⁸ This saying is trustworthy. I want you to insist on these things, so that those who have believed God might be careful to devote themselves to good works. These are good and profitable for everyone. ⁹ But avoid foolish debates, genealogies, quarrels, and disputes about the law, for they are unprofitable and worthless. ¹⁰ Reject a divisive person after a first and second warning, ¹¹ knowing that such a person is perverted and sins, being self-condemned.

READ

Read the passage.

PRAY

What parts of this passage do you react to more than others? Maybe an argument you've had comes to mind, or maybe you have trouble adopting the attitude toward authority described here. Perhaps you wish you could be given a "washing of regeneration" and made new. Try to summarize your primary thought. Express it to God.

THINK

Although being purified ("washing of regeneration and renewal by the Holy Spirit") is good for us and brings wonderfully satisfying results, the process often involves humbling, which isn't easy. Richard Foster said, "Humility means to live as close to the truth as possible: the truth about ourselves, the truth about others, the truth about the world in which we live."[25]

Think about Foster's statement, considering yourself, others, and the world around you. What elements of God's truth in this passage did you have trouble receiving? Maybe you're too hard on yourself and won't believe God's acceptance of you. Maybe you're afraid that if you admit the limitations of someone you look up to, it will unravel everything good you believe about that person. Or maybe you realize you don't want to get close to the real needs and problems of the world. Be open with God about the grime that keeps you from being clean and living closer to the truth.

LIVE

Now, keeping in mind how near or far you live from the truth about yourself, others, and the world, picture God as He's described in this passage: offering you the washing of regeneration, removing the grime that separates you from the truth. What do you think or feel about that? Whatever surfaces, share it openly with Him.

A DEARLY LOVED BROTHER

PHILEMON 8-20

8 For this reason, although I have great boldness in Christ to command you to do what is right, 9 I appeal to you, instead, on the basis of love. I, Paul, as an elderly man and now also as a prisoner of Christ Jesus, 10 appeal to you for my son, Onesimus. I fathered him while I was in chains. 11 Once he was useless to you, but now he is useful both to you and to me. 12 I am sending him back to you as a part of myself. 13 I wanted to keep him with me, so that in my imprisonment for the gospel he might serve me in your place. 14 But I didn't want to do anything without your consent, so that your good deed might not be out of obligation, but of your own free will. 15 For perhaps this is why he was separated from you for a brief time, so that you might get him back permanently, 16 no longer as a slave, but more than a slave — as a dearly loved brother. He is especially so to me, but even more to you, both in the flesh and in the Lord.

17 So if you consider me a partner, accept him as you would me. 18 And if he has wronged you in any way, or owes you anything, charge that to my account. 19 I, Paul, write this with my own hand: I will repay it — not to mention to you that you owe me even your own self. 20 Yes, brother, may I have joy from you in the Lord; refresh my heart in Christ.

READ

Read the passage and, if possible, the entire book of Philemon. (Don't worry — it's only twenty-five verses long!)

THINK

Here Paul writes a letter to Philemon concerning a slave named Onesimus. Paul has grown to see this man as a friend and — more specifically and importantly — as a brother in Christ. So Paul encourages Philemon to accept Onesimus in the same way.

Paul is saying that the greatest label we can have for one another is "dearly loved brother" or true Christian sister.

What Christians do you have a hard time accepting as brothers or sisters in Christ? Why is it hard to think of other believers this way? Explore your heart: Is it their backgrounds, ethnicities, behaviors, cultural differences, theological differences, or something else? What would need to change in you for you to accept these people, seeing them as Christian brothers and sisters?

PRAY

Talk to God about this. Tell Him about your struggle to accept others. Thank Him that He accepts you, and thank Him that He sees you and other believers as no less than His very own children. Ask God to help you see others with the same eyes.

LIVE

As you encounter people who are different from you, be reminded that God sees them with the label "My children" — and that means you, too.

SUSTAINING ALL THINGS

HEBREWS 1:3

[3] The Son is the radiance of God's glory and the exact expression of His nature, sustaining all things by His powerful word. After making purification for sins, He sat down at the right hand of the Majesty on high.

READ

Read this verse over and over again. Let it resonate in your heart. Become familiar with the words. Memorize it before moving to the next section.

THINK

Though the authorship of Hebrews is uncertain, we can be certain of the message of the book: God's plan to redeem history came in the form of His Son, Jesus.

Spend time meditating on the passage. First, consider the purpose of a mirror: to display in perfect clarity a faithful representation of an object or person. How incredible to realize that Jesus' role was to be a mirror of God to the world! Second, consider the monumental act of "sustaining all things." How amazing to know that Jesus does this, that He is vital to the vast scope of human history!

In what ways does the significance of Jesus in the world impact your view of Him?

PRAY

Stand in front of a mirror and consider Jesus, who mirrors God. While looking at your reflection, ask God for the courage and guidance to help you mirror Jesus to the world, reflecting Him as you go about every day.

LIVE

Consider how you might reflect Jesus today — and do it.

DAY 329

GOD ENCOUNTERS

On this seventh day, review and reflect on all you have read this week. Take the time to revel in the ways you've encountered God in the past six days.

RICHES OF GLORY

HEBREWS 2:6-10

⁶ But one has somewhere testified:

> What is man that You remember him,
> or the son of man that You care for him?
> ⁷ You made him lower than the angels
> for a short time;
> You crowned him with glory and honor
> ⁸ and subjected everything under his feet.

For in subjecting everything to him, He left nothing that is not subject to him. As it is, we do not yet see everything subjected to him. ⁹ But we do see Jesus — made lower than the angels for a short time so that by God's grace He might taste death for everyone — crowned with glory and honor because of His suffering in death.

¹⁰ For in bringing many sons to glory, it was entirely appropriate that God — all things exist for Him and through Him — should make the source of their salvation perfect through sufferings.

READ

Read the passage aloud slowly.

THINK

Read the passage again, noting the diverse themes of death and suffering versus angels and glory. What words or phrases fascinate you most? Pause a moment and ask God to help you understand them and continue to be absorbed by them. Why do you think those words or phrases fascinate you? What is going on in your life right now — feelings, circumstances, decisions — that they might correspond to?

PRAY

Ask that you will be continually fascinated by God's glory, God's well-deserved honor and brightness.

LIVE

Sit in the quiet and reflect on how you would feel if God were degrading, dishonoring, and not at all beautiful. Why is it better to live and breathe on an earth created by such a magnificent God?

SHARPER THAN A SWORD

HEBREWS 4:12-13

[12] For the word of God is living and effective and sharper than any double-edged sword, penetrating as far as the separation of soul and spirit, joints and marrow. It is able to judge the ideas and thoughts of the heart. [13] No creature is hidden from Him, but all things are naked and exposed to the eyes of Him to whom we must give an account.

READ

Read these two verses. Then read verse 13 first and verse 12 next. Finally, read the verses in their proper order again.

THINK

Most of us believe that God's message, His Word, is important. In fact, you probably wouldn't be reading these words right now if you didn't believe God's Word is significant. But if you're like many people, reading it sometimes feels like a chore — less than enjoyable.

Most Jewish children in the first century would memorize the first five books of the Bible (the Pentateuch) before their thirteenth birthdays.[26] They were taught to believe that the words were a love letter to them from God Himself.

Think now about how important Scripture is to *you*. What if you were unable to read or hear anything from the Bible for twelve months? Would you miss it? Why or why not? What do you think "no creature is hidden from Him" means? In what ways have you experienced God's Word to be precise and powerful, "sharper than any double-edged sword"?

PRAY

Start praying by thanking God for the gift of His Word. Ask Him to give you more passion and desire for it. Give God permission to let His Word work in your life in the days and weeks ahead.

LIVE

Memorize these verses, and pray them regularly as a way of asking God to make Scripture increasingly important in your life.

HEIRS OF THE PROMISE

HEBREWS 6:13-19

¹³ For when God made a promise to Abraham, since He had no one greater to swear by, He swore by Himself:

¹⁴   I will indeed bless you,
      and I will greatly multiply you.

¹⁵ And so, after waiting patiently, Abraham obtained the promise. ¹⁶ For men swear by something greater than themselves, and for them a confirming oath ends every dispute. ¹⁷ Because God wanted to show His unchangeable purpose even more clearly to the heirs of the promise, He guaranteed it with an oath, ¹⁸ so that through two unchangeable things, in which it is impossible for God to lie, we who have fled for refuge might have strong encouragement to seize the hope set before us. ¹⁹ We have this hope as an anchor for our lives, safe and secure. It enters the inner sanctuary behind the curtain.

READ

Read the passage aloud slowly.

THINK

Read the passage aloud again, noting the emphasis on promises and hope. Consider what part hope has played in your life. Its opposites are despair, suspicion, doubt, and cynicism. What does this passage tell you about hope?

Read the passage aloud one more time. What words or phrases stand out to you? Why are those words or phrases important for you today?

PRAY

Pick out phrases that you'd like to pray and converse with God about, such as:

- ☐ "guaranteed it with an oath"
- ☐ "it is impossible for God to lie"
- ☐ "seize the hope set before us"
- ☐ "this hope as an anchor"

LIVE

Walk through this day trying on an attitude of greater hope — expectancy, anticipation, trust. This is what everyday life in the kingdom of God looks like.

A NEW COVENANT

HEBREWS 8:1-2,6-12

¹ Now the main point of what is being said is this: We have this kind of high priest, who sat down at the right hand of the throne of the Majesty in the heavens, ² a minister of the sanctuary and the true tabernacle that was set up by the Lord and not man. . . . ⁶ But Jesus has now obtained a superior ministry, and to that degree He is the mediator of a better covenant, which has been legally enacted on better promises.

⁷ For if that first covenant had been faultless, there would have been no occasion for a second one. ⁸ But finding fault with His people, He says:

> Look, the days are coming, says the Lord,
> when I will make a new covenant
> with the house of Israel
> and with the house of Judah —
> ⁹ not like the covenant
> that I made with their ancestors
> on the day I took them by their hands
> to lead them out of the land of Egypt.
> I disregarded them, says the Lord,
> because they did not continue in My covenant.
> ¹⁰ But this is the covenant
> that I will make with the house of Israel
> after those days, says the Lord:
> I will put My laws into their minds
> and write them on their hearts.
> I will be their God,
> and they will be My people.
> ¹¹ And each person will not teach his fellow citizen,
> and each his brother, saying, "Know the Lord,"
> because they will all know Me,
> from the least to the greatest of them.
> ¹² For I will be merciful to their wrongdoing,
> and I will never again remember their sins.

READ

Read the passage from the perspective of someone living in Old Testament times, hearing the promise of a "better covenant" that has no form yet. What would life be like without Jesus? Sit and take in this picture of life. Let yourself imagine what it would be like to sin in that context and to relate to God.

THINK

Read the passage again, this time from your present-day perspective, noting contrasts with the Old Testament perspective. What does it mean to you to hear God say He will make a new covenant, not like the old covenant that expects you to perfectly obey Old Testament laws? How does this reality make you see Jesus differently? What's it like to have such an approachable High Priest who will "never again remember [your] sins" and who will show you what God is like?

PRAY/LIVE

Talk with Jesus about what stands out to you from this time of meditation. Perhaps a new desire to be obedient arises in contrast to previous discouragement over trying to change. Maybe you want to thank Jesus for being near you, or maybe you feel like singing a song of praise to Him. Maybe you just want to sit in quiet gratitude because God threw out the old plan and created a new plan, writing it on your heart.

WHAT WE CAN'T SEE

HEBREWS 11:1-3,39-40

[1] Now faith is the reality of what is hoped for, the proof of what is not seen. [2] For our ancestors won God's approval by it.

[3] By faith we understand that the universe was created by God's command, so that what is seen has been made from things that are not visible. . . .

[39] All these were approved through their faith, but they did not receive what was promised, [40] since God had provided something better for us, so that they would not be made perfect without us.

READ

If possible, read all of Hebrews 11, but focus on verses 1-3 and 39-40.

THINK

This familiar passage of Scripture is often called the Faith Hall of Fame. It lists people of the Bible who exhibited the faith — sometimes at extreme personal cost — that made God famous. Talking about faith is much easier than living it out every day, but we can turn to these people's lives for inspiration.

You've heard, and possibly even uttered, the saying "Seeing is believing." The writer of Hebrews begins with a definition of faith that he connects to eyesight. Faith, he writes, is "the reality of what is hoped for, the proof of what is not seen." So, really, *not* seeing is believing.

What do you have a hard time believing because you can't prove it by seeing or touching it yourself? Would faith be easier if you could physically see the object of your faith? (Would faith still be faith if you could see the object, or would faith cease to be faith and become fact?)

PRAY

Thank God for godly people who inspire you to the kind of faith described in this chapter of the Bible.

LIVE

Sometime today, choose one of the people mentioned in the Faith Hall of Fame and read his or her story in Scripture. (If you need to, use a concordance to find the story.)

SUBMIT TO DISCIPLINE

HEBREWS 12:7-11

[7] Endure suffering as discipline: God is dealing with you as sons. For what son is there that a father does not discipline? [8] But if you are without discipline — which all receive — then you are illegitimate children and not sons. [9] Furthermore, we had natural fathers discipline us, and we respected them. Shouldn't we submit even more to the Father of spirits and live? [10] For they disciplined us for a short time based on what seemed good to them, but He does it for our benefit, so that we can share His holiness. [11] No discipline seems enjoyable at the time, but painful. Later on, however, it yields the fruit of peace and righteousness to those who have been trained by it.

READ

Read the passage aloud slowly.

THINK

Read the passage again.

How might God use "suffering" to discipline, or train, you? Don't jump on the first thing that comes to mind. Sit quietly for a while and see what God brings to you.

How might you cooperate better in this training? Once again, the first thing that comes to mind might not be God, but an old tape from the past. So take time to listen.

PRAY

Tell God what sort of disciplined person you'd like to be. What would you look like? Express confidence that this picture would be a much better life for you.

LIVE

Try to crawl into the persona of whom you'd like to become. How would your burdens in life be lighter?

DAY 336

GOD ENCOUNTERS

On this seventh day, review and reflect on all you have read this week. Take the time to revel in the ways you've encountered God in the past six days.

BE SATISFIED WITH WHAT YOU HAVE

HEBREWS 13:5-9

[5] Your life should be free from the love of money. Be satisfied with what you have, for He Himself has said, I will never leave you or forsake you. [6] Therefore, we may boldly say:

> The Lord is my helper;
> I will not be afraid.
> What can man do to me?

[7] Remember your leaders who have spoken God's word to you. As you carefully observe the outcome of their lives, imitate their faith. [8] Jesus Christ is the same yesterday, today, and forever. [9] Don't be led astray by various kinds of strange teachings; for it is good for the heart to be established by grace and not by foods, since those involved in them have not benefited.

READ

Read the passage aloud.

THINK

Spend time pondering the connection the writer is making between obsession with material possessions and the belief that God might leave us or let us down. What do you make of this? How are the two ideas related to each other?

PRAY

Take several minutes to explore your life in light of this instruction. How do you relate to material things? Do you often wish you had more? Do you feel that nothing can harm you because of what you have? What fears do you have about God letting you down? What would it be like to "be satisfied with what you have"? Talk with Him about this subject. Attentively listen for His input.

LIVE

Continue praying by personalizing the verses, pausing frequently to notice your internal reaction to what you're saying. For example, *God, help me avoid being obsessed with getting more material things. I want to be satisfied with what I have, since You assured me . . .*

When you're finished, look through the passage one more time, honestly confessing the contrary reactions, if any, you experienced when praying. With each, become aware of the possibility that your contrary feeling or belief could change. (Don't try to force that change; just be aware of the possibility.) For example, you could repeat to your soul that "The Lord is my helper," or you could ask God to increase your belief that He will "never leave you or forsake you."

A DOER OF THE WORD

JAMES 1:19-27

¹⁹ My dearly loved brothers, understand this: Everyone must be quick to hear, slow to speak, and slow to anger, ²⁰ for man's anger does not accomplish God's righteousness. ²¹ Therefore, ridding yourselves of all moral filth and evil, humbly receive the implanted word, which is able to save you.

²² But be doers of the word and not hearers only, deceiving yourselves. ²³ Because if anyone is a hearer of the word and not a doer, he is like a man looking at his own face in a mirror. ²⁴ For he looks at himself, goes away, and immediately forgets what kind of man he was. ²⁵ But the one who looks intently into the perfect law of freedom and perseveres in it, and is not a forgetful hearer but one who does good works — this person will be blessed in what he does.

²⁶ If anyone thinks he is religious without controlling his tongue, then his religion is useless and he deceives himself. ²⁷ Pure and undefiled religion before our God and Father is this: to look after orphans and widows in their distress and to keep oneself unstained by the world.

READ

Meditate on this passage. Underline words or phrases that stick out to you. Circle repeated words.

THINK

Consider what roles specific body parts have in your spiritual formation. James says here that our lives as followers of Jesus can be shaped by how we choose to use (or refrain from using) our ears and our tongue.

How have your ears and tongue been beneficial or damaging to your interactions with others recently? Be specific. When have you been a hearer of the word but not a doer? Think about what James says about that.

PRAY

Start your time of communication with God by putting your hands on your ears and saying aloud, "God, I desire to listen to what You want me to hear."

Remain in the silence. (You can lower your hands.)

Now put your hands over your mouth and say aloud, "God, I desire to use my tongue to speak words that are helpful and to refrain from speaking words that are hurtful."

Remain in the silence.

Confess those times when you have not listened and when you have spoken unnecessary and harmful words.

Remain in the silence.

LIVE

In conversations today, be mindful of the percentage of time you are speaking compared to the time you are listening to others. Then ask yourself whether the percentage is healthy.

338

SHOWING FAVORITISM

JAMES 2:1-9

¹ My brothers, do not show favoritism as you hold on to the faith in our glorious Lord Jesus Christ. ² For example, a man comes into your meeting wearing a gold ring and dressed in fine clothes, and a poor man dressed in dirty clothes also comes in. ³ If you look with favor on the man wearing the fine clothes and say, "Sit here in a good place," and yet you say to the poor man, "Stand over there," or, "Sit here on the floor by my footstool," ⁴ haven't you discriminated among yourselves and become judges with evil thoughts?

⁵ Listen, my dear brothers: Didn't God choose the poor in this world to be rich in faith and heirs of the kingdom that He has promised to those who love Him? ⁶ Yet you dishonored that poor man. Don't the rich oppress you and drag you into the courts? ⁷ Don't they blaspheme the noble name that was pronounced over you at your baptism?

⁸ Indeed, if you keep the royal law prescribed in the Scripture, Love your neighbor as yourself, you are doing well. ⁹ But if you show favoritism, you commit sin and are convicted by the law as transgressors.

READ

Read the passage aloud slowly. Who are the people who receive favoritism in your life? (They don't have to be wealthy, but just people you want to impress or want to think highly of you.)

THINK

Read the passage again, noticing these words: *dishonor, discriminate, favoritism, oppress.* James is urging us to love people and use things (as opposed to loving things and using people).

1. Whom do you "use" to entertain you? To help you? To make you feel better?
2. What does it look like to love others as you love yourself? To give others the same amount of time, energy, and attention you give yourself?

Set aside these thoughts and read the passage one more time. What comes to you from this passage? What might God be saying to you today?

PRAY

Pray for those in your life you are tempted to use. Ask God to show you how to care for them the way you already care for yourself.

LIVE

Sit quietly, picturing Jesus greeting people He encountered with great love (He never used anyone). What feeling did each person have in His presence? Feel that. You are in His presence now.

WISDOM FROM ABOVE

JAMES 3:13-18

[13] Who is wise and has understanding among you? He should show his works by good conduct with wisdom's gentleness. [14] But if you have bitter envy and selfish ambition in your heart, don't brag and deny the truth. [15] Such wisdom does not come from above but is earthly, unspiritual, demonic. [16] For where envy and selfish ambition exist, there is disorder and every kind of evil. [17] But the wisdom from above is first pure, then peace-loving, gentle, compliant, full of mercy and good fruits, without favoritism and hypocrisy. [18] And the fruit of righteousness is sown in peace by those who cultivate peace.

READ

Stand up and read the passage. Then read it a second time.

THINK

Defining something accurately involves stating what it is and what it is not. James does just that, telling us what wisdom is and is not. Review the passage again. Make two columns on a piece of paper, and in your own words write in one column what James says wisdom is not. Then in the other column write what James says wisdom is.

How do these characteristics of wisdom (and the lack thereof) line up with your actions recently? If James followed you around and observed your life for a week, what comments might he make about the presence — or absence — of wisdom?

PRAY

Tell God your desire to become wise, to sow the "fruit of righteousness." Ask Him to help you.

LIVE

Ask a friend or family member you trust to give you honest feedback for the next few weeks about wisdom in your life. Give them permission to affirm wise areas of your life and wise decisions you make, as well as to point out unwise areas of your life and unwise decisions you make.

RESIST . . . DRAW NEAR

JAMES 4:7-10

[7] Therefore, submit to God. But resist the Devil, and he will flee from you. [8] Draw near to God, and He will draw near to you. Cleanse your hands, sinners, and purify your hearts, double-minded people! [9] Be miserable and mourn and weep. Your laughter must change to mourning and your joy to sorrow. [10] Humble yourselves before the Lord, and He will exalt you.

READ

This is a short passage of contrasts. Read the entire thing aloud. Read it again, this time reading every other sentence aloud. Read it again, this time reading the other sentences aloud. Then read it again in its entirety.

THINK

Someone has said that we usually think of Satan in one of two ways: We either give him too much credit for his work in the world or we don't give him any credit at all. Neither view is right. James tells us to "resist the Devil, and he will flee from you." So this means the Devil is active, but it also means that resisting him by Jesus' power in us is enough to scare him away.

In what ways have you seen Satan work destructively in your life, in the lives of others around you, and in the world? What do you think your practical response should be to the Devil's work?

James also says to "draw near to God, and He will draw near to you." Think about the times you need God to come near to you.

PRAY

Are you tempted to sin? Resist Satan and be assured that he will leave you alone.

Are you in need of God's comfort and promises in your life? Draw near to Him and be assured that He is at your side.

Rest in God's promises in Scripture.

LIVE

Remember the power that God has in your life and over the Devil. Live confidently that in Christ we always win, which means we don't have to be afraid. Utilize the tools of "resisting" and "drawing near" in your walk with Jesus.

HEALED INSIDE AND OUT

JAMES 5:13-18

¹³ Is anyone among you suffering? He should pray. Is anyone cheerful? He should sing praises. ¹⁴ Is anyone among you sick? He should call for the elders of the church, and they should pray over him after anointing him with olive oil in the name of the Lord. ¹⁵ The prayer of faith will save the sick person, and the Lord will restore him to health; if he has committed sins, he will be forgiven. ¹⁶ Therefore, confess your sins to one another and pray for one another, so that you may be healed. The urgent request of a righteous person is very powerful in its effect. ¹⁷ Elijah was a man with a nature like ours; yet he prayed earnestly that it would not rain, and for three years and six months it did not rain on the land. ¹⁸ Then he prayed again, and the sky gave rain and the land produced its fruit.

READ

Read the passage aloud slowly.

THINK

Read the passage aloud again. What is God inviting you to do or be in this passage? How does this invitation resonate with what's going on in your life right now? Where are you hurting or sick or in need of forgiveness? Where do you need to sing?

PRAY

Offer a "prayer of faith" — one that trusts God. Confess your sins to God, and ask Him if there is someone you could confess to so "you may be healed." If there is, ask God for the courage to speak to the person about it.

LIVE

Try to live in the reality that you are freshly confessed — whole and healed inside and out. What does that look like in your life today?

DAY 343

GOD ENCOUNTERS

On this seventh day, review and reflect on all you have read this week. Take the time to revel in the ways you've encountered God in the past six days.

A DEEP CONSCIOUSNESS OF GOD

1 PETER 1:13-22

¹³ Therefore, with your minds ready for action, be serious and set your hope completely on the grace to be brought to you at the revelation of Jesus Christ. ¹⁴ As obedient children, do not be conformed to the desires of your former ignorance. ¹⁵ But as the One who called you is holy, you also are to be holy in all your conduct; ¹⁶ for it is written, Be holy, because I am holy.

¹⁷ And if you address as Father the One who judges impartially based on each one's work, you are to conduct yourselves in fear during the time of your temporary residence. ¹⁸ For you know that you were redeemed from your empty way of life inherited from the fathers, not with perishable things like silver or gold, ¹⁹ but with the precious blood of Christ, like that of a lamb without defect or blemish. ²⁰ He was chosen before the foundation of the world but was revealed at the end of the times for you ²¹ who through Him are believers in God, who raised Him from the dead and gave Him glory, so that your faith and hope are in God.

²² By obedience to the truth, having purified yourselves for sincere love of the brothers, love one another earnestly from a pure heart.

READ

Read this passage, and the expanded passage, if possible.

THINK

Peter, the young apostle who denied Jesus during the last hours of Jesus' life, is now a grown man and mature Christ follower. Here he writes words of encouragement and wisdom to other followers of Jesus.

Peter talks about being holy, meaning different, separate, set apart. He encourages followers to live differently from how the world lives — conducting yourselves "in fear." What would it mean to travel your life's journey with that fear of God?

What does it mean practically to "be holy in all your conduct"? What would it mean to really live that way?

Peter instructs, "Love one another earnestly from a pure heart." What would loving others this way require of you?

PRAY

Let these phrases guide your prayer life right now:

- "Be holy, because I am holy."
- "Conduct yourselves in fear during the time of your temporary residence."
- "Be holy in all your conduct."
- "Love one another earnestly from a pure heart."

LIVE

Ask God for a way to live separately, differently, and uniquely from the way the world lives.

344

FOLLOW IN HIS STEPS

1 PETER 2:11-17,21

[11] Dear friends, I urge you as strangers and temporary residents to abstain from fleshly desires that war against you. [12] Conduct yourselves honorably among the Gentiles, so that in a case where they speak against you as those who do what is evil, they will, by observing your good works, glorify God on the day of visitation.

[13] Submit to every human authority because of the Lord, whether to the Emperor as the supreme authority [14] or to governors as those sent out by him to punish those who do what is evil and to praise those who do what is good. [15] For it is God's will that you silence the ignorance of foolish people by doing good. [16] As God's slaves, live as free people, but don't use your freedom as a way to conceal evil. [17] Honor everyone. Love the brotherhood. Fear God. Honor the Emperor. . . .

[21]   For you were called to this,
         because Christ also suffered for you,
         leaving you an example,
         so that you should follow in His steps.

READ

Read the passage aloud slowly.

THINK

Read the passage again aloud, noting "for you were called to this . . . so that you should follow in His steps."

1. What, if anything, in this description of the life "you were called to" surprises you?
2. What, if anything, in this description fits with what you've been doing lately?
3. What, if anything, in this description challenges you?
4. Consider the day you have in front of you. How might the ideas of respect, honor, and living Christ's life fit into it?

PRAY

Thank God for the rich example Christ gave us so we could "follow in His steps." Ask God to draw you more deeply into that ongoing, vibrant life of Christ. Add anything else that came to you during today's meditation.

LIVE

Rest and delight in living a Christ-honoring life today. Consider that you won't be bored; rather, it will be an adventure.

HONOR HIM IN YOUR HEARTS

1 PETER 3:13-18

[13] And who will harm you if you are deeply committed to what is good?
[14] But even if you should suffer for righteousness, you are blessed. Do not fear what they fear or be disturbed, [15] but honor the Messiah as Lord in your hearts. Always be ready to give a defense to anyone who asks you for a reason for the hope that is in you. [16] However, do this with gentleness and respect, keeping your conscience clear, so that when you are accused, those who denounce your Christian life will be put to shame. [17] For it is better to suffer for doing good, if that should be God's will, than for doing evil.

[18]　For Christ also suffered for sins once for all,
　　　the righteous for the unrighteous,
　　　that He might bring you to God,
　　　after being put to death in the fleshly realm
　　　but made alive in the spiritual realm.

READ

Read this passage a few times, slowly and meditatively.

THINK

Mull over Peter's exhortation to honor Christ in every kind of circumstance. Do you agree with the link he makes between honoring Christ and doing good to others? When you're relating to others, what kinds of things do you give your attention to, if not to honoring Christ? Do you have other goals, like giving the person a good impression of you or making useful connections? In what ways does this approach to relationships leave you satisfied or dissatisfied?

PRAY

Share with Jesus what has surfaced for you, remembering that the Righteous One already knows the unrighteousness in you, and suffered for you anyway: He loves you.

Sit with Him in silence. Even if you don't sense Him saying anything, that's okay. Just stay there, open to Him. If you are led to genuine adoration of Him, go ahead and take time to tell Him what you think of Him. If not, just receive His acceptance of you.

LIVE

Douglas Steere, a leading Quaker of the twentieth century, once said, "In the school of adoration the soul learns why the approach to every other goal has left it restless."[27] Think back to how you relate to others and notice any dissatisfaction or restlessness in that. What would it look like for you to give Peter's idea a shot: to walk through today "honor[ing] the Messiah as Lord in your hearts"? Try it.

346

NO LONGER FOR HUMAN DESIRES

1 PETER 4:1-2,14,19

¹ Therefore, since Christ suffered in the flesh, equip yourselves also with the same resolve — because the one who suffered in the flesh has finished with sin — ² in order to live the remaining time in the flesh, no longer for human desires, but for God's will. . . .

¹⁴ If you are ridiculed for the name of Christ, you are blessed, because the Spirit of glory and of God rests on you. . . . ¹⁹ So those who suffer according to God's will should, while doing what is good, entrust themselves to a faithful Creator.

READ

Read the passage aloud slowly.

THINK

Read verses 1-2 again slowly. How does any suffering (which may be more like disappointment or frustration) you're going through relate to how "Christ suffered in the flesh," for example, wanting your own way but not getting it? In what ways do your "human desires" need to be invited to change?

Read verses 14 and 19 again slowly. Are you being ridiculed because you're living a selfless, Christlike life? If so, in what ways? If not, how might that happen to you at some point?

PRAY

Ask the Holy Spirit to fill you and help you change the deep desires inside you. If you're being mistreated because of Christ, ask the Holy Spirit to help you absorb the truth that the "Spirit of glory and of God rests on you."

LIVE

Picture yourself as one who has "the Spirit of glory and of God" on you. Consider that such a suffering life is intimately linked with God and provides the companionship of the Spirit.

SUPPLEMENT YOUR FAITH

2 PETER 1:3-9

[3] His divine power has given us everything required for life and godliness through the knowledge of Him who called us by His own glory and goodness. [4] By these He has given us very great and precious promises, so that through them you may share in the divine nature, escaping the corruption that is in the world because of evil desires. [5] For this very reason, make every effort to supplement your faith with goodness, goodness with knowledge, [6] knowledge with self-control, self-control with endurance, endurance with godliness, [7] godliness with brotherly affection, and brotherly affection with love. [8] For if these qualities are yours and are increasing, they will keep you from being useless or unfruitful in the knowledge of our Lord Jesus Christ. [9] The person who lacks these things is blind and shortsighted and has forgotten the cleansing from his past sins.

READ

Go into a room by yourself and close the door behind you, then read the passage aloud.

THINK

His divine power has provided everything we need for life and godliness. And Peter reminds us of the "great and precious promises" so we may share in His all-encompassing plan to redeem the world! Peter says we should supplement our faith with the following:

- goodness
- knowledge
- self-control
- endurance
- godliness
- brotherly affection
- love

Take time to ponder each character trait. Then think about those you are doing well in. Think about those you need to grow in.

PRAY

Admit your need for God's guidance and help in your growth in Him. Ask Him to help you grow in those areas where you recognize you need the most improvement.

LIVE

On a small sheet of paper, write down the character traits you desire to develop. Review often what you wrote.

Ask the Holy Spirit for encouragement — to illuminate and reveal areas of your life that show these character traits when they become evident.

DESTRUCTIVE HERESIES

2 PETER 2:1-3

¹ But there were also false prophets among the people, just as there will be false teachers among you. They will secretly bring in destructive heresies, even denying the Master who bought them, and will bring swift destruction on themselves. ² Many will follow their unrestrained ways, and the way of truth will be blasphemed because of them. ³ They will exploit you in their greed with deceptive words. Their condemnation, pronounced long ago, is not idle, and their destruction does not sleep.

READ

Read the passage aloud slowly.

THINK

Read the passage again slowly, noticing what causes destructive heresies. Keep in mind that the people who cause divisions rarely realize they're doing it. They may have good intentions (or *think* they have them) because they believe they're right about something.

1. Where have you witnessed destructive heresies within the body of Christ lately?
2. How might you grieve over having witnessed people:

   - bringing destruction on themselves
   - denying the Master who bought them
   - exploiting others with deceptive words

3. In what ways do such destructive heresies give a false representation (see verse 1) to the world of who God is and what He is like?
4. What might God be leading you to pray? What sort of person might He be leading you to *be*?

PRAY

Thank God for doing what He promises in this passage: "Their condemnation, pronounced long ago, is not idle, and their destruction does not sleep." Ask God to show you how you are to be one who prays for the injured as well as the "false prophets" — for both to grasp truth and love and to find healing.

LIVE

Grieve with God over people's willingness to create divisions within the church, which embodies the noncompetitive unity of the Trinity.

DAY 350

GOD ENCOUNTERS

On this seventh day, review and reflect on all you have read this week. Take the time to revel in the ways you've encountered God in the past six days.

IF ANYONE DOES SIN

1 JOHN 1:6–2:2

[6] If we say, "We have fellowship with Him," yet we walk in darkness, we are lying and are not practicing the truth. [7] But if we walk in the light as He Himself is in the light, we have fellowship with one another, and the blood of Jesus His Son cleanses us from all sin. [8] If we say, "We have no sin," we are deceiving ourselves, and the truth is not in us. [9] If we confess our sins, He is faithful and righteous to forgive us our sins and to cleanse us from all unrighteousness. [10] If we say, "We don't have any sin," we make Him a liar, and His word is not in us.

[1] My little children, I am writing you these things so that you may not sin. But if anyone does sin, we have an advocate with the Father — Jesus Christ the Righteous One. [2] He Himself is the propitiation for our sins, and not only for ours, but also for those of the whole world.

READ

Read the passage.

THINK

Truth. Grace. The two sides of a fence we often fall off of when responding to sin. In going to one extreme, we might rebuke sin but leave the sinner feeling condemned or rejected. In going to the other extreme, we might communicate acceptance to the sinner but minimize the sin, leaving the sinner in its bondage. John's perspective is different.

Look at the two halves of the problem presented in this passage: our attitude toward sin and our expectations of how God views sin. Notice what John points out about the role the Father and Jesus each play in the situation and the choice we have in how we view ourselves. Take a few moments to let John's statements about these things sink into you.

PRAY

What is your attitude toward the sins with which you struggle? What deeper desire lies beneath the draw that particular sin has on you? Does your guilt hold you back from Jesus? Talk to Him about this.

Now sit silently, listening for Jesus' response to you. What is His desire for you?

LIVE

Consider a situation that holds temptation for you. Ask Jesus to remind you of His presence as the Righteous One the next time you're faced with that temptation.

LOVE WITH TRUTH AND ACTION

1 JOHN 3:16-24

[16] This is how we have come to know love: He laid down His life for us. We should also lay down our lives for our brothers. [17] If anyone has this world's goods and sees his brother in need but closes his eyes to his need—how can God's love reside in him?

[18] Little children, we must not love with word or speech, but with truth and action. [19] This is how we will know we belong to the truth and will convince our conscience in His presence, [20] even if our conscience condemns us, that God is greater than our conscience, and He knows all things.

[21] Dear friends, if our conscience doesn't condemn us, we have confidence before God [22] and can receive whatever we ask from Him because we keep His commands and do what is pleasing in His sight. [23] Now this is His command: that we believe in the name of His Son Jesus Christ, and love one another as He commanded us. [24] The one who keeps His commands remains in Him, and He in him. And the way we know that He remains in us is from the Spirit He has given us.

READ

Read the passage slowly and carefully until you understand the crux of John's argument: "even if our conscience condemns us, that God is greater than our conscience."

PRAY

How does your conscience condemn you in your life? Maybe there's that voice in your head constantly telling you what you *should* have done. Maybe you can instantly think of six aspects of yourself that you'd change if you could. Maybe receiving compliments or affirmation from others is hard for you. Explore this with God, and talk with Him about what you find. Be open to what He might want to show you about yourself.

THINK

Why do you think John so firmly ties together loving other people and freedom from a condemning conscience, or self-criticism? Ponder this connection. In what ways are the two related?

Become aware of how much you do and do not believe John's argument. Be honest with yourself and with God, remembering that it's okay to admit that, while you think something sounds true, you aren't sure you believe it.

LIVE

Pay special attention today to how much you criticize yourself or minimize praise given by others. Notice what runs through your head when you look in the mirror or if you beat yourself up over mistakes at work. Jot these things down if you need help remembering. Then, sometime later in the day, talk to God for a few minutes about what you are noticing. Recall what John says about loving others and self-criticism, and ponder it some more.

GOD'S INDWELLING LOVE

1 JOHN 4:7,11-13,16-18

[7] Dear friends, let us love one another, because love is from God, and everyone who loves has been born of God and knows God. . . . [11] Dear friends, if God loved us in this way, we also must love one another. [12] No one has ever seen God. If we love one another, God remains in us and His love is perfected in us.

[13] This is how we know that we remain in Him and He in us: He has given assurance to us from His Spirit. . . . [16] And we have come to know and to believe the love that God has for us. God is love, and the one who remains in love remains in God, and God remains in him.

[17] In this, love is perfected with us so that we may have confidence in the day of judgment, for we are as He is in this world. [18] There is no fear in love; instead, perfect love drives out fear, because fear involves punishment. So the one who fears has not reached perfection in love.

READ

Read the passage aloud slowly.

THINK

Read the passage again slowly, pausing after the word *love* each time you read it aloud. While the command to love one another can be difficult, consider also these things that empower people to love one another:

- "Love is from God."
- We are born of God and know God.
- We receive love from God, so we're turning that love around to others.
- "God remains in us."
- God's love is perfected in us.
- God gives us assurance from the Spirit.
- God lives in us and we live in God.
- The love we've already experienced is driving out fear, which often keeps us from loving others.

1. Which of the above ideas is the easiest for you to grasp? Why?
2. Which one is the most difficult for you to grasp? Why?

Draw a little stick figure of yourself as the recipient of what is being given (love or relationship or God's own life or the Spirit).

3. How does it feel to receive like this?

PRAY

Thank God for pouring into you such things (your answers to 1 and 2, the entire list, or other phrases in the passage). Express your desire to be saturated with God's love so it overflows in you and pours out to others. (Or express the desire to have that desire.)

LIVE

Contemplate yourself as an absorber and container of God's love.

PROOF THAT WE LOVE GOD

1 JOHN 5:1-3

¹ Everyone who believes that Jesus is the Messiah has been born of God, and everyone who loves the Father also loves the one born of Him. ² This is how we know that we love God's children when we love God and obey His commands. ³ For this is what love for God is: to keep His commands. Now His commands are not a burden.

READ

Read the passage three times slowly.

THINK

What do you think of this connection between loving God and loving others? Does one or the other feel more difficult for you? Which one? What about it is difficult?

PRAY

Talk to God about the difficulties you experience in this area. Openly share with Him your feelings about your struggle. Listen for what He might have to say.

LIVE

C. S. Lewis wrote, "It may be possible for each of us to think too much of his own potential glory hereafter; it is hardly possible for him to think too often or too deeply about that of his neighbor. . . . The dullest and most uninteresting person you talk to may one day be a creature which, if you saw it now, you would be strongly tempted to worship. . . . There are no ordinary people."[28] How does this suggestion alter the way you view others you know? How does it alter the way you view yourself? As you go through your day, ponder these ideas more, but also be ready to ponder in practice. As you come across "God's children" during the day, look for small ways to love them.

WALKING IN THE TRUTH

2 JOHN 4-6

[4] I was very glad to find some of your children walking in the truth, in keeping with a command we have received from the Father. [5] So now I urge you, dear lady — not as if I were writing you a new command, but one we have had from the beginning — that we love one another. [6] And this is love: that we walk according to His commands. This is the command as you have heard it from the beginning: you must walk in love.

READ

Focus on these verses, but read all of 2 John, if possible.

THINK

If you grew up in the church, you know that love is a critical ingredient in the life of a follower of Jesus. This ingredient may seem elementary, and believers often talk about love. But that's for good reason: Love is the very nature of God! John reminds us: "This is love: that we walk according to His commands. This is the command as you have heard it from the beginning: you must walk in love."

On a scale of one to ten (with one being the lowest and ten being the highest), how would you rank your "love quotient"? How might your friends rank your love quotient? What is needed for you to grow in your understanding and expression of love to others?

What would your life look like if you were "walking in the truth"?

PRAY

Ask God to help you see the direct correlation between love and following His commands.

LIVE

Love God. Study His commands. Follow them.

SHOWING FAITHFULNESS BY WHAT YOU DO

3 JOHN 5-11

5 Dear friend, you are showing faithfulness by whatever you do for the brothers, especially when they are strangers. 6 They have testified to your love in front of the church. You will do well to send them on their journey in a manner worthy of God, 7 since they set out for the sake of the Name, accepting nothing from pagans. 8 Therefore, we ought to support such men so that we can be coworkers with the truth.

9 I wrote something to the church, but Diotrephes, who loves to have first place among them, does not receive us. 10 This is why, if I come, I will remind him of the works he is doing, slandering us with malicious words. And he is not satisfied with that! He not only refuses to welcome the brothers himself, but he even stops those who want to do so and expels them from the church.

11 Dear friend, do not imitate what is evil, but what is good. The one who does good is of God; the one who does evil has not seen God.

READ

Read the passage carefully, imagining that John is writing specifically to you.

THINK

What opportunity have you had recently to show someone hospitality or in some way help someone who is trying to do good? How did you respond to that opportunity? What do you notice about the motives and priorities behind your action (or nonaction)?

PRAY

Lay before God what you have remembered about that opportunity and what you have discovered in your heart. Maybe you will rejoice with Him about the victory you experienced in overcoming a temptation to be greedy or mean-spirited, or perhaps you will feel sadness at a missed opportunity.

LIVE

Brainstorm with God what it might look like for you to take steps toward showing faithfulness and being more hospitable to others. Think about some gifts you have to offer to others (such as your good cooking, your listening ear, your encouragement). Perhaps some of your gifts you are glad to share, while others you're hesitant to offer to others. Regardless of how you feel about each gift, write down what you have that could be helpful to someone.

Now think of a specific person who would be helped by your hospitality. Offer your list to God, and ask Him what He would have you offer to this person. Don't force yourself to give something you can give only grudgingly; remember, "God loves a cheerful giver" (2 Corinthians 9:7). Be open to take this small step toward hospitality, and be open to how God may change your heart as you do it.

DAY 357

GOD ENCOUNTERS

On this seventh day, review and reflect on all you have read this week. Take the time to revel in the ways you've encountered God in the past six days.

GRACE VERSUS LAWLESSNESS

JUDE 3-8

³ Dear friends, although I was eager to write you about the salvation we share, I found it necessary to write and exhort you to contend for the faith that was delivered to the saints once for all. ⁴ For some men, who were designated for this judgment long ago, have come in by stealth; they are ungodly, turning the grace of our God into promiscuity and denying Jesus Christ, our only Master and Lord.

⁵ Now I want to remind you, though you know all these things: The Lord first saved a people out of Egypt and later destroyed those who did not believe; ⁶ and He has kept, with eternal chains in darkness for the judgment of the great day, the angels who did not keep their own position but deserted their proper dwelling. ⁷ In the same way, Sodom and Gomorrah and the cities around them committed sexual immorality and practiced perversions, just as angels did, and serve as an example by undergoing the punishment of eternal fire.

⁸ Nevertheless, these dreamers likewise defile their flesh, reject authority, and blaspheme glorious ones.

READ

Read these verses aloud, including all the passion you sense from Jude.

THINK

Think about the meaning of *promiscuity,* or *lawlessness.* Now compare that to what you know *grace* to be. What differences do you see between them?

PRAY

Sit in silence and think back on experiences you've had with lawlessness — times you've done whatever you felt like, turning your back on what was right. Now consider experiences you've had with grace. Ask God to show you one of these experiences to focus on. Recall the details: What was it like for you? What was going on around you? What were you feeling about what you'd done wrong?

If you focus on an experience of grace, recall how God made that grace known to you — maybe through another person or through something you read. What did it feel like to be presented with that option? What was it like to take God up on His grace?

If you focus on an experience of lawlessness (when you did not open up to God's grace), were you aware of any other options at the time? What motivated you to choose the route you took? What did you feel later, after the dust had settled?

LIVE

Ask God what He wants you to take away from this time with Him and His Word. Be assured that "all things work together for the good of those who love God" (Romans 8:28). This doesn't mean that we'll feel happy right away or all the time but that God does want to see us restored. Walk through today pondering the grace of this reality.

THE COMING ALMIGHTY

REVELATION 1:4-8

[4] John:

To the seven churches in Asia.

Grace and peace to you from the One who is, who was, and who is coming; from the seven spirits before His throne; [5] and from Jesus Christ, the faithful witness, the firstborn from the dead and the ruler of the kings of the earth.

To Him who loves us and has set us free from our sins by His blood, [6] and made us a kingdom, priests to His God and Father — the glory and dominion are His forever and ever. Amen.

[7]   Look! He is coming with the clouds,
        and every eye will see Him,
        including those who pierced Him.
        And all the families of the earth
        will mourn over Him.
        This is certain. Amen.

[8] "I am the Alpha and the Omega," says the Lord God, "the One who is, who was, and who is coming, the Almighty."

THINK

Revelation is a surreal book, full of visions and events that usually stir up more questions than answers. But from one perspective, the book is not as complex as it seems. Revelation displays the final piece of God's magnificent and victorious story for people. In short, the book could be summarized with two words: God wins. And because of this, it propels us into overwhelming gratitude. Revelation is about worship.

READ

Read the passage aloud, noting the characteristics and actions of God.

PRAY

Lie on your back in stillness (outside, if possible, where you can see the sky). Focus on the magnificence of God's character and how He brings victory to humanity. As you think about who God is, whisper these words to Him:

> God, You are the Alpha and the Omega.
> God, You are the One who is.
> God, You are the One who was.
> God, You are the One who is coming.
> God, You are the Almighty.

Express your gratitude to God in whatever heartfelt way you wish.

LIVE

Live your life today in complete and total thankfulness for who God is and for the plan He's had in mind all along. Use your life as a palette to display your grateful response to Him as the victorious Almighty.

LISTEN

REVELATION 2:7,10-11,17

[7] "Anyone who has an ear should listen to what the Spirit says to the churches. I will give the victor the right to eat from the tree of life, which is in God's paradise. . . .

[10] "Don't be afraid of what you are about to suffer. Look, the Devil is about to throw some of you into prison to test you, and you will have affliction for 10 days. Be faithful until death, and I will give you the crown of life.

[11] "Anyone who has an ear should listen to what the Spirit says to the churches. The victor will never be harmed by the second death. . . .

[17] "Anyone who has an ear should listen to what the Spirit says to the churches. I will give the victor some of the hidden manna. I will also give him a white stone, and on the stone a new name is inscribed that no one knows except the one who receives it."

READ

Read the passage aloud slowly.

THINK

Sit down (if you aren't already sitting). Read the passage aloud again, standing up each time you read, "Anyone who has an ear should listen to what the Spirit says to the churches."

When you're finished, stand up again and ponder what God might have been trying to say to you recently about your life with Him, about your behavior toward others, about your deepest self, about how you could be salt and light in the world. What recurring themes have you noticed in Scripture? Among friends? From wise Christians you've read about? At church gatherings?

Now lie down on the floor with your arms outstretched above you, if you can. Ask God what He wants to say to you today. Wait expectantly. Don't be bothered if nothing specific comes to you. Consider this practice as one of the most important things you'll ever do: listening to God and inviting Him to speak to you.

PRAY

Talk to God about learning to listen to Him. Ask God to show you how He speaks to you most frequently.

LIVE

Sit in the quiet, and lavish yourself with the thought that God seeks you out to speak to you. You get to live an interactive relationship with God.

THE THRONE ROOM

REVELATION 4:2-8

² Immediately I was in the Spirit, and a throne was set there in heaven. One was seated on the throne, ³ and the One seated looked like jasper and carnelian stone. A rainbow that looked like an emerald surrounded the throne. ⁴ Around that throne were 24 thrones, and on the thrones sat 24 elders dressed in white clothes, with gold crowns on their heads. ⁵ Flashes of lightning and rumblings of thunder came from the throne. Seven fiery torches were burning before the throne, which are the seven spirits of God. ⁶ Something like a sea of glass, similar to crystal, was also before the throne. Four living creatures covered with eyes in front and in back were in the middle and around the throne. ⁷ The first living creature was like a lion; the second living creature was like a calf; the third living creature had a face like a man; and the fourth living creature was like a flying eagle. ⁸ Each of the four living creatures had six wings; they were covered with eyes around and inside. Day and night they never stop, saying:

> Holy, holy, holy,
> Lord God, the Almighty,
> who was, who is, and who is coming.

READ

Read the passage once aloud, and get a feel for what is happening. As you read it a second time, do you notice a common theme? Write it down.

THINK/PRAY

Close your eyes and imagine what's described here: the rainbow and the emerald, the thunder and the lightning, the torches and the sea of glass. See if you can sense the awe of the place. What does it feel like to be there?

Listen as the four living creatures begin to chant, "Holy, holy, holy." Speak these words to God a few times. Share with Him what they express for you. Think about what holiness means to you, but not for long. Return your attention to "who was, who is, and who is coming." Join the four living creatures in their worship again: "Holy, holy, holy."

LIVE

What is one way you could worship God today? Perhaps you know a poem or song that puts words and emotion to your love for Him today; read it, play it, sing it. Perhaps you have a special skill like dancing, surfing, or art; perform that for Him today. Maybe there is a specific action you could take that would honor Him. Do it. Maybe you'll want simply to tell Him what you like about Him.

BEFORE THE THRONE

REVELATION 7:9-12

⁹ After this I looked, and there was a vast multitude from every nation, tribe, people, and language, which no one could number, standing before the throne and before the Lamb. They were robed in white with palm branches in their hands. ¹⁰ And they cried out in a loud voice:

> Salvation belongs to our God,
> who is seated on the throne,
> and to the Lamb!

¹¹ All the angels stood around the throne, the elders, and the four living creatures, and they fell facedown before the throne and worshiped God, ¹² saying:

> Amen! Blessing and glory and wisdom
> and thanksgiving and honor
> and power and strength
> be to our God forever and ever. Amen.

READ

Stand up and read this passage aloud in a loud and excited tone of voice, imagining yourself before the throne of God.

THINK

Have you heard it said that our sole purpose in life is to worship God? Read again the words that the worshipers sing in this scene. How does this relate to your worship of God?

"Salvation belongs to our God." What has God saved you from, specifically?

"Blessing and glory and wisdom and thanksgiving and honor and power and strength." What comes to mind when you think about these words? What are you feeling about the God described by them? Why?

What might this passage have to do with shared worship in church each week?

PRAY

Why is God worthy of your worship? Consider lying down on your face before Him as you tell Him (with specifics), just as the angels, elders, and animals do in this passage.

Go on to worship God as you communicate with Him. Respond to Him with thankfulness, authenticity, honesty, and passion.

LIVE

Take out a piece of paper or your journal. Write down a few sentences or paragraphs telling God how grateful you are for Him and for what He has done, is doing, and will do. Include gratitude directed to the Lamb of God. Start and end with the word *Amen*.

Then read your writing aloud to God as an act of worship.

DEATH WILL NO LONGER EXIST

REVELATION 21:1-11

¹ Then I saw a new heaven and a new earth, for the first heaven and the first earth had passed away, and the sea no longer existed. ² I also saw the Holy City, new Jerusalem, coming down out of heaven from God, prepared like a bride adorned for her husband.

³ Then I heard a loud voice from the throne:

> Look! God's dwelling is with humanity,
> and He will live with them.
> They will be His people,
> and God Himself will be with them
> and be their God.
> ⁴   He will wipe away every tear from their eyes.
> Death will no longer exist;
> grief, crying, and pain will exist no longer,
> because the previous things have passed away.

⁵ Then the One seated on the throne said, "Look! I am making everything new." He also said, "Write, because these words are faithful and true." ⁶ And He said to me, "It is done! I am the Alpha and the Omega, the Beginning and the End. I will give water as a gift to the thirsty from the spring of life. ⁷ The victor will inherit these things, and I will be his God, and he will be My son. ⁸ But the cowards, unbelievers, vile, murderers, sexually immoral, sorcerers, idolaters, and all liars — their share will be in the lake that burns with fire and sulfur, which is the second death."

⁹ Then one of the seven angels, who had held the seven bowls filled with the seven last plagues, came and spoke with me: "Come, I will show you the bride, the wife of the Lamb." ¹⁰ He then carried me away in the Spirit to a great and high mountain and showed me the holy city, Jerusalem, coming down out of heaven from God, ¹¹ arrayed with God's glory. Her radiance was like a very precious stone, like a jasper stone, bright as crystal.

READ

If you can, skim the expanded passage once quickly to get a broader perspective on the context of these verses. Then read this excerpt three times slowly.

THINK

Among all the images and names given in this passage — for the believers, for God, for the way life will be then and what will happen — which stands out to you? Consider "God's dwelling is with humanity" or "He will wipe away every tear from [our] eyes." Can you believe that this will someday be reality?

PRAY

Offer God your belief or disbelief in the promise of His coming kingdom. Thank Him for the promise of it, even if you struggle to believe. Ask Him to help you hope in it. Sit in silence for a bit, and be aware of Him hearing you and looking at it all with you.

LIVE

What might be different in you (even if it's just the tiniest shift in perspective), knowing that a place "arrayed with God's glory" waits for you?

DAY 364

GOD ENCOUNTERS

On this seventh day, review and reflect on all you have read this week. Take the time to revel in the ways you've encountered God in the past six days.

LIVING DAILY FOR GOD

One year. Perhaps the beginning of a life lived for Him. What was it like? What did you discover that made you stop and really think about this almighty, all-knowing, paradoxical God? What fired your curiosity? What frightened you?

And as He revealed Himself to you, how did God work in your life? Where has He led you in this past year? Through the valleys or to the peaks of the mountains? A little of both? On the way, what did you discover about Him? About yourself? How has He changed who you are to make you more the person He wants you to be?

Take the things you have learned and put into practice this year and let them become part of the life God has planned for you. Don't let the discipline of reading and studying His Word languish. You're on a roll! Keep up the good work, because God is with you: "God is faithful; you were called by Him into fellowship with His Son, Jesus Christ our Lord" (1 Corinthians 1:9).

NOTES

1. *The Book of Common Prayer* (San Francisco: HarperSanFrancisco, 1983), 55.
2. Henri Nouwen, *The Inner Voice of Love* (New York: Image, 1999), 98.
3. C. S. Lewis, *Mere Christianity* (New York: Touchstone, 1996), 87.
4. *Book of Common Prayer*, 81.
5. Nouwen, 101.
6. Peter Kreeft, *Three Philosophies of Life* (San Francisco: Ignatius, 1989), 89.
7. Summarized from Richard J. Foster, *Prayer: Finding the Heart's True Home* (San Francisco: Harper Collins, 1992), 87–90.
8. William Johnston, ed., *The Cloud of Unknowing* (New York: Doubleday, 1973), 47.
9. W. E.Vine, *An Expository Dictionary of Biblical Words*, eds. Merrill F. Unger and William White (Nashville: Thomas Nelson, 1985), 18.
10. C. S. Lewis, *The Problem of Pain* (San Francisco: HarperSanFrancisco, 2001), 91.
11. David Jacobsen, *Clarity in Prayer* (Mills Valley, CA: Omega, 1979), 93.
12. Jan Karon, *These High, Green Hills* (New York: Penguin, 1996), 301.
13. C. S. Lewis, *The Lion, the Witch and the Wardrobe* (London: HarperCollins, 1998), 75.
14. Bruce L. Shelley, *Church History in Plain Language* (Nashville: Thomas Nelson, 1995), 3.
15. Oswald Chambers, *My Utmost for His Highest* (Uhrichsville, OH: Barbour, 2006), 52.
16. Teresa of Avila, *Interior Castle: The Collected Works of St. Teresa of Avila,* trans. Kieran Kavanaugh, OCD, and Otilio Rodriguez, OCD (Washington, DC: ICS Publications, 1980), 2:309.
17. These questions are adapted closely from Emilie Griffin, *Wilderness Time* (San Francisco: HarperSanFrancisco, 1997), 47.

18. Julian of Norwich, *Revelation of Love*, ed. and trans. John Skinner (New York: Doubleday, 1996), 13.
19. *Book of Common Prayer*, 337.
20. Margaret Silf, *Going on Retreat* (Chicago: Loyola, 2002), 40–41.
21. Chambers, 193.
22. Bernard of Clairvaux, in Foster, 168.
23. Ruth Haley Barton, *Sacred Rhythms* (Downers Grove, IL: InterVarsity, 2006), 117.
24. John Dalrymple, *Simple Prayer* (Wilmington, DE: Michael Glazier, 1984), 109–110.
25. Foster, 61.
26. That the World May Know Ministries, "Rabbi and Talmidim," *Follow the Rabbi*, March 7, 2007, http://community.gospelcom.net/Brix?pageID=2753.
27. Douglas V. Steere, *Prayer and Worship* (New York: Edward W. Hazen Foundation, 1938), 34.
28. C. S. Lewis, *The Weight of Glory* (Grand Rapids, MI: Eerdmans, 1965), 14–15.

INDEX

SOLO is intended to immerse you in the beauty and depth of the Bible through *lectio divina*. It is not a topical Bible or a concordance. However, if you are looking for a reading on a specific subject, the following index of topics and day numbers may be of assistance. It is not meant to be an exhaustive list of the topics covered by the Scripture passages discussed in this book.

ABOUT THE AUTHORS

Jan Johnson is a retreat leader and spiritual director and has written more than fifteen books, including *Invitation to the Jesus Life, Enjoying the Presence of God, Savoring God's Word,* and *When the Soul Listens* (all NavPress).

J. R. Briggs serves as cultural cultivator of The Renew Community and is the founder of Kairos Partnerships. As part of his time with Kairos Partnerships, he serves on staff with The Ecclesia Network and Fresh Expressions U.S. J. R. and his wife, Megan, have two sons, Carter and Bennett, and live in Lansdale, Pennsylvania.

Katie Peckham has an MA in spiritual formation and soul care from Talbot Seminary and works as a spiritual director in Orange County, California. She enjoys training for triathlons and traveling with her husband and daughter.

Choose your *SOLO* translation!

KJV: SOLO

Featuring passages from the King James Version, this 312-day devotional helps you read through the entire Bible and understand God's Word better. Using *lectio divina*, the ancient approach to studying Scripture, you'll learn how to Read, Think, Pray, and Live God's Word.

978-1-61291-342-1

KJV

KING JAMES VERSION: SOLO
AN UNCOMMON DEVOTIONAL

SOLO

OR . . .

The Message: SOLO
The Message text by
Eugene H. Peterson

This 312-day devotional uses text from *The Message* to take you through the entire Bible and discover how God's Word can impact your life. Using *lectio divina*, the ancient approach to studying Scripture, you'll learn how to Read, Think, Pray, and Live God's Word.

978-1-60006-105-9